T0127256

The Palace Letters

Jenny Hocking is emeritus professor at Monash University, Distinguished Whitlam Fellow at the Whitlam Institute at Western Sydney University, and Gough Whitlam's award-winning biographer. Professor Hocking first sought access to the Palace Letters from the National Archives in 2011 and again in 2015, but was refused. Aided by a crowd-funded money-raising campaign, and a stellar legal team prepared to work for her on a *pro bono* basis, she then took legal action to gain access to the documents. The Federal Court rejected her arguments in 2018, and the Full Federal Court rejected her appeal against this decision in 2019. She appealed this decision in the High Court on 4 February 2020, and the court's judgment in her favour was handed down on 29 May 2020.

The Palace Letters

Jenny Hocking

The Queen, the
governor-general,
and the plot
to dismiss
Gough Whitlam

SCRIBE

Melbourne • London

Scribe Publications
2 John St, Clerkenwell, London, WC1N 2ES, United Kingdom
18–20 Edward St, Brunswick, Victoria 3056, Australia
3754 Pleasant Ave, Suite 100, Minneapolis, Minnesota 55409, USA

Published by Scribe 2020

Copyright © Jenny Hocking 2020

All rights reserved. Without limiting the rights under copyright reserved
above, no part of this publication may be reproduced, stored in or introduced
into a retrieval system, or transmitted, in any form or by any means
(electronic, mechanical, photocopying, recording or otherwise) without the
prior written permission of the publishers of this book.

The moral rights of the author have been asserted.

Every effort has been made to acknowledge and contact the copyright holders
for permission to reproduce material contained in this book. Any copyright
holders who have been inadvertently omitted from the acknowledgements
and credits should contact the publisher so that omissions may be rectified in
subsequent editions.

Typeset in Adobe Garamond Pro by J&M Typesetting

Printed and bound in the UK by CPI Group (UK) Ltd, Croydon CR0 4YY

Scribe Publications is committed to the sustainable use of natural resources
and the use of paper products made responsibly from those resources.

9781913348472 (UK edition)
9781922310248 (Australian edition)
9781925938623 (ebook)

Catalogue records for this book are available from the National Library of
Australia and the British Library.

scribepublications.co.uk
scribepublications.com.au
scribepublications.com

To my mother, Barbara Hocking

Reporter: Do you think the Queen knew about this course of action?

Gough Whitlam: I shouldn't think so, but I don't know.

Reporter: Do you think the governor-general took any advice from Buckingham Palace?

Gough Whitlam: I don't know. I don't know. I was not informed that he had.

—11 November 1975

Contents

Foreword by Malcolm Turnbull   xi

Chapter One: 'In the shades of history'   1

Chapter Two: 'I never had any doubts'   15

Chapter Three: 'Australia owns its history'   31

Chapter Four: Archival manoeuvres in the dark   51

Chapter Five: 'Mr Whitlam ... would inevitably suspect the U.K.'s involvement'   75

Chapter Six: Fourteen minutes   97

Chapter Seven: 'Who cares what the Queen thinks?'   115

Chapter Eight: A royal whitewash of history   137

Chapter Nine: 'Constitutionally unthinkable'   157

Chapter Ten: 'My continued loyalty and humble duty'   169

Chapter Eleven: 'You will do it good'   195

Chapter Twelve: 'For the sake of the Monarchy'   221

Acknowledgements   233

Notes   235

Bibliography   257

Foreword

by Malcolm Turnbull,
prime minister of Australia, 2015–18

No less than Her Majesty the Queen was determined that the letters between Sir John Kerr and her private secretary should remain secret. By 2020, they were more than forty years old. If they had been cabinet documents, they would have been released in 2005. They concerned the greatest constitutional crisis in our history.

Had it not been for Jenny Hocking's tenacity, they would have remained secret for years to come. One of the other actors in this drama was to say, 'I owe nothing to history.' Certainly, history owes a great deal to Jenny Hocking.

I first became aware of the issue not long after the 2016 election. Professor Hocking's application to the Archives for access to the documents had been rejected on the basis that they had been deposited on terms they should remain confidential until 2027 and that they were 'personal' correspondence, as opposed to official government correspondence covered by the usual, timely rules for disclosure.

When I consulted the attorney-general, George Brandis, he told me that the Archives' position was supported by legal advice from the then solicitor-general, Justin Gleeson. While I had great respect for Mr Gleeson's erudition, I had no doubt that his advice must be wrong. The correspondence between the governor-general and the Queen is no more personal than correspondence between the governor-general and the prime minister.

However, it was very clear that the Queen, or at least her courtiers, were adamantly opposed to disclosure. Their concern, so we were advised, was not about the content of the correspondence, but that it could set a precedent for the disclosure of correspondence between Her Majesty and her viceroys in those remaining Commonwealth countries that, like Australia, retain the monarch of the United Kingdom as their head of state. Her Majesty's position was that the documents should remain confidential until the earlier of 2027 or the end of the Queen's reign.

When Professor Hocking challenged the Archives' decision in the Federal Court, I had no doubt that she would be successful. That seemed to offer an elegant solution. There would be no need for the Palace to break its own precedent, nor would the Australian government be obliged to take issue with Her Majesty's wishes.

While Justice Griffiths was considering the matter, I did explore the possibility of my formally advising Her Majesty that she should agree to release the letters. I was satisfied, however, that this advice would have been most unwelcome – better to await the resolution of the issue in the Federal Court.

However, the elegant solution was denied us when Justice Griffiths found in favour of the Archives in March 2018. Again, I had no doubt this would be reversed on appeal. By the time the Full Bench gave its decision in February 2019, I was no longer prime minister, but its judgment was equally astounding. Two of the three judges upheld Justice Griffiths.

Happily, common sense prevailed in the High Court, and Professor Hocking was triumphant in May 2020. The elegant solution was finally presented, but not without considerable trouble and expense for Professor Hocking, for which we should all be most grateful.

The letters are fascinating because they give a contemporaneous account of Kerr's thinking during the lead-up to the constitutional crisis and his sacking of Whitlam. But they are acutely dispiriting as well. Kerr's sycophantic grovelling is stomach-churning. But, worst of all, they show him bringing the Queen and her private secretary into his confidence in a manner he did not extend to the prime minister of Australia.

This was Kerr's greatest mistake. He should have taken Whitlam into his confidence and set out the course of action he would be obliged to follow if, indeed, Whitlam was not able to secure supply. He did not do so, as he acknowledges, because he was worried that Whitlam would ask the Queen to sack him. Even if this apprehension was a realistic one, it was no excuse. Kerr, in short, put the retention of his own job ahead of his duty to be honest and open with his own prime minister.

For many years, Australian monarchists have argued that the governor-general is the real head of state, and that the Queen's only role is to appoint, or remove, the governor-general on the advice of the prime minister. This correspondence shows the governor-general as an anxious country manager reporting back to head office, seeking not just approbation for, but guidance on, his conduct in a worsening political crisis.

The content of Kerr's letters did not surprise me, but the replies from the Palace did. I had expected Sir Martin Charteris would reply with little more than a brief, polite acknowledgement. That would have been the more tactful response. But, as Professor Hocking elaborates, Charteris and Kerr discussed the political and constitutional circumstances of the time in considerable detail.

Kerr had joined Prince Charles at independence celebrations in Papua New Guinea in September 1975, and had raised directly with Charles the possibility of Whitlam asking the Queen to sack him and appoint a more compliant governor-general. He was clearly seeking to find out what the Queen's reaction would be, and the answer came back in a letter from Charteris on 2 October. The Queen would, Sir Martin, wrote, 'take most unkindly to it. There would be considerable comings and goings, but I think it is right that I should make the point that at the end of the road The Queen, as a Constitutional Sovereign, would have no option but to follow the advice of her Prime Minister'.

This advice, no doubt, reinforced Kerr in concluding that, to forestall any risk of Whitlam sacking him, he would need to give him no, or very little, warning of his intention.

I was even more disappointed to find that, having elected to confer with Kerr about his situation, Charteris did not at any time advise Kerr to be upfront and transparent with his prime minister. Kerr made it very clear to Charteris that he was contemplating dismissing Whitlam, and Charteris did nothing to discourage him. In fact, some of his correspondence can be read as encouraging him to do so. How else to interpret his letter of 5 November, where Sir Martin commends to Kerr Arthur Meighen's spirited defence of Lord Byng, the Canadian governor-general who, in 1926, had rejected the advice of prime minister MacKenzie King to call an election?

Meighen, as Kerr knew well, had been the beneficiary when Lord Byng swore him in as prime minister after King had resigned.

A governor-general's duty, Meighen said, was 'to make sure that parliament is not stifled by government but that every government is held responsible to parliament, and every parliament held responsible to the people'.

Kerr wrote to Charteris on 17 November saying that 11 November 1975 had been the last practical date for an election of any kind to be called before Christmas, given that the last feasible election day was 13 December.

That being so, Kerr should have, and could have, privately and confidentially said to Whitlam a month beforehand, 'If supply is not obtained by 11 November, and if there is no prospect of obtaining it without an election being called, then you must call an election. If you are not prepared to do so, I will dismiss you and appoint Mr Fraser as caretaker prime minister to do so.'

Such an approach would not have been free from controversy, but at least it would have been open and honest.

It is worth comparing Kerr's conduct to that of Sir Peter Cosgrove a few years ago. In the course of 2017, the High Court found that Barnaby Joyce and Senator Fiona Nash were ineligible to sit in the Parliament because they were citizens by descent of other countries. As I describe in my memoir *A Bigger Picture*, this cast a shadow over the eligibility of dozens of Members of Parliament. My government had a majority of one on the floor of the House.

Questions were being raised over many other Coalition MPs, and eventually another, John Alexander, had to resign and also go to a by-election. For the few weeks, while both Joyce and Alexander were out of the House, the government had 73 seats (not counting the Speaker), Labor 69, and the crossbench five. We were a minority government. And at least one of the Nationals MPs threatened to take the opportunity to vote with Labor to bring down the government.

One possible option for us was to advise the governor-general to prorogue the sittings of the Parliament for long enough for the by-elections to be held. If, as it transpired, Joyce and Alexander held their seats, the status quo would be restored. If they lost, we would have been off to a general election.

Cosgrove told both the attorney-general and me that he would decline to prorogue the Parliament if I advised him to do so. (See *A Bigger Picture*, p. 554.) In my view, he would have been wrong not to follow such advice, had I given it, and I was confident that, however unhappily, he would have done so.

Cosgrove did not know we had already decided not to seek a prorogation, but had correctly surmised that such a request would be one way of dealing with a temporary loss of a majority. He wanted to give me a heads-up as to how he would react. He was, in my view, constitutionally mistaken, but at least he was upfront with me in a way that Kerr was not with Whitlam.

I said at the outset that I was surprised by how engaged Charteris became in his correspondence with Kerr. I shouldn't have been. Sir Martin was charming, witty, and very political, as Lucy and I learned when we met him and his wife in London in 1988.

Sir Martin was then the Provost of Eton College – a comfortable sinecure he had been appointed to in 1978 after he had retired as the Queen's private secretary.

'Mr Turnbull', Sir Martin said, 'I am very much obliged to you for your cross-examination of Sir Robert Armstrong.'

Only eighteen months before, Lucy and I had successfully represented Peter Wright in the *Spycatcher* case. Lord Armstrong, Thatcher's cabinet secretary, had been the UK government's main witness, and in the course of my cross-examination he had had to apologise for misleading the court, and tried to justify a misleading letter he had written as not being a lie, but 'perhaps being economical with the truth'.

'Mrs Thatcher had promised Armstrong he would be Provost. He couldn't wait to turn me out and get into my nice house. But, thanks to you,' Charteris said, raising a glass, 'he is disgraced, and I am still the Provost.' And so he remained until 1991!

Jenny Hocking's book is a thrilling tale of politics and intrigue, all the way to Buckingham Palace. But, above all, it is a reminder of how absurd it is that an Australian governor-general reports to Buckingham Palace in a manner not much different from that of a colonial governor in the century before last.

Australia's head of state should be one of us.

Chapter One

'In the shades of history'

I first caught a glimpse of the Palace letters in 2006, although I did not know it then. *AA 1984/609* was a catalogue entry for a file that did not exist. There was a quantity, 0.36m, a date range, 1974–1977, and an indeterminate name, 'Personal Records', and yet there was no content: 'Number of items: 0'. It was an empty record of the cryptic existence of what we now know as the Palace letters. That confused entry, simultaneously acknowledging and denying the existence of one of its own files, would be emblematic of all my dealings with the National Archives of Australia about its royal secrets.

I had spent months in the Archives, buried in Sir John Kerr's sprawling papers, shocked, dismayed, and enthralled in turn at the depth of political deception they revealed and the distortions of history they laid bare. Kerr's papers were a treasure trove of historical revelation, a vast untapped source of original material about the most dramatic and controversial vice-regal action in our history – his 1975 dismissal of the Whitlam government – and when I first began to open them, they had barely been touched.[1] Kerr's contemporaneous notes and reflections would refute his most significant public pronouncements about those tumultuous events, and would overturn decades of established dismissal history.

Kerr's papers unmasked a parallel history, a secret history, of the dismissal of the twice-elected Whitlam government that had been carefully erased from public view for decades. Yet here they were, an archival time-bomb, forgotten among the thousands of files in the National Archives in Canberra, unremarked, unopened, and unexplored.

I asked to see the *AA1984/609* file, and was told only that it was 'personal and confidential' and not for public access. It remained a mystery.

Kerr's papers had come to the Archives in two parts. The first of these, smaller and containing the apparently empty *AA* file, had been deposited by the governor-general's official secretary, David Smith, after Kerr's resignation as governor-general. These were largely mundane, formal records, including the extensive correspondence, both critical and supportive, received by Kerr in the wake of his dismissal of the Whitlam government, and records of functions, speeches, and invitations. Although there were some 'personal records' among them, most of these were considered 'Commonwealth records' from Kerr's term as governor-general. With the passage of the *Archives Act* in 1983, these records were routinely released after thirty years, beginning in 2005, more than thirty years after Kerr was appointed governor-general by prime minister Gough Whitlam.

It was the second, larger, part of Kerr's papers that was historically more compelling, for this included an extraordinarily important collection on the dismissal of the Whitlam government. These were Kerr's 'personal' records, many of them accrued after his term as governor-general and catalogued in 2005, fourteen years after his death. As 'personal' papers, they did not come under the *Archives Act* – a distinction that later assumed immense significance in my efforts to gain access to the Palace letters. Instead, personal records have their own conditions of access set by the depositor in an Instrument of Deposit.

To my astonishment, when I began to examine Kerr's papers in detail, the two critical series in the 'personal' collection covering the dismissal remained largely unexplored, although their significance could not have been clearer from their National Archives catalogue entries:

M4523
Private and confidential papers relating to the constitutional crisis of 1975
Documents in this series were packaged together in an envelope marked 'Private and Confidential'. Notes by Sir John Kerr relating to the constitutional crisis of 1975 are included. A number are handwritten by Kerr with typescript copies attached. A personal journal for 1980 is also included.

M4524
Notes and papers on the constitutional crisis of 1975 and the political events that followed
The documents in this series were packaged together in an envelope marked 'the contents of a light brown case'. Handwritten and typescript notes by Sir John Kerr on the constitutional crisis of 1975 and events that followed are included together with official documents, correspondence and relevant journal and newspaper articles.

When I eventually tracked down the envelope marked 'the contents of a light brown case' in another unrelated file, it was empty. What became of that light brown case is another archival mystery – one of many.

The simple admonition of the forensic journalist-biographer Robert Caro is to 'Turn every page'.[2] Mine became 'Open every file'. Keep opening, keep reading, keep searching. For the next three years, I worked through hundreds of dismissal files in Kerr's papers and elsewhere, opening every one with an intriguing title, an ambiguous title, or even just a suggestive title – so many of them had nothing more than an anodyne description revealing little about their content and nothing about their significance, and eventually I opened them, too. It was a mix of long hours, guess work, experience, and luck until I began to feel a disconcerting archival affinity with Sir John Kerr, a growing sense of how he had put his papers together, those he wanted to be found, and those most likely to give up his secrets.

One of these personal files was of immediate and obvious interest – *M4513 Personal papers (copy of AA1984/609)* – a copy of the closed 'personal papers' file right there in the open-access catalogue: 'The record consists of personal and private correspondence between the Governor General and Her Majesty the Queen. It was copied for Sir John Kerr at his request in 1977 by the Official Secretary as a means of refreshing his memory during his stay in Europe while writing *Matters for Judgement* [sic] published in 1978.'[3]

The little we knew of the letters was thanks to a brief mention in *Matters for Judgment,* in which Kerr described his correspondence with the Queen as his 'regular despatches' to the monarch and as part of his 'duty' as governor-general. Beyond that, we knew only that they were in the Archives, closed to the public, and with no means of seeking access to them.[4] The existence of the copy file had revealed the duplicate set, and had given more detail about their contents.

But the best was yet to come. Sometimes among a mass of files, with budget cuts, down-sizing, over-worked staff, and a loss of organisational memory, something unexpectedly slips through the archival net, to the consternation of the Archives but to the great benefit of history. Although this was a copy of the closed, unidentified *AA* file, the *M* file containing copies of those same letters was listed in the catalogue as available for public access, and a door to accessing the Palace letters had unexpectedly opened.

So now we knew. There were two sets of 'the Palace letters': the *AA* file, being the originals of Kerr's letters to the Palace, together with the Palace's replies deposited by David Smith in 1978; and the *M* file, being a 'near complete' copy made for Kerr and deposited with his personal papers. The Palace letters were closed until at least 2027, and their release after that date had to be 'authorised' by the Official Secretary of the Governor-General and the Queen's Private Secretary.

The copy file had slipped through the National Archives' protective net when it was deposited decades later, and, most importantly for access, it had been listed in the public NAA catalogue as open – not closed or embargoed, as the originals were. The unexpected existence of a copy of the Palace letters was an extraordinary opportunity, a rare chance to thwart the efforts of Government House, Buckingham Palace, and the National Archives to keep those letters secret by accessing their copies instead. Were it not for the copy file, the Palace letters would have remained closed and hidden from history, locked away in our own National Archives.

Unlike the originals, the copies of the Palace letters were among Kerr's personal papers deposited later by his family, not by David Smith, and they carried their own conditions of access set by the family, not by Smith or the Queen, and not by the Archives, which has no power over the conditions governing personal records. Since the copy file was *already* open and available through the catalogue, the Archives could not deny me access to it in defiance of the terms laid down by the Kerr family, which had placed them on open access. The copies of the Palace letters would have to be released.

And so, on 10 July 2011, I requested access to the copies of the Palace letters, fully expecting that the terms laid down by the Kerr family over his personal papers would be adhered to, and that the copy file would be made available to me. Barely a month later, the National Archives responded, denying my request, in the first of many surprises and disappointments in my efforts to have these historic letters between the governor-general and the Queen at the time of the dismissal released, despite the fact that, under the Kerr family's own conditions, they were already on open access. The biggest shock was that, not only had the Archives denied me access to the copy file, but it had now retrospectively 'closed the file from public access', following 'advice from the Governor-General's official secretary'.[5]

Both versions of the Palace letters were now completely closed to public access as 'personal' records, simply and solely because they were letters between the governor-general and the Queen. We were being denied access to our own history about one of the most controversial and polarising episodes in our history. The obvious question was why?

History is never fixed. It is a process, a continuing cycle of investigation, revelation, and reconsideration that is repeatedly transformed as new details emerge and historical certainties crystallise, or crumble and dissolve into the next iteration. In the unfolding history of the dismissal, Kerr's papers provided just such a moment of transformation.

It was an oddity in the title that caught my eye. 'Conversation with Sir Anthony Mason during October–November 1975'. '*Conversation*', singular, across two months? What 'conversation' lasts for two months? Why was Kerr speaking extensively with a justice of the High Court, unknown to the prime minister, over those crucial politically charged two months? And why was there a file about that 'conversation' in Kerr's 'Private and confidential papers relating to the constitutional crisis of 1975'? *It must have been some kind of conversation*, I thought, requesting access and nervously hoping that this file, with its intriguing title, would actually be released.

The Mason file was not only unopened; it was unexamined. This meant a frustrating wait while it was checked by nameless 'agencies' for possible exemptions under the *Archives Act* on the grounds of national security, confidentiality, or other broad exclusions that give the Archives its formidable power to deny public access to its records. When I sought access to Kerr's conversation with Sir Anthony Mason, nobody on the other side of that imposing 'exemptions' curtain realised the file's significance, or the furore its publication would cause. Not then, anyway.

I requested access, and I waited – not too long, as it turned out, certainly not when compared to the nine years I'd been waiting for numerous files – while the file was examined by 'agencies' and opened for public access, photocopied, and sent to me in Melbourne.

There's a moment, a sensation, that only the ardent archival researcher can know, of hitting 'archival pay dirt'. It's a moment of recognition – not a moment of discovery, but a moment of recognition of the significance of that discovery, which is a different thing – that the file you have just opened and just read and are still holding will transform the history of its time. That was the Mason file. I opened it impatiently as I turned from the letterbox, and began reading it as I entered the hallway, where I remained, utterly transfixed, as the words seemed to rise off the page and swim towards me:

> If this document is found among my archives, it will mean that my final decision is that truth must prevail, and, as he played a most significant part in my thinking at that critical time, and as he will be in the shades of history when this is read, his role should be known.

For once, Kerr's usual melodramatic language – *'in the shades of history'*, *'his role should be known'* – matched the significance of his words. It was not until the second page that it became clear who 'he' was and just how significant his role in the dismissal had been. The High Court justice Sir Anthony Mason, later to become an esteemed chief justice, was now revealed as Kerr's secret confidant and guide, as the long-term legal eminence behind the governor-general's deliberations and eventual decision to dismiss the elected government – all of it kept secret from the prime minister, Gough Whitlam, with none of the meetings announced in the vice-regal notices. Together, in several discussions over those months, Kerr and Mason arranged the timing of Kerr's approach to the chief justice of the High Court of Australia, Sir Garfield Barwick, to secure Barwick's imprimatur for the dismissal of the Whitlam government.

This single archival record revealed Mason not only as Kerr's *éminence grise* in the dismissal, but also as having carefully and insistently kept his role secret, allowing a false historical narrative of the dismissal to take hold. For thirty-seven years, Mason had maintained his silence and that historical deception, refusing to comment publicly, despite Kerr's pleas that he do so – ensuring the continuing public ignorance of his role in the dismissal of the Whitlam government.

Mason had not only advised Kerr on his decision to dismiss, but he had walked with him every step of the way for months beforehand, in meetings and conversations that began in August 1975, 'fortifying me for the action I was to take', as Kerr described it. Mason's role was more than mere fortification; it was an active one, and Mason himself later admitted that he had drafted a letter of dismissal for Kerr. As *The Australian* noted, 'the only tenable conclusion is that he [Mason] was implicated in Kerr's dismissal of Whitlam'.[6]

The breach of the separation of powers that this secret involvement of a High Court justice in the dismissal of a government constitutes is profound. Yet Mason later claimed that he did not give Kerr 'encouragement to dismiss the Prime Minister', which not only defies all understanding of the English language but also abrogates any personal responsibility for his own actions.[7]

Every justice of the High Court takes a judicial oath of office at their swearing in. Chief Justice Gerard Brennan QC described its great significance at his own swearing in: 'It is rich in meaning. It precludes partisanship for a cause, however worthy to the eyes of a protagonist that cause may be. It forbids any judge to regard himself or herself as a representative of a section of society. It forbids partiality and, most importantly, it commands independence from any influence that might improperly tilt the scales of justice.'[8]

Mason and Kerr had ensured that Mason's involvement remained hidden for the next thirty-seven years, until I located this remarkable file in Kerr's papers. There is surely no better example of the significance of original archival documents, and of public access to them, to understanding history than this. *The Australian* described it as 'a discovery of historical importance'.[9]

The discovery of the 'significant part' played by Mason in Kerr's dismissal of the Whitlam government transformed that history, pointing to the collusion, secrecy, and planning behind it that had never been previously acknowledged. It was the final blow to the foundational dismissal narrative so assiduously promulgated by Kerr and Malcolm Fraser: that Kerr had acted alone, that he had 'made up my mind, for my own part', that he had consulted no one, received no advice, and had reached 'an agonising decision' in lonely solitude.[10]

The insistent circulation of a flawed 'dismissal narrative' was more than just a collation of errors, misinterpretations, historical amnesia, or even conscious bias – although it was all of those things. This was a carefully crafted historical construction, an intervention in the process of history formation itself, through the deliberate withholding of information that would tell us otherwise and the repeated circulation of a version of events *that was known to be false.*

I went to see Sir Anthony Mason, twice. When I first approached him, while I was working on *Gough Whitlam: his time*, he replied cautiously, wanting to know exactly what I intended to raise with him: 'It is by no means clear to me why my recollections "would form an important part of the biography".' He agreed to see me, with one proviso, 'I am not willing, however, to discuss the events leading up to the Dismissal of the Whitlam government, including the advice given by Sir Garfield Barwick to the Governor-General'. By the time of our second meeting, I had found Kerr's record of their 'conversation', and so I knew why he had placed that firm condition before agreeing to see me. I asked him anyway.

Mason was charming, sharp, erudite, and wary. He was one of only two people still alive who could speak about the remaining secrets of the dismissal, and I found his refusal to discuss, much less acknowledge, his own role in the dismissal and his urge for self-protection, despite the immense public impact of his secret actions, deeply disturbing.[11] And so I asked him 'in the interests of history' to speak to me about those events. He refused, with the resounding words, 'I owe history nothing.'[12]

It struck me then, as it does now, as a statement of the most remarkable moral cowardice. Both Kerr and Mason were public officials, senior judicial and vice-regal figures, paid for by the public for much of their working lives, and yet they felt no compunction about misleading and dissembling even to the highest levels of elected government – to the prime minister, Gough Whitlam, at the time – and to the Australian public and our history since. Most shamefully, and it was this that shocked me most, these bearers of historical deception were prepared for the truth to come out, eventually, 'but not until after our deaths'.

Perhaps the best, or worst, example of the deliberate contrivance of history revealed in these archives are letters between Barwick and Kerr, seven years after the dismissal. As they recall their shared intervention, Kerr and Barwick reflect on the need to keep Mason's name and role in the dismissal from the public, thereby allowing this distorted and incomplete history to continue unchallenged. They write on the seventh anniversary of the dismissal, on 11 November 1982, reminiscing about their actions and about their knowledge of Mason's role. Barwick says to Kerr, 'I am not minded ... to disclose my conversation with Mason ... I feel strongly that the younger man [Mason] should not be involved'. Kerr replies: 'I have no desire to bring forward Mason's name, certainly not at this stage, though I feel that it may be desirable, before the history is finally written, for it to be known, ... *but not until after our deaths*'. [my emphasis][13]

I met the director-general of the National Archives, David Fricker, at a Whitlam Institute event in Sydney not long after the publication of the Mason 'conversation' in *Gough Whitlam: his time*, and he told me something quite remarkable. Having realised the significance of this history-changing document, the Archives had considered withdrawing it from public access, and with it my authority to publish from it. Had they done so, Mason's role would still remain secret today, and the flawed history of the dismissal would have continued unabated.

In the end, Fricker told me, the Archives recognised that withdrawing from public access a file that I had already been given access to, and had a copy of, would only have created an even greater furore than the document itself. I could only imagine the invidious position this would have placed me in. Had the Archives withdrawn the Mason file from public access, I would have been expected and required not to reveal it, to maintain the secrecy and the circulation of an historical narrative that I now knew to be false. The prospect was unthinkable.

This exchange was unsettling on several levels: in whose interests would a retrospective withdrawal from access of such a significant historical document have been? Not the Australian public, in whose name the Archives is meant to 'preserve, manage and make public' our historic archival records, and certainly not the history of the dismissal.[14] The only interests this could have served were the now-flawed legacies of Sir John Kerr and Sir Anthony Mason. And what role should that have in a decision by the Archives over public access to its most significant records?

It was the first hint of the conflicting pressures the Archives might face from requests to access its most important records about the dismissal.

After Mason, the floodgates opened as Kerr's dismissal deceptions tumbled from the archives. As every one of Kerr's claims about the dismissal collapsed into fiction, so too did its history: Kerr and Fraser *were* in secret telephone contact in the weeks before the dismissal, arranging the terms under which Kerr would then appoint Fraser as prime minister. 'Complete nonsense' Fraser had said on the day of the dismissal; 'false and ridiculous', according to Kerr. Whitlam *had* decided to call the half-Senate election, for which, the archives show, Kerr had finalised the paperwork and confirmed Whitlam's announcement to be made in the House of Representatives on the afternoon of 11 November 1975. And, finally, Whitlam had not 'raced to the Palace' to seek Kerr's recall as governor-general on hearing of his dismissal.[15]

I began to wonder whether there was anything about the dismissal of the Whitlam government that Kerr had been truthful about.

As the months stretched into years, this research was all-consuming, and the moral disorder of Kerr's papers was draining. I had become a captive of the archives, searching for something – and I didn't know what – that would make sense of the 'scraps of writing, scraps of cloth' as Hilary Mantel describes the lacunae from which we fashion a history.[16] Kerr's obsessive reworking, over and over, of the same incidents; his repeated versions of events, conversations, and episodes; and his search for vindication and validation were book-ended by his erratic denigrations of Whitlam, the prime minister towards whom he had maintained the constitutionally preposterous policy of 'silence', and against whom he decided to act in 'stealth'. Whitlam was 'dangerous', 'not open to reason', 'waging psychological warfare against me', 'the enemy'. The sheer banality of it, the moral torpor, told me to stop.

By the time I finished what I thought would be my last foray through Kerr's disturbed and disturbing papers, six years later, I was happy never to go back there.

What brought me back was a rare moment of archival reconstruction – finding a path to the Palace letters.

Chapter Two

'I never had any doubts about the Palace's attitude'

In 1980, from his lonely exile in England, Sir John Kerr began a journal. It was, like Kerr himself, fixed on his dismissal of the Whitlam government five years earlier, which he now cast as an inevitability of Gough Whitlam's own making, with Kerr himself the victim of Whitlam's 'euphoric megalomania', his 'lying and viciousness'.

The *Journal* was hand-written, self-absorbed, and short-lived. There were less than three months of scattered entries in Kerr's sloping hand across 158 pages, and, despite its brevity, it did not disappoint. What Kerr wrote was riveting. Those few entries dramatically contradicted his unfailing public stance that the Queen had known nothing about the dismissal, nor even about his planning for it, and raised again the lingering question of just what Kerr had told the Palace before he dismissed the Whitlam government, and what the Palace had said to him in return.

Kerr's fleeting *Journal* would become one of the most significant documents in the search for the Palace letters. It provided the first details of the content of the letters, and gave a window onto Kerr's relationship with the key players at the Palace – Charles, the Prince of Wales, the Queen, and in particular the Queen's private secretary, Sir Martin Charteris.[1]

The National Archives of Australia is housed in the understated elegance of the old art deco 'East Block', one of Canberra's earliest government buildings, which, together with its prosaically named bureaucratic twin, 'West Block', accommodated its first public servants, including Gough Whitlam's father, the Commonwealth crown solicitor Fred Whitlam. I sat for days in the calm of the light-filled reading room, its tall windows overlooking the changing autumn leaves, completely absorbed in the nondescript, red-bound, lined exercise book that served as Kerr's journal. It began on 1 January 1980 with an evocative, lyrical description of recently acquired snow-covered village life for Kerr and his second wife, Lady Anne (Nancy) Kerr:

> New Year's Day 1980. It is very cold in Surrey. Our second winter here. I sit writing this in the study Nancy created for me in our house in Oxshott. It is warmed by central heating but the frost lies thick outside, on the lawns and paths. Inside I wear my heavy navy blue guernsey which Nancy bought for me last year on the Island of Alderney when we went there for two weeks to revise the manuscript of Matters for Judgment. The cold welcomed us here on Saturday night when we arrived back here from the Amalfi Coast where we had a sparkling holiday for Xmas.

By the fifth page, Kerr had returned to his favoured theme, and the real reason for the *Journal*, his continuing preoccupations with Gough Whitlam, the dismissal, and his frequent letters to the Queen, which, he had been assured, were 'welcomed in the Palace'. The *Journal*'s legibility declined markedly after Kerr's numerous luncheons in select London clubs, invariably accompanied by the visiting Liberal–National Party identities tasked with keeping him happily ensconced in England, away from Australia and feeling part of the inner circle of political trust around the Fraser government. In reality, he was neither happy nor trusted. Their visits were strained, leavened only by lunch, and Fraser himself was always too busy, too rushed, to find the time to see the reluctantly retired former governor-general.[2]

Kerr's preferred tipple was at the exclusive Carlton Club, the foundation home of the British Conservative Party, whose approbation he craved and membership of which he was soon granted on the nomination of Lord Hailsham, the chancellor in the Conservative Margaret Thatcher government, and Lord Carrington, Thatcher's foreign secretary and a close friend of Malcolm Fraser. Kerr had been warmly welcomed by the titled and the entitled among the British Conservative establishment at a celebratory Britain–Australia Society Dinner in London, just two months after the dismissal. The Queen's private secretary, Sir Martin Charteris, was there, as was the former Conservative prime minister Edward Heath, who scribbled on the back of his place-card and pushed it across the table to Kerr. 'You are now revealed as being in the hands of the Establishment', wrote Heath to the insecure, intemperate son of a boilermaker; as if there could be no better place on all this earth than right there, at that moment, in *their* hands.

Oblivious to the condescension, Kerr placed the name-card with its precious six words of a gently mocking entrée to another world among his papers, as a memento for posterity to know his imagined place in the annals of conservative history. Now he was one of them. Oh, happy day!

From Kerr's first statement hours after the dismissal, it had been a foundational pillar of the dismissal history that he had had no prior contact with the Palace about the prospect of Whitlam's dismissal – not with the Queen, Prince Charles, or the Queen's private secretary, Sir Martin Charteris. As Sir William Heseltine, the Queen's assistant private secretary at the time, still insisted decades later, 'The governor-general gave no clue to any of us at the Palace what was in his mind'.[3] Kerr's *Journal* tells us otherwise.

The most startling entries concern Kerr's communications with the Palace in the months before the dismissal. Kerr recounts a series of exchanges, some of which were in the file of the embargoed 'Palace letters', in which the prospect of the dismissal of the government was canvassed. In his entry for 13 March 1980, Kerr describes a conversation with Prince Charles in Port Moresby where, in a tableau of Shakespearean proportions, all the key players in the dismissal were present at the invitation of the prime minister, Gough Whitlam, for the Papua New Guinea Independence Day celebrations. There, Kerr confided to Charles that he was considering dismissing the government and his great fear that Whitlam might recall him as governor-general if the prime minister became aware of Kerr's intentions – which would not have been an unreasonable response by Whitlam, had he known of Kerr's collusions and contemplation of his dismissal – yet which never transpired.

Kerr describes Charles's response to the prospect of this extreme vice-regal action against an elected government as one of concern – not for the fate of the elected government, but for Kerr's position: 'But surely Sir John, the Queen should not have to accept advice that you should be recalled ... *should this happen when you were considering having to dismiss the government*'. [my italics]

The impact of that single sentence was immediate and dramatic – what Atkins calls a 'syncopal kick' to the dismissal history as we knew it.[4] There were two aspects that shocked. First, Kerr had, by his own description, told Charles that he was 'considering having to dismiss the government' – and he had told him this in September 1975, two months before the dismissal and one month before supply was even blocked in the Senate. If this exchange had indeed taken place, then Kerr's planning for Whitlam's dismissal had been longer, more organised, and more extensive than anyone had previously imagined.

Second, and even more disturbing, was Charles's response. Kerr quotes Charles's solicitous reply that 'surely' the Queen 'should not have to accept' Whitlam's advice – that is, the monarch should not have to accept the advice of her Australian prime minister on the tenure of a governor-general, 'when you were considering dismissing the Prime Minister'. This was a startling proposition from our future monarch, a return to the imperial power of the Crown over the appointment of dominion governors-general not seen since the Imperial Conferences of 1926 and 1930, and a direct intervention in the Australian political process. Kerr writes that Prince Charles then relayed this critical conversation with Kerr to the Queen's private secretary, Sir Martin Charteris, and from Charteris the details were passed on to the Queen. From Kerr's own pen, the Palace knew of his planning, and they knew this was being kept secret from the prime minister, Gough Whitlam; yet they neither urged Kerr to speak to Whitlam, his constitutional advisor and responsible minister under the central tenet of the Westminster system, nor withdrew from this intensely political discussion. Instead, they engaged with it.

From this point on, by Kerr's own account, the Palace was a part of his considerations of options and planning. In this, they were not alone. Kerr's *modus operandi* throughout these months was to bring key institutions and individuals – Mason, Barwick, and Fraser – into his closely knit circle of those who gave advice and had prior knowledge of the possibility of dismissal, ensuring at least their quiescence and at best their support. Through this dendritic web of secrecy, Kerr ensured his own protection legally, politically, and royally. His journal *qua* royal reflections unmasked the extent to which he likewise drew the Palace into his planning, alerting them to the prospect of his dismissal of the Whitlam government and his imagined need for their protection.

Kerr's *Journal* came to a meandering end on 13 March 1980 with a lengthy entry reprising his one great obsession about the dismissal – that Whitlam might have recalled him as governor-general had he known that Kerr was planning to dismiss him. Kerr's continuing focus on this singular point years after the dismissal was a necessary *post facto* justification for the unjustifiable – his 'policy of silence' toward the prime minister, for which he had been roundly condemned. Kerr was at pains to present this not as fear but as fact, as real and 'not academic'. He insisted still, more than four years after the dismissal, that Whitlam *would have* recalled him – 'this he undoubtedly would have done' – even though by then it was clear that Whitlam had not. In this final rumination on his fear for his own position, and the correctness, courage, and inevitability of his actions, Kerr gave a rare insight into what he called 'my relationship with the Prince of Wales' and on the nature of his correspondence with the Queen, through Charteris. The contents of the Palace letters were beginning to emerge.

In his lengthy final entry, Kerr quotes directly from Charteris's response to the concern he had raised with Prince Charles regarding his recall. Not for the first time with Kerr's papers, I could scarcely believe what I was reading. I returned again and again to those final pages in Kerr's sprawling, sloping hand, checking every word of the scenario he presented. When a document is so completely at odds with every public statement made by those involved, belief is suspended, if only for a moment, and it takes time not only to read it, but to shift the historical frame and *see* it.

With the Palace now aware of the possibility of Whitlam's dismissal, it then became a part of Kerr's planning, as he described it. Early in October 1975, the Queen's private secretary, Sir Martin Charteris, wrote to Kerr setting out a means of dealing with the contingency Kerr had first raised with Charles, to salve his concerns and to deal with the prime minister's possible advice to recall him. I checked the name, Sir Martin Charteris, and the date, October 1975, and realised that this critical letter detailed by Kerr in his *Journal* was one of the embargoed Palace letters, locked in the National Archives, to which I had been denied access. And here it was, described in detail in Kerr's *Journal.*

From that letter alone, it was obvious that the Palace letters would have an extraordinary story to tell about the dismissal, if only we could see them. Until then, I would have to make do with this snippet from Kerr's description of Charteris's letter of October 1975 about his fear of recall: 'When the Prince of Wales was home he talked to Sir Martin Charteris about it, and Martin wrote me a letter early in October. ... [Martin said that] ... if the kind of contingency in mind were to develop ... the Queen would try to delay things.' I let these words sink in, *'the Queen would try to delay things'*, unpacking them piece by piece like a jigsaw in reverse, and let them fall, to be put back together once all the other pieces had been found, to tell a new story, a new history: one of intrigue, deception, and dismissal. As a senior government source put it to me, that letter from Charteris, if it existed, was not only shocking; it 'would show that they were complicit'. Only the Palace letters could tell us whether this was so; but with the Queen's embargo firmly in place, that was impossible to know.

Certainly, this critical advice from Charteris was seen by Kerr as giving him support and protection. He later confided to Sir Walter Crocker, the arch imperialist *manqué* lieutenant-governor of South Australia, that he knew exactly how the Palace would deal with his consuming fear of recall by Whitlam: *'entre nous,* for good reasons, I never had any doubt about what the Palace's attitude was on this important point'. Because, '*entre nous*', the Palace had already told him.[5]

From Kerr's account in his *Journal*, the Palace had re-entered the Australian domestic political space as though it were still the imperial master and Australia a mere colonial upstart, despite all the former dominions being 'equal and autonomous communities' in the Commonwealth. At the heart of this, formalised at the 1926 Imperial Conference, is the 'constitutional practice' that the monarch 'acts on the advice of responsible Ministers' in the dominion concerned. So much of this political relationship, both within Australia and residually between Australia and the United Kingdom, remained in the realm of 'convention' – inevitably disputed in law and presumed in politics. However, the imperial conferences at which the dominions passed to full autonomy set out precisely, neither by convention nor law, but by specification, what the relationship was between the Queen and the prime minister in relation to the tenure of the governor-general. The appointment and recall of a governor-general was unambiguously prescribed at the 1930 Imperial Conference as 'a matter in regard to which His Majesty is advised by His Ministers in the Dominion concerned'.[6]

In 1975, for the Queen to discuss the question of the governor-general's tenure with anyone other than her 'Minister in the dominion concerned' – the Australian prime minister – let alone to determine in advance not to act immediately on the prime minister's advice, was an unassailable breach of that elemental relationship, and an affront to our national autonomy. It belied the royal insistence that the Queen is always 'strictly neutral' and plays no part in political matters.

This arrangement was for Kerr both an affirmation and a facilitation, smoothing his way towards the dismissal free of his greatest concern, over his own possible recall.

By the time I had finished unpacking Kerr's *Journal* in 2012, I was in no doubt about the extraordinary historical significance of the Palace letters, and perturbed by their embargo by the Queen, which was preventing us from knowing the full story of the dismissal, even forty years later. The Palace letters were integral to our history, and yet I had met an absolute dead-end. Original documents are fundamental to historical research – none more so than for contested histories. Returning to those contemporaneous records strips away the patina of error and distortion built up over years and cemented into written, received history, and enables a powerful historical corrective to emerge. That this bedrock of historical information, the original documents themselves, were still being kept hidden from us decades later was disheartening.

As 'personal records', the Palace letters did not come under the *Archives Act*, so I could not appeal to the Administrative Appeals Tribunal. There was simply no way to challenge the Archives' designation of the letters as 'personal' other than by undertaking a prohibitive Federal Court action. It was a powerful legal Catch-22.

I was working through the last of Kerr's papers in 2015 while finishing my book *The Dismissal Dossier*, which was an encapsulation of every forgotten, ignored, contested, and newly uncovered element in the transformation of the dismissal history. The book brought together every essential detail about that much misunderstood and misrepresented episode through an archival research trail that had now hit an impenetrable road-block set up around these vital, unattainable Palace letters.

Both as a historian and as an Australian whose history these letters tell, this was a personal affront and a national humiliation. I wanted to access the letters, to read them, to write about them. I wanted to know our history. Kerr's *Journal* had given me just a hint of their explosive content, a portent of the political storm that would accompany their release if ever it were secured. The

Queen's embargo over the Palace letters was beginning to make perfect sense.

The name of the file, 'Miscellanous handwritten notes', gave no hint of its significance. I requested it cold, from the title alone, never knowing, as with all these files, whether it would bring another piece to the puzzle, or just the latest iteration of Kerr's rotating preoccupations with long-past conversations, meaningless asides, incidents, and individuals still ghosting his past.[7]

The slim white folder emerged at the window of the reading room, and from it a single, slightly crumpled sheet of foolscap paper – on which, handwritten on both sides, and much amended with numerous scratchings, Kerr had listed fourteen points. The top five of these, under the simple heading 'Dismissal', all related to his discussions with the Palace, matching the chronology set out in his *Journal*.

The first point was his conversation with Geoffrey Yeend, the deputy secretary of the Department of Prime Minister and Cabinet, about Kerr's recurrent preoccupation, his possible recall by Whitlam – the conversation that Kerr claimed set him on the path of seeking to protect his position as governor-general. The points then cascaded in chronological order through his contacts with Prince Charles, and the conversations within the Palace about it, to Charteris's contact with him. 'New Guinea – Prince of W', and 'my relations with the Prince of Wales' at point 3 were followed by 'Prince's conversation with MC' [Martin Charteris] at point four.

Then came six of the most important words in the history of the dismissal, which, if true, would finally render untenable the claim of royal ignorance and passivity about the dismissal. At point number five, Kerr had written: 'Charteris' advice to me on dismissal'. There was simply no way around the dramatic implications of those six very precise words. Not only did the Palace know about the prospect of Kerr's dismissal of the Whitlam government, but the Queen's private secretary, Sir Martin Charteris, had given Kerr 'advice' about it. The chain of communication from Kerr to the Palace and back to Kerr could hardly have been clearer.

The critical factor is that all these vice-regal exchanges took place *without the knowledge of the prime minister*, Gough Whitlam, towards whom Kerr had determined on the unthinkable path of 'remaining silent', of 'playing his cards close to his chest'. What these notes reveal is that, while keeping the prime minister, his chief advisor, in the dark, Kerr was discussing the possibility of the government's dismissal with the Queen, her private secretary, and Prince Charles, all of whom, as the Palace itself insists, must play no role in Australian politics. And yet there it was: *'Charteris' advice to me on dismissal'*.

In February 1980, Kerr contacted Buckingham Palace, seeking a meeting with the Queen's then private secretary, Sir Philip Moore, to discuss the Palace letters. Specifically, he wanted them to be released. Kerr had always wanted his letters to the Queen published, believing they would support his disputed version of those events and his decision to dismiss Whitlam.

The letters had been lodged by the official secretary, David Smith, in 1978 on Kerr's behalf, with the conditions specified by Smith accepted by the National Archives as Kerr's own conditions of access. If these were indeed Kerr's conditions, he had soon changed his mind. Just two years later, over the same months that he was writing his *Journal*, Kerr was trying to change those conditions and have the release of the letters brought forward.

This parallel timing makes the few months of *Journal* entries particularly illuminating. When I first tried to gain access to those letters, I had been denied by the Archives on the grounds that they were Kerr's 'personal' records, and that access was controlled by the conditions set by him and could therefore only be changed by him. It was completely baffling, then, to see from his *Journal* that Kerr had had no more success in getting his own 'personal' correspondence with the Queen opened than I had.

An anomaly had now emerged about the 'personal' nature of these letters. The National Archives claimed they were embargoed under the Instrument of Deposit governing access set by Kerr himself. Yet how could this be Kerr's own instrument if Kerr himself did not agree with its terms, could not change it, and did not even seem to be aware of its terms?

Kerr wrote in his *Journal* that he was 'most anxious' that the Palace letters be released during his children's lifetime – 'If it is possible I should like access to be given to the letters during the lifetime of my children and Nancy's' – as he came under increasing criticism for his failure to either warn or consult with Whitlam. He was not about to give up on making them public.

First, Kerr contacted Geoffrey Yeend, head of the Department of Prime Minister and Cabinet, and Sir Robert Menzies' former private secretary, 'who had become a friend', to discuss 'the Palace correspondence'. Kerr suggested the release of only his letters to the Queen, and not her replies, and of these he sought to release only 'relevant extracts'. Yeend was unmoved:

> He could see no way in which the relevant extracts from that correspondence could be published. His view was that the Palace would never agree and said that even if the Palace did the PMs department never would agree.[8]

Kerr persisted. His determination to see the Palace letters released had made him something of a loose cannon, and he then did the unthinkable – he made a direct approach to the Palace, visiting Sir Philip Moore to discuss the letters and plead his case. Moore was horrified at the suggestion that any part of this correspondence, whether Kerr's or the Queen's, might be published, and dismissed it out of hand.

So here's the perplexing thing – according to the Archives, these letters were Kerr's 'personal' records and he had set the access conditions for them, and yet Kerr obviously had no control over the release even of extracts from them. He could not publish them, he could not expedite their release, and they could remain closed against his wishes at the insistence of others. How could any of this be the case if the letters were indeed his 'personal' records and his personal property?

History is an endless tussle with the past and what we know about it – and what we don't yet know about it. These documents – the *Journal*, Kerr's notes and his reflections, and his 'points on dismissal' – are a self-referential archival story. They link together in such a way that the meaning of any one of them only becomes clear when each of them is known, reconstituted, and reconsidered. This additive process exemplifies the mosaic nature of archival research: several files when pieced together can reveal a picture that no single file could explain alone, as these files eventually did.

Not long after I began my excursion into Kerr's papers, I opened an unidentified file, simply titled 'Extracts from letters'.[9] Such vague, equivocal files in the papers could also be the most instructive, their secrets hidden behind inconsequential titles. The extracts were unidentified – just seven short extracts with six different dates, typed – and each one described meetings, conversations, and incidents about political developments in Australia in the weeks before and the week after the dismissal. All that I could tell with certainty was that these were extracts of letters between 20 September and 20 November 1975. There was no indication on its face of who had written them, or to whom.

However, my identification of Kerr as their author was straightforward. That was apparent at once from the second extract, dated 17 October, which recounted a short exchange between Gough Whitlam and Kerr at an official dinner for the visiting Malaysian prime minister, Tun Razak. Kerr had written about this in his memoirs, as had Whitlam in *The Truth of the Matter*. Kerr had felt aggrieved and offended by Whitlam's jocular aside in relation to the stand-off over supply in the Senate, when he had said, 'It could be a question of whether I get to the Queen first for your recall or you get in first with my dismissal.' Kerr would cite this quip as evidence of Whitlam's intention to recall him; Whitlam would cite it as evidence of nothing more than an after-dinner joke.

The penultimate extract, of 11 November 1975, set out Kerr's version of his dismissal of Whitlam in his Yarralumla study, just as he had described it in *Matters for Judgment*.

Identifying to whom it was that Kerr was writing was more difficult. From the extracts alone it was impossible to tell, and for a time I was stumped. The tone of the letters provided a clue – it was deferential rather than familiar, and almost nervous. This was someone to whom Kerr was in thrall. The content of the extracts provided another clue: the recipient had to be someone to whom these bland details of otherwise insignificant episodes involving Kerr and various political identities would be of interest, and there couldn't have been too many of them. Who would be interested in Kerr's prosaic descriptions of conversations with the prime minister, with the leader of the opposition, an after-dinner joke, details of his attendance at an official reception at Government House in Victoria, or a brief exchange with the prime minister regarding Papua New Guinea? *Not many people*, I thought. That narrowed it down appreciably. From the tone and their focus, I wondered whether they might have been written to Sir Robert Menzies. Whatever they were and whomever they were to, the extracts revealed little that was not already on the public record. I put them aside and opened another file.

It was a year later, as I read Kerr's *Journal* describing events at Port Moresby, that those words kept coming back to me in a persistent, irritating echo of something I had read before. I searched back through my notes and, sure enough, there they were. Kerr's direct quotations from his letters to the Palace written up in his *Journal* matched two of these unidentified extracts – from 17 October 1975 and from 11 November 1975. So the unidentified 'extracts of letters' were extracts from the secret Palace letters.

Duplicitous to the end, and desperate to have these extracts released, Kerr had circumvented the Palace's strictures against publication by leaving a copy of them among his papers for someone – in this case, me – to find and release, despite the insistence of the Palace that they were to remain closed. In his own way, Kerr had also avoided the 'personal' label placed on these letters by David Smith and accepted by the National Archives, by ensuring their availability should they be located and identified.

Having identified the extracts as seven short extracts of Kerr's letters to the Palace, their description as 'personal' seemed entirely insupportable. There was no part of these extracts that could be described as anything other than official – in their nature, their tone, and their style. None revealed even a moment of informality, of light-hearted or private reflection. Each considered in some way the prospect of the unprecedented vice-regal action of removing the government that Kerr was to take. These were clearly Commonwealth records masquerading as personal ones.

It seemed that the Queen's correspondence was sacrosanct and that it remained closed neither because it was genuinely personal, nor because Kerr wanted it, but simply because the Queen had instructed it. The imperial presumption of royal secrecy was alive and well, even in the former colonies. So, as I faced the brick wall of archival intransigence over the elusive *AA1984/609* file and its twin copy, *M4513*, *'Personal and private correspondence between the Governor-General and the Palace'*, I had no doubt that the Palace letters were of the greatest historical importance, and I had no hope of ever being able to see them.

Then I read Sydney barrister Tom Brennan's blog, 'Australia owns its history'.

Chapter Three

'Australia owns its history'

Tom Brennan was affable, curious about what I had found in Kerr's papers, and convinced of the possibility of a legal challenge. I had called in to see him on 10 December 2015, just days after reading his article 'Australia owns its history', which called for the release of the Palace letters. 'We Australians do not need to ask the British Monarch for her consent to our accessing that history: our Parliament secured that for us in 1983', Tom had written.[1] At last! Here was a call to apply Australian law, our own *Archives Act*, to the Palace letters – and not a quasi-colonial plea to the Queen to release them.

I was so surprised to read Tom's article, given the popular view circulating at the time that the prime minister should go cap in hand and deferentially ask the Queen's permission to access our own historical records, that I wrote to him at once: 'I read your very interesting piece on the question of the status of the embargoed "Palace letters" from and to the Governor General Sir John Kerr … which I agree with entirely.'[2] I happened to be in Sydney, another coincidence, and we arranged to meet the next day. From this serendipitous, almost accidental, contact, there would follow five years of legal argument, royal intrigue, Archival obstruction, and court hearings to secure the release of the Palace letters.

Tom was in his chambers on the thirteenth floor of Wentworth Chambers in the heart of Sydney's legal precinct. Law courts, chambers, and cafés with lawyerly names like 'Legal Grounds' and 'Silks' ran the length of Phillip Street from the miraculously preserved, now incongruous paean to colonial austerity and ingenuity of St James' Church, dwarfed by the Law Courts building dominating it all, to the angular glass tower of Chifley Square on Bridge Street where the old Tank Stream once ran down to Sydney Harbour. Tom was optimistic and inquisitive, and seemed always on the verge of laughter, at which his shoulders would move up and down in silent synchronicity. It was difficult not to be as excited about the legal possibilities as he was.

So many basic questions remained unanswered about the letters. We knew that there were two versions of them in the Archives – the *AA* file with the originals, and the *M* file with the copies, each deposited at different times and each termed 'personal'. Each of these should therefore also have had its own Instrument of Deposit made at the time they were lodged with the Archives. The perplexing thing was that the Archives had only ever referred to one Instrument, which it called 'Sir John Kerr's Instrument of Deposit', provided by David Smith in 1978 with the original letters. How could we be certain that this also covered access to the copies of the letters that were deposited nineteen years later?

The inadvertent catalogue entry for the copy file had given me a way into the Archives' record system that I had been unable to penetrate through the closed *AA* file of originals. The catalogue entry had given me the sliver of light I needed – an open copy of a closed file. By requesting access to the open copy file in 2011, I had entered an all-important bureaucratic tangle, a way through the maze of Archival obfuscation. The Archives now had to provide me with reasons for its shock decision to peremptorily close the copy file.

The only reason given to me in 2011 for this startling shift from 'open' to 'closed', had been a simple assertion – 'these letters are personal and private correspondence between the Governor-General and Her Majesty the Queen, not subject to the *Archives Act*'. In other words, with marvellously circular reasoning, the Palace letters were closed because they were royal letters, and royal letters were personal, and therefore they were closed. Critically, the Archives had failed to inform me of my review rights, to which I was entitled.

On Tom's advice, I again wrote to the Archives in December 2015, requesting a review of the decision four years earlier denying me access to the copy file.[3] This began a chain of new material from the Archives about the Palace letters, with each new detail pointing to another document, another file, some previously unknown 'advice' or arrangement that we could follow up to keep the search alive. And then, bingo! Some other documents emerged. Archives replied, confirming its decision to close the copy file and remove it from public view, entirely as expected. What was far more important was that this time it also referred to two documents in support of that decision – each of which I could now request and pursue.[4] I felt like I had finally grasped the end of a piece of thread that was unravelling fast as the edifice of royal secrecy slowly began to fall.

In again denying me access to the copies, Archives referred to two documents: advice from the governor-general's official secretary to the Archives in 1991, and 'Sir John Kerr's Instrument of Deposit which sets out conditions of access to personal letters'. No other Instrument of Deposit was mentioned. It was now claimed that what Archives termed 'Kerr's Instrument of Deposit', provided and signed by David Smith in 1978, had covered *both* the originals and the copy file. This sounded reasonable enough at first glance, but actually made no sense. The copy file had been lodged with the Archives nearly a decade after Kerr's death and two decades after the original Palace letters had been lodged – so how could Kerr's

Instrument of Deposit, written in 1978, also apply to documents lodged after his death by someone else?

It would be six months before the truth of the access conditions governing the Palace letters and their copies was finally confirmed, and with it the real reason why Archives had kept those conditions hidden from me until legal proceedings forced their hand.

Meanwhile, information sent to me from Government House told a different story again. In September 2015, I had decided to pursue one final avenue to secure the letters. I wrote to the official secretary to the governor-general of Australia, Sir Peter Cosgrove, and submitted a Freedom of Information request seeking the release of 'Correspondence during 1974–5 between Sir John Kerr and members of the Queen's family and staff – including Queen Elizabeth II herself, Charles, Prince of Wales and the Queen's Private Secretary, Sir Martin Charteris'.

The official secretary's response brought another surprise and further confusion, and introduced a vital new element into this morass of bureaucratic twists by directly contradicting the advice I had received from the Archives. Archives had always claimed that it was Kerr himself who had embargoed the Palace letters, according to his own 'Instrument of Deposit' in 1978. My FOI request elicited something quite different. According to Government House, it was not Kerr who had embargoed the letters at all; it was the Queen.

'The files are under strict embargo', the official secretary informed me, 'at Her Majesty The Queen's instruction.'[5] I stared at this for some time, wondering whether I had misread it or misunderstood it, and not for the first time I was momentarily shocked, perplexed, and increasingly angry. So intent were these two major public institutions on denying access to the Palace letters, at any cost and on any grounds, that they hadn't even bothered to get their stories straight. You could be forgiven for thinking, as I did then and still do, that in relation to royal matters, Government House and the Archives believe they should defer to the wishes of the monarch.

Suddenly, Kerr's 'personal' documents were not so personal at all – since it now appeared that he didn't even control them. The implications of this remnant imperial control over our historical records were profound: Australia did not control access to key historical documents in our National Archives; the Queen did, even though those documents related to the extent of prior knowledge of the Queen and the Palace regarding Kerr's dismissal of the government. This unassailable conflict of interest lies at the heart of the Palace letters case.

So, whose conditions were they – Sir John Kerr's or the Queen's? At the time, this question seemed academic. Whoever had put the conditions on the original letters or the copy file, the outcome was the same – there would be no access. However, the response to my FOI request was the first indication to me that these were not Kerr's personal conditions blocking access to the letters, but the Queen's. This made the central claim that the Palace letters were Kerr's personal records and not Commonwealth records far more difficult to sustain, since it was now clear that, even before his death, Kerr did not have control over either the letters or his own Instrument of Deposit. That would be a critical point in any legal challenge.

From my first meeting with Tom Brennan, things had moved quickly. Every new document strengthened his view that the denial of access to the letters could be challenged and that a legal case had a genuine chance of success. The only way was to initiate proceedings in the Federal Court of Australia. This was an expensive, onerous, and extremely risky process, particularly for a self-funded litigant facing an organisational behemoth of the National Archives, Government House and Buckingham Palace.

Brennan didn't hold back on the severity of the prospect of costs in any legal action against the Archives: 'Costs can be awarded against you if you lose … You would want to be confident of winning if you were to incur the risks of costs.'[6] Winning such a case would in turn depend on 'whether there was evidence to establish that the [Palace letters] file contains material which is official and not personal … My sense is that there is plenty of material of that kind.' It was made very clear to me that regardless of how positive we assessed the chances of success to be, I faced the risk of a significant adverse cost order, directing me to pay at least part of, and possibly all, the Archives' costs should I not succeed. The prospect of this risk stretched beyond the Federal Court since, even if I succeeded, we fully expected that the National Archives would appeal the case all the way to the High Court.

Although the question of legal action was on the table from the outset, I pushed it aside for as long as I could, to be dealt with when the decision absolutely had to be made. For now, there were documents to collect, records to search for, and a case to be made.

I spent the new year of 2016 putting together a report on the Palace letters. Tom Brennan had asked me to prepare a short document setting out the main evidence from my researches that the letters were Commonwealth records and not personal. I drew on the key documents I had identified from Kerr's papers: sections from his *Journal*, including his discussions with Prince Charles; the 'contingency' arrangement with Charteris dealing with Kerr's concern about his own recall, and his fruitless visits to Sir Philip Moore urging the release of the letters; the 'Extracts of letters' file containing extracts from some of the Palace letters; and a chapter from Kerr's autobiography, *Matters for Judgment*, in which he described the letters in clearly official terms as 'despatches' and as his 'duty' to the Queen.[7] I sent the document and its attachments to Wentworth Chambers, and waited.

By late January, while most lawyers were still enjoying their summer break, Tom was preparing a formal legal Opinion, arguing that the Palace letters were Commonwealth records and assessing the prospects of success for a case against the National Archives that challenged its denial of access to them. The Opinion, which Tom had prepared on a *pro bono* basis, rested on the key definition of 'Commonwealth record' in the *Archives Act* – 'property of the Commonwealth or a Commonwealth institution' – and centred on the identification of the letters as the property of the Commonwealth. Our case never veered from this key definitional argument: the letters were prepared in the course of Kerr's duties as governor-general, they were the property of the Commonwealth, and therefore they were Commonwealth records.

The legal arguments about the nature of the property – the paper on which the letters were written or copied, the photocopier on which the copies were made, the fact that the official secretary had made the copies in Yarralumla – detailed in the Opinion all remained central to the case as it later unfolded. The fact that the letters had been lodged by the official secretary, David Smith, after Kerr had left office also pointed to their official nature.

The Archives' view, by contrast, rested essentially on a claim of British practice – a 'convention' of royal secrecy over the Queen's correspondence.[8] Here was a colonial relic, if ever there was one: the British practice of retaining royal documents separate from the public National Archives, in their own Royal Archives in the 'round tower at Windsor', was unproblematically mapped onto the Australian Archives. This essence of the Archives' case would also remain largely unchanged as the case unfolded, augmented with claims of longstanding convention, but essentially just as the National Archives had put it to me in its initial denial of access to the Palace letters.

Tom's detailed knowledge of the difficult legislative history of the *Archives Bill* under the Fraser government was critical. Having run several cases focusing on FOI law and the *Archives Act*, he knew the intricacies of the passage of the Bill as it became bogged down in committee over the very issue of access to the governor-general's correspondence with the Queen. Perhaps unsurprisingly, Malcolm Fraser had worked with Government House and David Smith in an effort to ensure that the Palace letters would not come under the terms of the *Archives Bill*: they would be excised from public access under a proposed exemption of the governor-general's records. In a reflection of the lingering divisions within conservative circles over the dismissal, Liberal senator Alan Missen, who had strongly opposed the blocking of supply and Kerr's dismissal of the Whitlam government, and was chair of the Senate standing committee considering the Bill, refused to accept the total exclusion of the governor-general's records.

The Bill remained in limbo as amendments were put forward and compromises proposed, all of them trying to insulate the governor-general's records from public access, until, in 1982, Missen announced that he intended to support the Labor opposition's amendments to bring all records of the governor-general under the *Archives Bill* in order for it to pass. Rather than risk the amendment succeeding, the Fraser government chose not to proceed with the Bill. And there the *Archives Bill* remained until 1983, when Fraser called an ill-advised snap election.

Soon after the election of the Labor government led by Bob Hawke, the *Archives Act 1983* was finally passed, five years after it had first been introduced. With the change of government, the Bill had also undergone a highly significant change: in its final version, the *Archives Act* made no express exemption for the records of governors-general. If the Act had been passed as Malcolm Fraser had intended, none of the transformative revelations from Kerr's papers could have been released, and Sir Anthony Mason's role would still be unknown today.

I was in the middle of an extraordinary process in which my archive-driven historical research was being transformed into a legal case, and it was fascinating. Part of me wanted to sign up there and then just to see how this rare alchemy of law, politics, and history would come together and where it would end up.

My greatest hesitation was the simple and pedestrian one of cost: it was huge. The prospect of a Federal Court action, opposed by the National Archives with its vast organisational resources, including its own legal department, the government solicitor's office, the solicitor-general, and Government House, with likely input from Buckingham Palace, and the possible intervention of the federal attorney-general, was impossible for me even to contemplate.

Although the public interest in the case was clear, this was not the usual type of matter that was more commonly the subject of public-litigation funding arrangements. Our concern was with history and public access to key primary documents; it was closer to matters of open government, accountability, and transparency, and neither litigation funders nor court orders for public-interest protection were likely to cover it. While there was a good chance the court would acknowledge the public-interest dimension and set aside any adverse costs should I not succeed, that was by no means certain. In which case, I could still be left with enormous adverse costs. That was a risk I couldn't take.

There was no rush to make a final decision, and there were other documents still to come from the Archives. I would wait, gauge our final chances of success, based on all the relevant documents, and then decide. At least that's what I kept telling myself, all the way to the Federal Court.

It was Tom Brennan's offer to work on the case *pro bono* that convinced me. As he later described it, 'The proposition that there's a slice of history we could never read, simply because it's between the Queen and the governor-general, seemed to me profoundly anti-democratic and inconsistent with the Australian Constitution's system of responsible government. It's of profound public interest.'[9] This was not only a great act of generosity, but it was a rare opportunity – to take on an historic case that had come together through an unexpected confluence of circumstances and interests unlikely to occur again, to secure the release of royal letters about the dismissal, to apply Australian law over infuriating residual imperial presumptions, and to know our history and the full details of the dismissal of the Whitlam government. Walk away from that? Not a chance.

Within a week we had secured the interest of Antony Whitlam QC, Gough Whitlam's eldest son, and James Whittaker, managing partner of Corrs Chambers Westgarth, one of the largest law firms in Sydney. They were interested and prepared to take the case on a *pro bono* basis, and wanted to meet before making a final decision. This was not my usual field, and I felt strangely untethered as things moved quickly around me, as if they were happening to someone else and I was watching on with great interest, my knees knocking under the table.

On 5 February 2016, we all met by email, the first time the legal team came together, and laid some critical groundwork. An important decision was to take action under s39B of the *Judiciary Act*, which had the distinct advantage of operating with no time limit on the commencement of proceedings. This would give us much-needed time to gather more documents and more archival evidence. We all agreed that the more documents we could get from the Archives, both here and from the UK National Archives, the better our chances would be of finding something that would help show that the letters were Commonwealth records. Antony Whitlam suggested that the first step was to follow the trail of documents, to write to the Archives and request each of the documents referred to in its decision to close the copy file: 'Kerr's Instrument of Deposit', and the 1991 advice to Archives from the official secretary to the governor-general.

On 18 February, James Whittaker, partner at Corrs Chambers Westgarth, wrote to the National Archives requesting a copy of those two documents. The letter began, 'We act for Professor Jennifer Hocking'. I felt myself sliding ineluctably, frictionless and heedless, into the vast legal vortex of a Federal Court action.

After everything I had found in Kerr's papers, I thought I had long since ceased to be shocked by any new deception or falsehood relating to Whitlam's dismissal, and yet I would be shocked again at every turn. The Archives' response to James's letter would be the latest in a long line of responses to cause me dismay and confusion: it now presented us with yet another version of the Instrument of Deposit governing access to the Palace letters and their copies. The Archives had told me in 2011, and had confirmed in 2015, that the letters were governed by 'Sir John Kerr's Instrument of Deposit'; Government House had told me they were embargoed on the instructions of the Queen; and the Archives now produced a different Instrument of Deposit altogether, and claimed that this was the reason for the denial of access to the copies of the Palace letters.

This latest Instrument of Deposit was dated 29 March 2004, a decade after Kerr's death. The name of the person who had deposited the copy file of letters with Kerr's personal papers in the Archives, and the signatory to the Instrument, had both been redacted by Archives. It was not even clear, therefore, who had deposited the copies, nor who had responsibility for them.

Astonishingly, this Instrument of Deposit simply stated that *all* of Kerr's personal papers were to be opened after thirty years, directly contradicting Archives' previous reason for denial of access. There were no exceptions and no qualifications.

This was completely different from the advice I had twice received from the Archives. The latest documents did not support what the Archives had told me in 2011 and confirmed in 2015, namely that the copies of the letters were covered by 'specific instructions' and were to remain closed under the same conditions as the originals of the Palace letters. It was now clear that this was simply untrue. The file should have been released to me when I first requested it in 2011, let alone when I asked again in 2015.

'These documents significantly improve your prospects', wrote Tom Brennan with excellent legal restraint. They did more than this; they made the likely success of our case as close to definitive as could be. There was now no basis for the denial of access to the 'personal' copy file of the letters. If the court found the letters to be 'personal', the copies would have to be opened according to the terms of the latest Instrument; on the other hand, if they were found to be Commonwealth records, the originals would have to be opened, as the 30-year public-access period for Commonwealth records had already long passed.

If it sounded like a rare win-win scenario, that's because it was.

On the strength of this dramatic development, we all met for the first time in person at Corrs Chambers Westgarth in Sydney. I took the lift to the 17th floor, gasped as the doors opened onto a spectacular proximate view of Sydney harbour and the harbour bridge, and was shown to a conference room with Antony Whitlam QC, Tom Brennan, and James Whittaker and Tim Bunker from Corrs. I had met Antony some years before when I interviewed him as I was working on my biography of Gough Whitlam. He was, like his father, methodical, erudite, and extremely well read and, less like his father, measured and temperate.

We all agreed that this latest material from the National Archives seemed almost too good to be true. Was it possible that the copy file had come into the Archives by some other route, and that these terms did not apply to them? Or that there was some other document that the Archives had not yet sent us that affected access to the copy file? If so, Archives had not sent it to us, despite our requests for all relevant documents.

Although I had twice sought confirmation from the Archives about access to the copy file, we would write to them once again to ascertain that there were no other relevant documents lurking among their records that they had somehow neglected to send us. We sent two letters, the first seeking confirmation of the chronology and details from the limited material we had for each of the two files – the *AA* originals and the *M* copies – and specifically asking the Archives to confirm that there were no other documents affecting access, other than those provided to us to date. The second letter would again request access to the original Palace letters on the basis that they were Commonwealth records, setting out the key arguments that Tom had put together in his legal Opinion.

Those two letters were sent by James Whittaker at the end of March 2016. It would be nearly two months before the National Archives responded.

'Dear Sir John, The task is done', wrote the official secretary, David Smith, to the former governor-general Sir John Kerr in June 1978. The file began, as Archive files do, at the end. I had turned to the beginning, and read the file from back to front as another part of this endlessly fascinating story emerged.

Still uncertain about the access conditions over the two versions of Palace letters, I had decided to return to the National Archives while we waited for the Archives' response, and was working through a different set of files: the Archives' own negotiations with Kerr and Government House over the acquisition of Kerr's personal papers after he left office. There I found some answers, and some bizarre instances of arcane Yarralumla ritual, in letters between Smith and Kerr, then resident in the south of France, where he was working on his book, *Matters for Judgment*.

In the reading room of the National Archives, with *M4520 2 Archives [Arrangements relating to the disposition of Sir John Kerr's Records]* spread out in front of me, a new element in the story of the elusive Palace letters unfolded. I didn't know it then, but these letters would turn out to be of the greatest significance for our case. We had known from the outset, from the Archives' catalogue entry, that the copy file had been made for Kerr 'at his request in 1978 by the Official Secretary as a means of refreshing memory during his stay in Europe while writing *Matters for Judgement*'. This small file, just seven letters between Kerr and Smith, written at the time the copying was being done, was a window onto a lost vice-regal world.[10]

Smith was in the photocopy room at Yarralumla, waiting for a time 'when no-one else was about' so that he could complete his final secret mission for his favourite governor-general – hours of photocopying reams of Palace letters, so large that they had been divided into six parts and had taken Smith weeks to copy. 'I badly under-estimated the number of hours needed to do the job', Smith wrote, struggling with the sheer volume of material before him.[11] Pile after pile of letters from Kerr to and from the Queen, through Sir Martin Charteris, some hand-written and most neatly typed on Government House letterhead, with extensive attachments and press clippings, together with the equally numerous royal replies, were all waiting to be photocopied and sent to Kerr 'to refresh his memory' as he worked on his book.

The file contained all of Kerr's correspondence with the Palace during his entire term as governor-general, from July 1974 to December 1977, with his first letter sent on 15 August 1974. The attachments alone were so large that 'just dismantling the files, removing the staples, unfolding the large press clippings and adjusting the reduction mechanism to copy the larger pages took even more hours than did the straight copying', Smith lamented. Kerr's replies to the overwhelmed Smith revealed a critical aspect of the nature of the letters, as Kerr expressed his gratitude for Smith's work, 'participating in the preparation' of the letters and his assiduous checking and contribution to them; 'suggestions which you made from time to time as to its contents were very valuable to me as well as your comments on the replies from the Palace'.[12] The official secretary had clearly played a notable role in writing Kerr's 'personal' letters to the Queen, and that seemed to me important.

Although Kerr had left office the previous year, his slurring and swaying top-hatted appearance at the Melbourne Cup having formed a lasting image, his relationship with the fiercely loyal Smith remained as tight and as seigneurial as ever. 'I am very much in your debt for doing the enormous amount of work involved in letting me have the copy', Kerr wrote. 'I am grateful and honoured to have served you during this most interesting period in our nation's political history', Smith replied.[13] In order to continue to serve the man who was no longer governor-general, Smith had resorted to secretly copying the Palace letters on the Yarralumla photocopier in the dead of night to avoid detection.

I found the absurd scenario of the official secretary waiting for nightfall before sneaking into the Yarralumla photocopy room with the Queen's letters, to make copies for the former governor-general, rather unsettling. There was a sense of self-deprecation, of humiliation, about it. Besides, if the Palace letters really were Kerr's personal property, as the Archives kept insisting, why would he need to have copies made for him when he could have just taken the originals with him?

With 'the task done', Smith sent the file containing the copies of the letters to Kerr in France. After Kerr's death in 1991, this file travelled a circuitous route: first to Kerr's second wife, Lady Anne (Nancy) Kerr, and then, after her death, to her executor, before finally coming to the National Archives, twenty years after the original Palace letters had been lodged there. The originals meanwhile, and this would be critically important, were in the Yarralumla 'strong-room under absolute security until the task is completed and the original file is in Archives'.[14] This was the provenance of Kerr's copies of the Palace letters, the *M* file, 'the copy file', as it came to be called, which would confuse and confound lawyers and even judges all the way through this case, and which I greatly enjoyed reading about on that cold autumn day in Canberra.

I sent these letters to the legal team who were putting together our submissions for the Federal Court application, uncertain whether they would be of any use in the case, but confident that we were building a composite picture of the Palace letters and their copies. They went straight into our bundle of material, and became part of our growing collection of documents to be used in evidence.

Weeks had passed since we wrote to the Archives asking for confirmation that we had been sent all relevant documents relating to access to the Palace letters, and still we had heard nothing. Finally, nearly two months later, in May 2016, the Archives replied with a brief and unhelpful restatement of its previous assertions. Then came a bizarre abrogation of accountability and responsibility: 'Archives is not able to confirm or deny the correctness or otherwise of the statements in your letter.'[15] This was the arrogance of an organisation that had lost its way, and which felt no obligation to the public, to legal inquiry, or the presumption of public access. The National Archives of Australia, whose key function is to collect, preserve, and provide access to our most important historical records, had refused to confirm or deny its own access conditions and practices relating to the Palace letters – some of the most significant records in the nation's recent political history. Whatever had become of this trusted repository of 'our national memory'?

With this dismissive, delayed response, the Archives had refused to confirm or deny that there were any other documents governing access to the Palace letters, despite our repeated requests for clarity. There was no point in engaging further on these questions of fact. We had to accept that when I requested access to the copy file for the third time, Archives had finally given me the correct details about the conditions of access, and that the latest Instrument of Deposit, specifying that Kerr's personal records were to be opened after thirty years, was the only relevant one.

If Archives later tried to produce yet another Instrument of Deposit once the case was under way, it would undoubtedly face 'adverse costs consequences', as Tom Brennan put it, for its failure to produce it to me when requested. How prescient that turned out to be.

'Focus on the things you can control', the great Australian Rules St Kilda coach Allan Jeans always said. And so I did. The only way to think about the Federal Court action was to break it down into manageable stages and take each one step by step. If at any point the next stage was untenable, I would reconsider, and if it really was impossible to continue, withdraw. I was under no illusions about the risks involved; they had never been downplayed to me, and I knew they were significant.

If I took the case, I would have to raise funds to cover the extensive non-legal costs – court costs, filing fees, hearing fees, and transcript fees – and to provide some degree of protection against the prospect of an adverse cost order. I set up a crowd-funding campaign, 'Release the Palace letters', to run alongside the court case, and if it was going to work, media interest would be essential. From this point on, we would work together to co-ordinate a schedule involving fund-raising, media coverage, and the preparation of submissions for filing in the Federal Court. The aim was to have each of these three elements perfectly timed, so that the media interest would come just as the crowd-funding campaign opened and the legal action commenced. Each would then build on the other: the media would report on the case and the crowd-funding campaign, the legal team would file in the Federal Court, journalists could read the filed documents, and the media coverage would generate public interest. That was the plan, and we had six months to get there. The reason we did get there was Terri King.

Terri, a longstanding publicist, had worked with me on three books. Calm, organised, well-connected, and greatly respected, if anyone could bring public interest and media coverage to this, it was Terri. There were so many serendipitous moments on this path, and here was another one – Terri was soon to strike out on her own with other colleagues in a new media and publicity company called Pitch Projects. 'Can I be your first client?', I asked. Working with Terri King would be one of my best decisions in the whole campaign.

For the next two months I worked on developing the crowd-funding campaign that we ran on the Chuffed platform – the text explaining the project, a pitch to capture attention, images for visual interest, and details explaining the importance of the case and why the Palace letters still mattered more than forty years after they were written. In short, I had to convince people to support this case among the thousands of no less urgent and far more compelling crowd-funding pleas and imprecations on the internet. My head was swirling with platforms, delivery dates, targets, and 'perks' to offer for donations, text to write, and images to source. And every word had to be read and checked by the legal team.

I felt a wave of relief when, just days before we were due to file in the Federal Court, we made the first test donation and everything worked perfectly. The donation buttons clicked through, the payment appeared, and our fund-raising had begun. It was bolstered by news from Terri King that the ABC's *7.30* programme wanted to cover the case as its lead story later that week. All our hard work could come together if everything was ready in time – the crowd-funding site, the *7.30* story, and our filing in the Federal Court, all on the same day.

I did an interview with the ABC in my office, firing up about the National Archives' denial of public access to such significant letters, describing the dramatic transformation of the dismissal history in recent years, and the development of the legal case to secure the release of the letters; 'They are absolutely pivotal to our history, and it's galling that the Queen … should retain any sort of veto over our access as Australians to critical documents in our history'. Australians should own their own history![16]

As the story went to air, we opened the Chuffed site, and I watched in astonishment as donations poured in. Hundreds of people across Australia, even some in the UK, donated whatever they could, and by the end of the weekend nearly half the target amount had been raised.

On Friday 20 October 2016, I commenced action in the Federal Court of Australia against the director-general of the National Archives of Australia, seeking the release of the Palace letters.

Chapter Four

Archival manoeuvres
in the dark

On Australia Day 1987, a young Brisbane barrister, George Brandis, wrote to his friend and mentor, Sir John Kerr, about the 'problem' of compassionate policies. 'Dear Sir John, ... I agree that there is a problem in paying for "compassionate policies" – indeed, there is a greater problem in determining what "compassionate policies" in fact are.'[1] Nearly thirty years later, Brandis seemed no closer to knowing just what compassionate policies were when, as attorney-general in the Abbott conservative government, he proclaimed that all people 'have a right to be bigots'.[2]

Brandis had befriended Kerr in England some years earlier as a young student at Oxford. Together with his close friends and fellow Queensland Young Liberals Don Markwell and Tom Harley, and the future Director of the National Gallery of Victoria Timothy Potts, this 'very bright group of young Australians' regularly entertained Kerr, whom Brandis considered 'the real victim of the dismissal'.[3] At picnics, drinks, dinners, and luncheons, their get-togethers were conversational, sometimes intellectual, and always gossipy, if slightly boozy, affairs in London, Oxford, at the Kerrs' Surrey house, and later at the Australian Club in Sydney. Kerr referred to his little group affectionately as 'the Gang'.[4]

In 1985, 'the Gang' would be particularly important to Kerr when, with the tenth anniversary of the dismissal looming, he became extremely concerned about the inevitable 'rehash of 1975' that the anniversary would bring. Public approbation and validation of his actions had been a central theme in Kerr's life in exile, and he prosecuted it vigorously, casting around for scholars, lawyers, and journalists who might write articles in support of his dismissal of the Whitlam government. Among the names put forward as prospective columnists, along with Brandis, Markwell, and Harley, were Liberal Party and conservative luminaries such as Sir John Atwill, Sir Garfield Barwick, Robert Ellicott, and Sir Walter Crocker, and *Quadrant* magazine heavyweights Peter Coleman, J.B. Paul, and Richard Krygier. The former governor-general's pretence at 'political neutrality' was no longer even affected as his diminishing circle of contacts moved ever rightward. In regular contact with 'the Gang', Kerr drew up a 'strategy plan' to have his own version of events feature prominently in the public domain, fearing that Whitlam's version had caught the public imagination and was fast becoming more credible and established than his own.

As Kerr sought support from all quarters, Sir Anthony Mason was becoming nervous. His own role in the dismissal was still unknown, and over lunch in Sydney in March 1985, Mason pleaded with Kerr to 'let things rest now' just as Kerr was rattling the dismissal cage again, excited that a series of articles by Barwick was to be published in *Quadrant*.[5] Mason was a likely candidate to become the next chief justice of the High Court and, as Whitlam's attorney-general Kep Enderby later told me, were Mason's role in the dismissal to have become known to the Hawke Labor government, that appointment would never have been contemplated.[6] Mason urged Kerr to remain silent, but of that there was no chance.

Kerr was determined to have his story told, and he was willing to use anything, even the surreptitious release of the Palace letters, to do this – if only he could find a way to publish them. He knew from his discussions with the Queen's private secretary, Sir Philip Moore, that the Palace would never agree to their release, and he could hardly reveal them himself. At their strategy meeting in July 1985, Kerr arranged to give Don Markwell a copy of some of the Palace letters, 'at least Volume I, perhaps without the press clippings'. This volume of the letters, part of the copy file that was then in Kerr's personal possession, was to be photocopied for Markwell, who was also to be given complete access to Kerr's personal files in order to draft an article to be published on the tenth anniversary of his dismissal of Gough Whitlam, on 11 November 1985.[7]

This support-and-admiration network was not all one-way, and Kerr in turn used his connections to promote 'the Gang' in legal and political circles. In July 1985, he introduced Brandis by letter to the former Liberal attorney-general, minister for external affairs, and immediate past chief justice of Australia, Sir Garfield Barwick, extolling Brandis's credentials and capacity just as he was setting out on his career as a barrister. The first action point in the Gang's strategy plan was for Kerr to speak to Barwick in person about Brandis, to put his 'strong view' that they should 'grab George now'. With their strategy in place, a celebratory, bibulous meal was arranged the following month: 'Sir John and Lady Kerr are very happy to be guests of the Gang to dinner on the night of Friday 2 August, and have kindly offered pre-dinner drinks at their home.'[8]

Brandis's personal connection with Kerr remained strong, with their contact continuing in Sydney until Kerr's death in 1991.[9] On the 25th anniversary of the dismissal in November 2000, it was his affection for Kerr and not the dismissal that focused Brandis's mind. '[E]ven today, so long after his death, I can scarcely speak of him without emotion', he told the parliament.

Their paths crossed again, figuratively and unexpectedly, in 2016, when I lodged my claim in the Federal Court, seeking the release of Kerr's royal correspondence. Brandis was now the federal attorney-general and the minister responsible for the National Archives. He could scarcely have been a less disinterested party in the proceedings.

With the case filed, apprehension made way for anticipation. This was now a defining legal contest between British imperial expectations and Australian post-colonial independence, overlain by centuries of an asserted convention of 'royal secrecy' over the monarch's correspondence. Not since a brash young barrister and future prime minister Malcolm Turnbull had scored an extraordinary legal victory against the British government and security establishment in the *Spycatcher* case had there been a legal challenge to claims of British secrecy operating in Australia.[10] It was also great media fare, propelled by the drama of the dismissal, the indignity of the Queen's embargo over our history, the mystifying secrecy of the Archives, and all of it fuelling the lingering questions over the Queen's prior knowledge of Kerr's actions. From its earliest days, the 'Palace letters' case, as it became known, was recognised as a landmark case to secure historic letters in our own National Archives from under the Queen's embargo, which the Archives was 'fiercely resisting'.[11]

The case itself was straightforward. I was challenging the Archives' decisions denying me access to the two files containing the Palace letters: the originals and the copies. This two-pronged approach was a unique and extremely welcome position to be in, giving us two possible avenues to success. It was this rare providence of the existence of two versions of the letters that, we felt, gave us the best chance of succeeding. The 'Originating Application' with which we had launched the action in October 2016 sketched our basic approach. First, the original Palace letters were Commonwealth records, and should therefore be released under the open-access provisions of the *Archives Act*; second, the copies were *either* Kerr's personal property – in which case they should be released, since the personal Instrument of Deposit stated that Kerr's personal files were to be opened after thirty years – *or* they were Commonwealth records, which should likewise be released. Either way, at the end of this case at least one of those files would have to be opened.

Our Statement of Claim setting out the key facts, the 'particulars', about the originals and the copy file, drew on Tom Brennan's earlier legal opinion: the *AA* file consisted of 'the originals of correspondence received by, and the original copies of correspondence sent by, Sir John Kerr in the discharge of the duties of his office of Governor-General'. Since the time Kerr left office, the letters had been 'in the possession and control of the official secretary to the Governor-General … At all relevant times Sir John Kerr treated the original bundle, and the letters which constituted it, as being the property of the Commonwealth and as not being his personal property'. The letters had been catalogued by the Archives, and they were in its care and possession.

As for the *M* file containing the copies, as we set out in the Statement of Claim, it consisted of copies made by the official secretary, David Smith, for Kerr in 1978 – as shown by the letters between them while Smith undertook his after-hours secret photocopying at Yarralumla. That copy file, we argued, was either Kerr's property or the property of the Commonwealth, and, if Kerr's personal property, it should be opened under what we now knew was the correct Instrument of Deposit just released to us showing that all Kerr's personal papers were to be open after thirty years. If they were Commonwealth records, then they, too, had to be released after thirty years under the *Archives Act*.

The next month was spent putting together every possible piece of documentary evidence supporting these twin arguments. These would form the backbone of the great Case Book containing every one of our supporting materials – copies of original archival documents; extracts from books, articles, legal texts, the *Archives Act 1983* and earlier iterations of the *Archives Bill*, Kerr's *Matters for Judgment*; and all of the archival documents I had already put together from Kerr's papers – the *Journal*, the extracts, and Kerr's 'notes on dismissal', among others. We arranged for typed transcriptions of the *Journal* entries to be done, since Kerr's handwriting was so difficult to read, together with detailed references, citations, and National Archives catalogue entries for every one of the archival documents, so that we had verifiable documentation attesting to their provenance at every stage.

Two chapters of *The Dismissal Dossier* also formed part of the evidence book, and I worked back through every footnote in those chapters, collecting images of the sources quoted and references cited for each of the footnotes and all of the statements I had made in them.[12] Professor Caroline Elkins describes that uneasy, apprehensive transition of archival research from written history into legal action as 'the moment where literally my footnotes are on trial'.[13] Finally, the letters between Kerr and David Smith in 1978 that I had located in the Archives only months earlier were also included, because they revealed the creation of the copy file by Smith on the Yarralumla photocopier, they showed that Smith had helped write some of Kerr's letters, and they also showed that Kerr was unaware of the terms under which the original letters had been lodged with the Archives. Kerr had wanted them to be released and 'available for future historians', yet had been unable to do so, since they were under the control of the Queen.[14] All of this, we felt, went strongly to our case that the Palace letters were Commonwealth records and not Kerr's personal property, as the Archives contended.

As the case got under way, the only remaining concern was that we did still did not know the identity of the executor of Lady Kerr's estate, the depositor of the copy file in 2004, whose name had been redacted by the Archives when it finally and reluctantly released the personal Instrument of Deposit to us. I had requested details of those access conditions three times, and still the identity of the depositor was missing from the material the Archives had sent me. What concerned me and the legal team was that since we still did not know who had signed the personal Instrument over the copies of the letters, it was always possible that there was another document that we hadn't yet seen, ultimately controlling access to the copy file. We would seek those details again as the case progressed.

Lawyers speak a kind of argot – a patois of in-jokes, gossipy asides, and knowing glances – weighing up their chances, not only in terms of the strength of their case and the weakness of the other side, but also in terms of the judge who will be hearing it. The inclinations and predilections of every judge at every level are raked over as a form of judicial relaxation, a private payback from the practitioners against those who grill and dissect their skills relentlessly every week. There was a sense of relief when our case was listed to be heard by Justice John Griffiths. Griffiths was not one of the big-named Sydney lawyers whose families had signposted their paths to the law for generations through private education, privilege, and personal connections. He was a graduate of the ANU, Harvard, and Cambridge, a former chair of the Human Rights Committee of the New South Wales Bar Association, and an expert on administrative law and matters of public access. Tom Brennan and Antony Whitlam thought Justice Griffiths was 'probably the best you could have hoped for'.

I didn't have to wait too long to find out, as the first case-management hearing was listed for 15 November 2016. These preliminary hearings deal largely with administrative matters, set some dates, and establish documents for filing. Although Corrs assured me there was no need for me to attend, there was no way I was going to miss the first hearing, no matter how small and insignificant it might be, in this epic struggle to unlock the Palace letters. In the days before the hearing, the media interest grew again: I did several interviews, and was still surprised to see a throng of journalists milling on the steps outside the cold façade of the Law Courts building as I walked up Phillip Street with Tim Bunker that morning.

The lift to the 21st floor was crowded with gowned and wigged lawyers, I knew only my own team by sight, and was surprised to see the young, pony-tailed barrister who had shared our lift enter the courtroom with us and make his way towards the Archives' lawyers' bench. This was Craig Lenehan, who would be presenting the case for the Archives.

For all the inevitable emotion of a court case, it was strangely clinical. Courtroom no. 21B was not unlike a small university lecture theatre, with little atmosphere, even less warmth, and an assigned seating plan that put everyone in their place, literally and metaphorically. A gap in the seating discreetly separated the public from the practitioners, perhaps the only nod to creating a less intimidatory public face of the courts. I sat at the front of the public seats, across the aisle from the journalists and a small group of supporters who had donated to the crowd-funding campaign. Tim Bunker and the Corrs' solicitor were in front of me, the Archives' solicitors from the Australian Government Solicitors' office were in front to my right, and in front of them was the bar table – Tom Brennan to the left appearing on his own, Craig Lenehan to his right also appearing alone. At the apex of this hierarchical theatre was the bench, elevated and empty. At 9.29 am precisely, the tipstaff left the room through a side door next to the bench, returning immediately just as two sharp knocks at the door heralded the arrival of Justice John Griffiths. 'All rise! This court is now in session'. *Hocking v Archives* had begun.

Justice Griffiths was relaxed and attentive, and I felt at ease at once when he queried the Archives' claims of a 'special relationship' between the monarch and the governor-general, and the necessarily 'personal' letters between them. 'Confidential yes, but not personal', Griffiths said, 'unless they were talking about going to the races'![15] I saw Tom Brennan's shoulders move up and down in silent laughter at this rare flash of judicial humour.

Three things were settled at this first hearing that would define the parameters of the case all the way to the High Court. First, it would turn on whether the Palace letters were 'Commonwealth records' under the *Archives Act 1983*, which was a 'jurisdictional fact' to be determined by the court and not at the Archives' discretion; second, the case would proceed on the basis of an agreed 'Statement of Facts' setting out the facts, dates, and particulars agreed by both my legal team and the National Archives. Tom Brennan suggested to Griffiths that since 'a distinguished historian and National Archives bureaucrats would not necessarily meet agreement' on all of these 'agreed facts', we should each prepare affidavits in support of the key points of evidence, which Griffiths then ordered we prepare along with the statement of agreed facts. Finally, and most significantly, we would seek further documents from the Archives through a 'Notice to Produce', which the Archives would then be bound to respond to.

The National Archives must have shuddered as Justice Griffiths asked the critical question – would we be asking for the Palace letters to be produced – and Tom Brennan replied, 'Yes.' We would call for the Palace letters and their copies to be provided to the court, to be read by Justice Griffiths, by my legal team, and by me. The Archives' barrister, Craig Lenehan, was on his feet at once, urging 'caution' on Griffiths as if the future of the monarchy itself depended on it. Lenehan foresaw international upheaval, a constitutional and Commonwealth fracas, and damaged international relations if the Palace letters were allowed into open court, even under a strict confidentiality agreement. The production of the Palace letters, he insisted, his pony-tail sliding in agitation, would raise significant 'international aspects' requiring consultation with the Department of Foreign Affairs and Trade, it would involve the Queen and her relations with other Commonwealth nations, and it would raise constitutional issues involving the federal attorney-general, George Brandis.[16] Whoever could have imagined that a historian simply seeking access to records from our National Archives could threaten the very fabric of the monarchy and the Commonwealth?

If this scarifying prospect was meant to deter Justice Griffiths, it seemed only to bemuse him, and even Lenehan seemed uncertain of just what the constitutional problem raised by bringing the letters into court would be, although he was sure there was one. Justice Griffiths seemed equally unmoved by the Archives' repeated assertion of a 'special relationship' between the monarch and the governor-general, which, it claimed, necessitated secrecy over all vice-regal letters and the monarch's lasting embargo over them. 'Could we see a return to the notion of Crown privilege?' Griffiths asked, appearing incredulous at the hint of a revival of the divine right of kings. By the end of the case-management hearing, I thought that Justice John Griffiths really was the best Federal Court judge I could have hoped for.

The attorney-general's office was involved from the outset. Within days of the commencement of proceedings, the Archives prepared an urgent ministerial submission to the attorney-general, George Brandis, in October 2016. It was sent to Brandis's special advisor, Don Markwell. Sir John Kerr's truncated 'Gang' had been reprised in the offices of the attorney-general.[17]

Two weeks later, on 25 November, we issued the Notice to Produce instructing the National Archives to produce the Palace letters in the Federal Court in order for Justice Griffiths, me, and my legal team to read them. It sent shock waves all the way from the National Archives across to Government House and on to Buckingham Palace.

With centuries of royal secrecy threatening to unravel, the governor-general's official secretary wrote to the Queen's private secretary soon after the case began:

> Dear Sir Christopher,
> I wish to advise that certain legal proceedings have been commenced in the Federal Court of Australia seeking orders that, in effect, may lead to the release of correspondence between Her Majesty The Queen and Sir John Kerr then Governor-General.[18]

Behind the scenes, and unknown to me, although not at all unexpectedly, Buckingham Palace was being kept well informed of the progress of the case. What I had not expected was just how far the Palace would work in tandem with Government House in support of the National Archives' efforts to maintain the Queen's embargo and prevent the release of the Palace letters.[19] The extent of that engagement has been revealed through Freedom of Information requests, which show that the Queen's lawyers, Harbottle & Lewis of London, were notified at every stage of proceedings.[20] The greatest royal consternation came from our Notice to Produce calling for the Palace letters to be produced in court.

Neither I nor any of the legal team had read the letters or knew what was in them, other than the brief extracts and *Journal* entries about them in Kerr's papers that had given us some clues. On the other hand, the director-general of the Archives, David Fricker, as we understood it, had read them all. The imbalance was profound, and it strained at the tenets of procedural fairness, since it gave Fricker and the Archives' lawyers the great benefit of knowledge of the letters as they formulated their legal response against their release – knowledge we did not and could not have.

It is a fundamental principle of natural justice that neither side in a claim be given privileged access to key documents. In this case, the Palace letters were not just key documents; they were *the* documents. If we were to meet the Archives on a judicial level playing field, we needed to see the letters and to read them, just as the Archives had. We were even prepared to accept an alternative position, that only Justice Griffiths and my legal team would view the letters and that I would not, so that we could at least finalise our submissions on this basis. The Notice to Produce would have redressed that imbalance.

The Archives, however, would have none of it, and the following month it applied to the court to set aside my notice to produce the letters, describing it as 'an abuse of process' and taking the extreme step of claiming a 'public interest immunity' over their release. The National Archives argued that the unquestionable public interest in the release of the Palace letters as significant historical documents had to be overridden by a greater so-called public interest in keeping the letters secret.[21] In an indication of how closely the Archives was working with Government House on this, the director-general, David Fricker, staked his claim to immunity without providing any public grounds for it himself. Fricker referred only to his secret, closed submission and to a submission from Government House in support, which claimed that the letters between Kerr and the Queen belonged to a 'unique class' of documents, 'that in the public interest ought not be disclosed'.[22] It was a deeply antithetical position for any National Archives to take.

The Archives' response was so extreme for a 'pro-disclosure organisation' that it could only fuel the view that the embargoed letters masked vice-regal intrigue in the dismissal of Whitlam on a scale never before imagined. Subsequent actions strengthened that view. The Archives' application to set aside the Notice to Produce was supported by three affidavits – two from Fricker, and one from the official secretary to the governor-general, Mark Fraser, at Government House, which included the letters from Buckingham Palace in support of the Archives' case that the Palace letters should be kept secret under the Queen's embargo.

This was where the real surprises began, and the National Archives revealed the tension between its concern for the impact of access decisions on international relations and its role as the national repository of our most significant historical records and as the holder of 'the memory of our nation'. Although Fricker provided the court with three submissions, only two of them were open to us. In a move more closely associated with his former role as a deputy director-general of ASIO, Fricker had provided a *secret* submission, a closed affidavit, unable to be seen by me or my lawyers, and later available only to Justice John Griffiths. Fricker's public affidavits were bolstered by his secret one, and was supported by a detailed, expansive affidavit tendered to the court by Government House, written by the governor-general's official secretary. The intersection of the Archives' interests so completely with the interests of Government House, and through it with Buckingham Palace, against the interests of public access and transparency, was now overt.

As soon as the case began, the Archives had contacted Government House, and Government House in turn had contacted the Queen's private secretary, in a series of letters that became part of the official secretary's own affidavit to the court. The letters show Government House operating with a level of subservience closer to that of a branch office of Buckingham Palace than a national, albeit arcane, institution of national Australian governance. The Queen's private secretary and the governor-general's official secretary confirmed in a series of mutual assertions that the Palace letters were indeed 'private and confidential', 'non-official correspondence', and subject to a 'long-standing convention' of 'confidence' over such letters – not only in Australia, but across all fifteen of 'her Majesty's realms'.

That these reciprocal assertions of a convention, conveniently written while the case was in progress, were then provided through the governor-general's official secretary's affidavit in support of the Archives' legal argument that the Palace letters were 'personal', and not Commonwealth records under the *Archives Act,* said a great deal about the nature and strength of the Archives' case. It rested on a series of presumptions and assertions presented as law, and a perplexing misreading of the trajectory of the *Archives Bill* through to its final form as the *Archives Act.* The duteous letters between the Archives, Government House, and Buckingham Palace as the case progressed were a reminder that the sun had not yet set on the pocket of empire still ensconced at Yarralumla.

The Queen's private secretary even presumed to interpret Australian law to the official secretary with the assurance that 'the records in question are not caught by the *Archives Act 1983*', pre-empting the Federal Court's first substantive hearing of the case, which would determine exactly that question. The official secretary declared that the secrecy of the Palace letters and all royal correspondence was necessary, 'to preserve the constitutional position of the Monarch and the Monarchy'. My troublesome legal action was now apparently threatening 'the constitutional position' of the monarchy itself.

It was like being stuck in a Victorian-era time-warp, the language and the deference reflecting another time and a different, essentially colonial, political system. The sophistry and hypocrisy of it was laid bare by the willingness of the Archives and Buckingham Palace to release some of the Palace letters – those same letters that it claimed could under no circumstances be released for fear of damaging the monarchy itself – if it suited their case to do so. At the same time that the Archives, Government House, and Buckingham Palace were insisting on an inviolable 'strict convention of confidentiality' over the Palace letters, the governor-general's official secretary and the Queen's private secretary had agreed to breach the 'strict convention of confidentiality' and release two of the Kerr–Charteris letters to the court in order to support the Archives' case, given 'the highly exceptional circumstances of the present legal proceedings'.[23] The Queen's control over Australia's national archives and historical records could not have been clearer – the Palace letters could be released in her interests, but not our own.

Early in the New Year 2017, I met again with Tim Bunker in the offices of Corrs Chambers Westgarth in Sydney. It was a stifling summer, and the sun streamed through the glass-panelled offices as we worked through every one of the Archives' documents that would be used as evidence during the case. For each of these, we identified where I had located it, how I had obtained it from the Archives, the record details, and the mechanics of the online catalogue system *RecordSearch* for submitting access requests, in preparation for the case book and my affidavit, both due the following week.

The case was to continue with a Directions Hearing set for 14 February. As we filed our key documents, and the Archives filed theirs in reply, it was clear that we had still not been sent all the relevant documents relating to my request to access the copy file, just as Antony Whitlam had suspected. So we served another Notice to Produce on the National Archives, the fourth attempt to get the full details of the access conditions over the copy file, this time asking for the 'complete and unredacted Instrument of Deposit' signed by the still-unknown executor of Lady Kerr's estate. Under the auspices of legal proceedings, that should finally tell us who had signed the Instrument of Deposit over the copy file.

The answer to this question would throw the entire case into disarray before it had even begun.

The unredacted Instrument of Deposit arrived on 27 January 2017, the day my affidavit was due to be filed, leaving me no time to incorporate it or to follow up the dramatic facts emerging from it.[24] The personal Instrument of Deposit over the copy file had been signed not by Sir John Kerr's daughter, Gabrielle Kibble, who had deposited the first of his personal papers with the Archives, but by Stephanie Bashford, the daughter from a previous marriage of his second wife, Lady Anne Kerr. This was a name we had not seen before. The obvious question was, why had Archives been so reluctant to reveal the identity of the signatory and the contents of the Instrument of Deposit for so long? To find that out, we served yet another Notice to Produce, this time asking for all correspondence between Bashford, Kibble, and the Archives about the Instrument of Deposit governing the copy file.

The day before the Directions Hearing, those letters were released to me. They showed conclusively, if there was ever any remaining doubt, that were no 'specific instructions' over access to the copies of the Palace letters, as the Archives had incorrectly told me there was in 2011 when it denied my requests for access to that file. There was no correspondence even hinting at the existence of specific instructions. Indeed, to the contrary.

It could hardly be suggested that Bashford and Kibble had somehow been confused about what was being signed when Kerr's personal papers were placed in the Archives. A 'File Note' released to us with this batch of documents showed that the Archives had encouraged Ms Kibble to consider placing special conditions over what it politely termed the possible 'unwarranted intrusion into personal affairs' that might arise from the release of the copies of the Palace letters. Kibble disagreed; her view, which mirrored Kerr's own desire that the letters be released, was that by the time of the release of any 'intrusive' papers in 2005, 'she did not see any real problem if the debate over her father's role in the dismissal was rekindled'.

Kerr's stepdaughter, Mrs Stephanie Bashford, had clearly felt the same; she had not placed any 'specific instructions' over the copy of the Palace letters in Kerr's personal papers, which she also had specified were all to be released after thirty years. Bashford had not shifted from this view, even when the Archives specifically pointed to the claimed 'exception to the 30-year rule [for] the private correspondence between Governors-General and the Queen' as one possible example of 'different conditions'.[25] The opportunity for the copy file of the Palace letters to be locked away under 'specific instructions' could not have been made clearer to the depositor. Yet Mrs Bashford had ignored these suggestions and had signed an unqualified Instrument of Deposit. *All* Kerr's personal records, including the copy file, were to be opened after thirty years.[26] The copy of the Palace letters would now have to be opened.

Not even the National Archives could continue to claim that there were any 'specific instructions' over access to the copy file. It was now unassailable that the file should have been opened for me in 2011, and inevitable that it would be opened for me now. We would return to the court armed with this new information, confident that whichever way the court ruled, whether the letters were deemed to be Commonwealth or personal records, the copy file at least would have to be opened. Tom Brennan turned to me as we walked past a crowd of journalists into the Directions Hearing the next day, and said, 'You've just won this case.'

***

The first thing that struck me was Justice Griffiths' demeanour. Gone was the relaxed, agreeable *persona* of the initial hearing; today he was agitated, even aggravated, by his very presence there. 'There's almost something bizarre about what's happening here today', he grumbled to no one in particular. 'Why are the parties here and not in the AAT [Administrative Appeals Tribunal]?'[27] My heart sank. *Surely he must know that we can't appeal this to the AAT. And why is this case and this hearing 'bizarre'?*

Antony Whitlam rose to speak, his voice, height, and bearing so like his father Gough Whitlam that it caught my breath. The veteran journalist Hugh Riminton leant towards me with a quizzical look, 'Son of?' he asked. I nodded, 'Eldest son of.' Whitlam focused at once on the need to bring the Palace letters before the court, stressing that the letters themselves were 'the essence of the case', that they had been 'seen by others' on the Archives team, including the director-general and his lawyers, which put both us and Justice Griffiths at a major disadvantage if we were to conduct our entire case without also seeing them. 'We suspect Your Honour would be assisted by at least counsel having access for the purposes of submissions and assisting the Court', he put to Griffiths. Without seeing the letters, which were 'the essence of the case', the scales would be as heavily tilted against us in evidentiary terms as they already were institutionally.

There was a momentary glimmer of light when Justice Griffiths conceded that we had a 'legitimate forensic purpose' in requesting access to the letters, only to quickly declare himself reluctant to look at them, and even more reluctant to let my lawyers look at them – and he clearly had no intention whatsoever of letting me look at them. It struck me again in this short hearing that Griffiths seemed unusually unnerved by this discussion, hesitant to make a decision, and on edge. 'I can see minefields', he said, 'the way in which this case is progressing is very unusual, very troubling'. These were strong words – 'minefields', 'something bizarre', 'very troubling' – and they caught me off-guard. I could scarcely imagine what was making the judge so uncertain, so cryptic, and so self-evidently nervous.

Even the words 'take a look at the letters' seemed to trip Griffiths up. He spoke instead in odd deflections, of taking a 'judicial peep' at the letters, and of my lawyers taking a 'counsel peep', in what seemed to me a form of legal baby-talk aimed at avoiding the critical issue at hand, which was the use of secret evidence in a case seeking public access to secret royal letters in the National Archives. And that really was 'bizarre'. Perhaps the letters could be tendered on the basis of a 'judicial peep', Griffiths said, although he conceded that he was 'very uncomfortable' with seeing something himself that my lawyers could not also see, implicitly acknowledging the breach of fairness that this would entail. Griffiths was here referring not only to the Palace letters, but also to David Fricker's secret 'closed' affidavit – another vital document that was apparently of such startling sensitivity that neither I nor my lawyers could see it.

What concerned me the most was Griffiths' suggestion that if he did look at the letters, that in itself could have implications for his 'ongoing involvement' in the case. It seemed to me that if we kept pressing Griffiths to look at the letters, he might feel obliged to excuse himself from hearing the case, with dire implications for me as a self-funded litigant dependent on the largesse of a *pro bono* legal team. I would then have to start over again, organise a new trial with a new judge, and at untold further expense. The implication was clear: it would be best if we stopped pursuing the need for a 'peep' at the Palace letters, and accepted the denial of procedural fairness that this entailed.

Thomas Howe QC for the Archives rehearsed again the

arguments about a claimed convention of royal secrecy and of the 'confidentiality' of the monarch's correspondence, of the need to preserve the dignity and 'political neutrality' of the Queen, and to protect the monarchy. This case would always circle around the unresolved tensions between Australia's post-colonial autonomy and the residual 'colonial relics' still tying us in the most unexpected ways to the demands and expectations of a fading empire and the Queen. 'It may be that the UK government, as a foreign country, has an interest in an outcome that may be seen to undermine the dignity and neutrality of the monarch', Howe proffered. Justice Griffiths shot back, 'I thought she was our head of state!'[28]

Although Justice Griffiths dismissed the Archives' claim of public-interest immunity over the letters, ruling that the Notice to Produce was not an abuse of process and that the letters should be produced, it was a Pyrrhic victory. Griffiths also ruled that the Palace letters and Fricker's secret affidavit would be available to him alone to view, and then only if he needed to: 'a judicial peep will be absolutely the last resort'. Neither I nor my lawyers could see the Palace letters or Fricker's secret affidavit, and the case would have to be run with that great imbalance between us remaining.

It was just after 5.00 pm on a Friday, 10 March 2017, one month after the official secretary at Government House had alerted Buckingham Palace that the case 'may lead to the release of correspondence between Her Majesty The Queen and Sir John Kerr', when an email from the Archives' lawyers arrived at Corrs. The covering letter gave no hint of its explosive content. It was the attachments that stung: two newly minted affidavits signed just days earlier, one from Kerr's stepdaughter, Stephanie Bashford, and one from the former acting assistant director-general at the Archives, Maggie Shapley.[29] Both of these affidavits now repudiated Bashford's 2004 Instrument of

Deposit governing access to the personal copy of the Palace letters, which, as we had painstakingly elicited from the Archives, had conclusively shown that the copies had to be released for public access.

Bashford now claimed in a newly sworn Instrument of Deposit arranged with the National Archives that when she had made the previous Instrument over the copy file in 2004, 'it was not my intention or understanding that it would apply to private correspondence between Sir John Kerr and Buckingham Palace or copies of such correspondence'. Mrs Bashford had sworn this despite the exchange of letters in 2004 showing that this very question had been raised with her by the Archives at the time. And, remarkably enough, word for word, Ms Shapley now also claimed that by her recollection of this signing of the Instrument of Deposit, which she had supervised, 'it was not my intention or understanding that it would apply to private correspondence between Sir John Kerr and Buckingham Palace', although she herself had raised questions about access to that correspondence with Mrs Bashford at the time.[30]

Bashford had signed the new Instrument of Deposit over Kerr's personal papers, annulling the previous Instrument and now specifying that the copy file of the Palace letters was to remain closed on the same terms as the originals: 'to remain closed until 50 years after the end of Sir John Kerr's appointment as Governor-General, ie: after 8 December 2027, and thereafter their release is subject to the approval of the Sovereign's Private Secretary and the Official Secretary of the Governor-General'. The new access conditions had been arranged with the Archives behind the scenes while we were preparing for the first substantive hearing, and we had been presented with it after the fact, as a *fait accompli*. We were all completely blind-sided.

Our case had always hinged on the fact that there were two

versions of the Palace letters and two Instruments of Deposit – one over the originals and another over the copies. They were at the heart of the case, the reason I had taken it, the basis for my assessment of the risk I faced and of our claim, and it had been torn apart in midstream. It was devious, artful, and devastatingly effective.

I was stunned. It was as if everything had suddenly turned upside down and I couldn't find my bearings. I simply could not comprehend how this could be done while the case was in progress. Surely it was *sub judice* or some equivalent to rewrite the central document governing access to one of the files that were the subject of the case while the case was in progress? I had taken the case precisely because of this second Instrument of Deposit, believing – correctly, as this extraordinary subterfuge now vindicated – that it meant the copy file would have to be released. How could it be changed during the case itself, before the hearings had even begun? Antony Whitlam was shocked: 'It was a very underhand thing for Archives to engineer once litigation was on foot.'

I was angry. I was viscerally angry – not just for myself, but for our supporters, for the donors who had contributed so much, from the smallest amounts that they could least afford, to the largest. Bad law was one thing; this was quite another.

Our chances had just been shredded, and there was nothing we could do about it. If we continued to argue that the copies were Kerr's personal copies of the Palace letters, we had to accept that the depositor, Mrs Bashford, could change the Instrument of Deposit at any point – since they were her personal property, and the terms were hers to determine – and we had no challenge to the fact that she had done just that. And if we argued that the copies were 'Commonwealth records', we would simply be duplicating our contention about the originals, which we had always argued were Commonwealth records. The changed Instrument of Deposit had rendered our claim over the copy file redundant.

I felt as if the case was over before it had even begun. What had started with such hope and exhilaration had been decimated, and not even by skilled, powerful reasoning or court-room drama – that, at least, I could accept – but by a cheap, tawdry, behind-the-scenes piece of legal chicanery. And to rub salt into that smarting wound, this very act of chicanery was a frank admission that we had been entirely correct, that the copy file should have been released, and that the National Archives had misled me when it had claimed that the copies were under 'specific instructions' forbidding their release.

By May 2017, six months after the case had been filed, we had little choice but to drop our pursuit of the copy file and to refocus the case on our core contention that the original Palace letters, the *AA* file, were Commonwealth records. The Archives' manoeuvres had derailed our two-pronged strategy and undermined our fail-safe case, all in the desperate hope that it would stymie our entire case. *Well*, I told myself, *it will not*.

Chapter Five

'Mr Whitlam ... would inevitably suspect the U.K.'s involvement'

The British National Archives rises like a concrete bunker behind a black steel fence from the rows of unremarkable terrace houses along the quiet suburban streets of Kew in London's south-west. High security permeates even into the reading room, where uniformed guards pace around the shared desks, checking over your shoulder, watching as you head to the photocopier, and a card-activated barrier lets you leave. Or not. It makes the National Archives in Canberra seem like a quaint old-fashioned curiosity.

The Federal Court hearing had been scheduled for 31 July 2017, and I was at the British Archives to spend three weeks immersed in the records of the Foreign and Commonwealth Office [FCO]. I had seen these records years earlier – notes, briefing papers, memos about the Whitlam government and its dismissal – and was working through them again for a new edition of *The Dismissal Dossier*, focusing on 'the Palace Connection'. Although they weren't new to me, I was astounded anew re-reading those files steeped in a deep-seated suspicion of the new 'republican' prime minister who was determined to end what he called the 'colonial relics' still entangling our relationship with the United Kingdom.

The records describing Whitlam's first official visit to London to discuss his core policies of ending remaining appeals to the Privy Council, ending the Imperial honours system in Australia, and bringing an independent stance to foreign affairs bristled with disbelief, disrespect, and even outright derision. Whitlam was 'wayward, arbitrary and doctrinaire', his policies 'foolish', and, in what the FCO considered the most abject lapse of all, he had failed to 'take account of British interests'.[1] This was Whitehall at its condescending, imperial best.

Within the FCO, the jaundiced view of Whitlam as 'evasive' and 'didactic' only escalated after the government's re-election in 1974 until, by October 1975, it was actively considering 'possible intervention' in Australian politics.[2] Memo after memo with headings like 'Australian domestic politics: Possible intervention' and 'Australian Constitutional Deadlock: Possible UK Involvement' not only canvassed British intervention in Australian politics, but stressed the need for secrecy while considering it: 'Mr Whitlam, if he heard of it, would inevitably suspect the U.K.'s involvement.' In October 1975, the FCO wrote, 'Any intervention by us (in effect in Australian domestic politics) could have serious implications and both the nature and the timing thereof would need very careful consideration'.[3] Whitlam, of course, knew nothing of these internal British discussions contemplating their foreign intervention in our domestic political matters, in a shocking betrayal of their constitutional role.

At the same time, the FCO and the British foreign minister considered whether the Queen's private secretary, Sir Martin Charteris, might 'get in touch with Sir John Kerr with a view to "blocking off" any attempt [by Whitlam] to involve The Queen in Australian domestic politics'.[4] This concern about the Queen's possible involvement stemmed from Whitlam's intended half-Senate election, which the FCO apparently feared might lead to the Queen being given conflicting advice from the prime minister and the state governors regarding the issuing of writs by the states for that election.[5] The paramount concern for the FCO and for Charteris at all times was that, 'In our dealings with Australian constitutional matters ... we very much try to bear in mind the possibility of embarrassment to The Queen.'[6] The FCO had determined that this potential for royal embarrassment of conflicting advice arising from the Senate election was to be avoided 'if at all possible'.[7] The problem for the FCO and Charteris was, first, that the timing of the periodic Senate election was constitutionally determined and was due at that time, and, second, that Whitlam had announced on 16 October 1975, when supply was first blocked, that if the obstruction continued he would call the Senate election.

These two strands of my work – on the dismissal in general and the Palace letters in particular – intersected at the point of those FCO files. At every spare moment, waiting for a file or searching the catalogue, I was also searching for clues to the Palace letters, anything that might point to the origins of the use of the label 'personal' or the nature of the letters themselves. I became a speed scanner as hundreds of pages of FCO files flicked through my hands like a flip-book cartoon, catching a word here and there, stopping and restarting, hoping I didn't miss something that might help the case.

With just a few more days left in the British Archives, I requested *FCO 24/1931, Changes in Constitution of Australia 1974*, one of a huge number within the FCO series on internal political matters in Australia. I was working through this series as fast as I could order them, and this 157-page file was just one more in a long list of innocuous generic titles, until I read the opening letter. I recognised its significance at once. And there it was: instructions from the FCO on the use of the term 'personal and confidential' in official despatches as a mechanism to ensure their secrecy: 'If these reports take the form of official despatches, they should be marked "Confidential", and should not be included in the ordinary numbered series of despatches. ... they should not take the form of despatches, but of personal letters marked "Personal and Confidential".'[8]

The file concerned Whitlam's intention that the communications of Australian states with the Queen should be channelled through the governor-general and not, as they then were, from the state governors to the FCO, and from there to the Queen. The states remained, in the eyes of the FCO, 'in a quasi-colonial relationship with the United Kingdom'; Whitlam sought to end that residual status and drag the states and the Commonwealth into the late twentieth century and genuine post-colonial independence.[9] The FCO was not at all happy about the prospect of being sidelined in this way.

Included in the file was a helpful table listing various communications from the governor-general and state governors, how they were sent, and how that would change if they were all to go through the governor-general, as Whitlam wanted. On that list were the regular despatches from state governors to the Queen, the 'personal and confidential' quarterly reports officially sent by the governors in exactly the same way the governor-general's despatches described by Kerr were sent. An 'informal note' detailed how these despatches were to be written, how they were to be sent, and, most importantly, how they were to be labelled.[10]

I sent a copy of the informal note and the file details to Tim Bunker at Corrs Chambers Westgarth, unsure whether this meant anything for the case or even whether it could be part of our evidence, since the date for lodging documents had passed. Tim replied at once, asking for a certified copy of the key pages and a copy of the entire file. The certified copy would be useful if the Archives later sought to dispute its provenance, he said – surely being overly cautious, I thought. I had spent hours photographing every page of the file, the cover sheets, and the accession details, on the Archives' clumsy imaging camera. This meant that we had them all as individual pages, 157 pdfs, each bearing the UK National Archives logo, and now we needed a certified copy as well? One thing was certain: for the legal team, this was clearly an important file.

The informal note perfectly revealed the sophistry of the term 'personal and confidential' to describe the governors' despatches to the Queen. It showed conclusively that its use was a sham, a subterfuge designed to avoid acknowledging these letters as official despatches, and to ensure their secrecy, by calling them something else. We sent them to the Archives' lawyers at the Australian Government Solicitors, and, two days before the Federal Court hearing was due to begin at the end of July 2017, it was agreed that the informal note on the governors' 'personal' despatches could be included in evidence.

I wondered then at history's remarkable circularities. Gough Whitlam's determination to recast the channel of communication between state governors and the Queen, to treat our royal relations at a national level – nation to nation, and not 'quasi-colonial' states to imperial monarch – had generated evidence that would be used decades later in a court case, argued by his son, about his dismissal.

On 20 July 2017, Federal Court Justice John Griffiths was in Canberra to deliver the keynote address at the National Administrative Law Conference, *Ripples of Affection: administrative law and communities*. It was a typical Canberra winter's day, with an icy morning and a crisp, blue sky, as Griffiths opened the prestigious legal conference with his address on 'access to administrative justice'. Among the other speakers at the two-day conference were the attorney-general and minister responsible for the Archives, George Brandis, and the director-general of the National Archives, David Fricker.

Fricker reprised some well-worn pronouncements on the importance of archives to good governance, accountability, and history – statements with which no one could disagree, and which bore little resemblance to my recent experience of Archival practice. It was odd, if not disorienting, to read Fricker's description of the role of Archives as 'ensuring that the actions of public officials are open to the scrutiny of the public they serve through the ... accessibility of government records', written at the very time he was leading the National Archives in contesting my efforts to hold the actions of the governor-general and the Queen 'to the scrutiny of the public they serve'.

Fricker's idealised representation of the Archives as a form of beneficent public-scrutiny monitor could not have been more different from the unashamed provocations of his minister, George Brandis. From his time as one of Sir John Kerr's London 'Gang', Brandis had never been shy about his own capacity, and as attorney-general he was brusque, often churlish, and always supremely confident of the correctness of his legal opinions, as his speech on 'Green Lawfare' exemplified. Brandis took aim at a favoured theme, the spectre of environmental groups using the courts to challenge mining-development approvals – and, worse, succeeding.[11] The case that had caused him particular angst was a 2015 Federal Court decision staying the government's approval of Adani's Carmichael coal mine in Queensland. In response to this judicial 'activism', the attorney-general had demanded changes to the legal standing of environmental groups, branding them 'green vigilantes' who were using the law as a form of 'legal sabotage' merely to disrupt development at the cost of 'thousands of mining jobs'.[12]

Brandis now repeated these familiar tropes, reducing environmental groups to a legal and political enemy, and decrying environmental legal proceedings as nothing more than 'vehicles for an ideological agenda' in which the law was virtually helpless in the face of public-interest litigation, which he saw only as 'a hapless vehicle for the extraneous ends of others, a weapon to be deployed'. As a public-interest litigant, I saw it otherwise. Never afraid to name names and point to what he considered errant judicial decisions, Brandis called out academics, politicians, and judges for recognising the 'so-called public environmental right' to engage in legal process, and criticised particular legal approaches and decisions for 'ignoring the human cost entailed by investment projects being forgone because of lawsuits ... with a cost in jobs and prosperity'.

What made this speech particularly abrasive was that it came at a time when the Full Federal Court was in the process of hearing an appeal against Justice Griffiths' rejection of a second Federal Court challenge to Adani's ministerial approval.[13] For a judiciary that had been assailed by its own federal attorney-general for years, this was nothing new, just another intimidatory ministerial irritant; however, Brandis's strident presentation to such a gathering was a marker of the politically charged atmosphere the judiciary was working in at the time.

During the week of this conference, my lawyers at Corrs Chambers Westgarth and the Archives' lawyers in the Australian Government Solicitor office were finalising the statement of agreed facts that Justice Griffiths had ordered at the directions hearing in February, setting out the key factual details about the Palace letters. The final version of these twenty-three facts, confirmed by both legal teams, was filed and sent to Griffiths on 20 July, the same day he delivered his keynote address. The most important and surprising fact conceded by the Archives was that the Palace letters 'address topics relating to the official duties and responsibilities of the Governor-General'. This acknowledgement surely pointed to the letters themselves as Commonwealth and not personal records, and I was considerably heartened by the unexpected concession. These agreed facts would now form the uncontested factual basis of the case, which Justice Griffiths was to hear on 31 July 2017.

As it curved towards St James Church, the top end of Phillip Street was bustling with barristers, lawyers, and clients pushing past the journalists, microphones, and cameras surging towards us as we approached the Law Courts building. If it was possible to be excited, apprehensive, and calm all at the same time, I was. Interest in the dismissal had been revived, first by my revelations of justice Mason's involvement four years earlier, and reinforced by the news that Kerr's extensive secret correspondence with the Queen was now under legal challenge. The Queen's continuing embargo over the Palace letters was fuelling the widespread belief that there were still more dismissal secrets to be told. The case was seen as historic, and its implicit challenge to claims of royal secrecy, which had dogged attempts to access British archival records for decades, was well recognised. *The Times*, the UK's *Daily Telegraph*, and *Deutsche Welle* all ran stories about the case that week.[14]

We shared the lift up to the 21st floor with the Archives' legal team, nodding politely like old friends. Courtroom 21B was crowded with reporters, supporters on both sides, and a scattering of interested members of the public as David Fricker headed towards the back. I sat at the front, behind the Corrs solicitors, glued to every word, watching for a look or even a glance from Justice Griffiths, hoping to get a 'judicial peek' of his view.

'All rise! This court is now in session!' I had thought about this day for months, anticipating this moment of the first day of the hearing, and never had I imagined what His Honour's opening words actually turned out to be. Justice Griffiths began by saying that he 'thought he should mention' that he had met Sir John Kerr and Lady Kerr when he was an academic at Cambridge University during the 1980s: 'I attended a social function in which I was introduced to Sir John and Lady Kerr, and apart from exchanging pleasantries we had no discussion about the events of 1975 ... we had no discussion about his journals or anything else, it was pure pleasantries'. It was not the opening I had expected.

Griffiths then disclosed that he had given the keynote address at the conference the previous week at which 'Mr Fricker or Dr Fricker, I'm not sure which, was also a speaker ... I made a point of not introducing myself to Dr/Mr Fricker ... and my paper was not on Archives legislation or anything like that.' There was no mention of the presence of the attorney-general, George Brandis, nor of Brandis's fierce denunciation of public-interest litigation.

Antony Whitlam's delivery was measured, patient, and unruffled; whenever Griffiths sought clarification, it was at his fingertips within seconds. Whitlam's approach to argument was to be respectful and constructive, and never to unsettle the judge. The occasional irritation, and there were some, was acknowledged by just the slightest pause and a barely perceptible sharp word. The ABC described him as, 'a strikingly tall man like his father, [who] made his arguments in a clear and even tone, without theatrics'.[15]

Whitlam began by working through the details of the Palace letters, their content, and how they came to be placed in the Archives, establishing the key facts and defining features about them, and my efforts to access them, and our central arguments. The case rested on the meaning of 'Commonwealth record', which in turn was defined in the *Archives Act* as the 'property of the Commonwealth or a Commonwealth institution'. The 'foundational criterion' of 'Commonwealth record', Whitlam argued, is ownership, and our efforts were directed towards showing that the Palace letters were the property of the Commonwealth and therefore Commonwealth records.

Whitlam was always restrained, even on the rare occasion when a retort might have been in order, as his exchange with Justice Griffiths over the agreed facts showed. Early in his presentation, Whitlam moved to dissecting the statement of agreed facts, which was part of the Evidence Book containing all the documentary evidence from both sides, asking Griffiths almost as an aside whether he had looked at it. To my astonishment, Justice Griffiths replied, 'No, I haven't.'

Griffiths himself had ordered at the Directions Hearing that the statement of agreed facts be prepared for the purposes of these proceedings. They were critical to the case, since they now formed its factual spine, the empirical basis on which we all proceeded, and they had been sent to Griffiths on 20 July – eleven days before the hearing. And yet he had not read them. Whitlam appeared taken aback by Griffiths' response, and he paused for just a moment before calmly suggesting that his Honour might take a look at the statement, 'because it is important'. Whitlam said, 'At the risk of wearying your Honour, it's relatively short, and I could just take your Honour through it, because it *is* important and it's not that long.' [my emphasis] It was an admirable lesson in legal restraint.

The agreed facts established vast details about the letters that had previously been merely speculated about, the most significant of which were that they addressed 'topics relating to the official duties and responsibilities of the Governor-General'; and that Kerr's letters to the Queen included 'attachments comprising photocopies of newspaper clippings or other items of correspondence, expanding upon and corroborating the information communicated by the Governor-General in relation to contemporary political happenings in Australia'. The Palace letters, taken together with these extensive attachments, were clearly more detailed and more frequent than the usual quarterly reports expected of governors and governors-general.

The agreed facts set out the key details about both the originals and the copies, and the changes made to their Instruments of Deposit – by the Queen over the originals after Kerr's death, and by Mrs Bashford over the copies just four months earlier. The fact that the Queen had changed Kerr's purportedly 'personal' Instrument of Deposit after his death had always seemed to me completely destructive of the Archives' claim that these were Kerr's personal records. As Antony Whitlam put it, it was 'inconsistent with the respondent's case' that the Queen could impose any conditions over access to documents that she did not own.

Although we had been forced to drop our pursuit of the copy file because of the sudden change to the Instrument of Deposit by Mrs Bashford, the fact that she had been able to change the access conditions over her *personal* copies of the letters exposed the danger to our documentary heritage of the Archives' position that the original Palace letters were also personal. For the corollary, as Whitlam argued, was that if the original Palace letters were found to be personal records owned by Kerr's family, then they too could be disposed of at the whim of Mrs Bashford. As personal records, the Palace letters could be withdrawn from access, destroyed, or sold to the highest bidder – which would mean the end of any national control or preservation of these highly significant historic archival records, and potentially their disappearance altogether.

Whitlam concluded, 'If the respondent is right about a government convention of confidentiality ... the consequence is that Mrs Bashford, or perhaps her heirs, are presently entitled to control the disposition or destruction of the official bundle ... And we submit confidently that that is a result which is so extraordinary as to suggest error in the respondent's approach'.[16]

As Tom Brennan had identified from the outset, the case would hinge on the meaning and interpretation of the *Archives Act 1983*, specifically the definition of a 'Commonwealth record' as the property of the Commonwealth. Our success or failure on this point would be the key to the entire case. It was here that the political and legal elements came together most clearly as Whitlam worked through the political machinations behind the protracted passage of the Act, which had stalled over the very question of whether the governor-general's records were to be excluded from it. In the end, the *Archives Act 1983* made no such exclusion for governor-general's records, and specifically included the records of 'the official establishment of the Governor-General'. This, we argued, must include the correspondence between the governor-general and the monarch. Our case rested heavily on the trajectory that Whitlam now described: the Fraser government's original *Archives Bill* sought to exclude *all* of the governor-general's records from its open-access provisions; however, the Senate Standing Committee on Constitutional and Legal Affairs had firmly rejected this, and instead recommended changes to the Bill in order to bring the records of the governor-general, and *specifically* his correspondence with the Queen, under its provisions.

'So it's significant', Whitlam continued, 'that the committee, at the end of 1979, considered and rejected the exclusion of so-called Palace records'. As prime minister, Malcolm Fraser rejected the committee's recommendations, and after three years of fruitless negotiation, dropped the Bill from further consideration. This impasse remained unresolved at the time of the election of the Hawke Labor government in 1983, and a new *Archives Bill* was presented that made no exemption for the governor-general's records. Antony Whitlam concluded on the final terms of the *Archives Act*, 'The Parliament rejected any special provision for Palace correspondence, and substituted a comprehensive regime of accountability and publication.'[17]

Without any specified exemption, the governor-general's

'personal' records are only excluded from the *Archives Act* in the same way that *all* personal records of individuals are excluded. As Whitlam described it, 'for example, bank records, medical records ... correspondence with family, birthday cards' were all 'personal records': 'things that are unrelated to the performance of the office'.[18]

Whitlam argued that the relationship between the governor-general and the Queen is not a 'personal' one in any sense but a constitutional one, 'created and governed by the Constitution and, regardless of any personal connections between the occupants of those offices, communications engaged in in connection with the performance of their offices are not personal'. Kerr had been appointed governor-general only the previous year, and 'it couldn't seriously be suggested that there was a personal relationship between the Queen and Sir John Kerr', Whitlam said, to a ripple of laughter through the court.

For more than two hours, Whitlam was on his feet. All the material we had put together over the previous twelve months found its way into his evidence that day as he took the court through Kerr's descriptions of the Palace letters as his 'duty' and as 'despatches' in *Matters for Judgment*; the details about and direct quotes from the letters in his 1980 *Journal*; Kerr's journal entry stating that the letters should be 'preserved as part of the archives and will be a good record of my Governor-Generalship'; David Smith's secret nocturnal photocopying to create the copy file for Kerr in France; and the identification of the extracts of the Palace letters, of which, as Whitlam noted, 'there's not a word of a personal nature in those extracts'.[19]

When it came to the extract from Kerr's letter to the Queen describing the official dinner for the prime minister of Malaysia, Antony Whitlam pointed out a major error in Kerr's description of that event. Kerr wrote in his *Journal* that he had described this dinner, which took place on the day that supply was blocked in the

Senate, in some detail to the Queen because the prime minister, Gough Whitlam, had joked to the assembled dinner guests that, 'it could be a question of whether I get to the Queen first for your recall or you get in first with my dismissal'. While acknowledging that 'we all laughed', Kerr proclaimed in his *Journal* that Whitlam's jocular remark was, in fact, something far more sinister – of such significance that 'I considered it to be my duty to report exactly what Mr Whitlam had said in the letter to the Queen … the Queen was entitled to know what Mr Whitlam had said because it indicated that he had said *in the presence of one of her other Prime Ministers* that he could in some circumstances be asking for my recall'. [my italics] That is, because of a joke.

Antony Whitlam paused there: 'It's a curious thing for a former president of Law (Asia) [as Kerr was] to say. Malaysia is a kingdom, but the Queen is not the Queen … Abdul Razak was not one of the Queen's prime ministers.' It was indeed an extraordinary error for the governor-general to make regarding a letter to the Queen purporting to indicate that her Australian prime minister was considering recalling him. Kerr's claimed pretext for writing to the Queen, as he described it in his *Journal*, was incorrect. In his haste to construct his preferred scenario about the political situation in Australia, one in which his own position was presented as under threat, Kerr had informed the Queen of Whitlam's joke since, as he wrote in his *Journal*, 'I didn't dismiss such a statement made in such circumstances as a mere joke.'

Antony Whitlam then turned to the Foreign and Commonwealth Office material that I had sent from the UK Archives the previous month, describing the FCO's instructions to the state governors to use the label 'personal and confidential' on their reports to the Queen:

> If these reports take the form of official despatches they should
> be marked confidential and should not be included in the

ordinary numbered series of despatches ... it may however be found convenient that they should [take the form of] personal letters marked personal and confidential.

Whether sent as official despatches, reports, or letters, these 'undoubtedly official communications' were to be marked 'personal and confidential', he told the court, not because they dealt with any 'personal' matters, but because this was the designation prescribed by the FCO in order to ensure their secrecy. There could be no sense in which a governor-general's communications with the Queen in carrying out their official duties could be 'personal'.

After more than two hours of argument, Whitlam concluded by reminding the court of the defining convention of a constitutional monarchy: the governor-general acts on the advice of the prime minister, and reports to the Queen in that capacity.

In an indication of the competing conventions at the heart of these divergent legal arguments, Thomas Howe QC and Craig Lenehan for the Archives began with a different convention altogether – the claimed 'constitutional convention' that royal correspondence with the governor-general is 'personal and confidential'.

The Archives' legal approach had always centred on arguments linking British archival practice with the unquestioned expectation that Australia would do the same: first, an essentially British convention of royal secrecy over the Queen's correspondence; second, a correlating Australian 'constitutional convention' that the governor-general's Palace letters were 'personal and confidential'; third, an interpretation of the *Archives Act 1983* as excluding the 'personal' records of the governor-general, including the Palace letters; and finally, a 'mirror' provision in the UK placing the Queen's copies of this correspondence out of public reach in the Royal Archives.

I had always found this approach of 'reciprocity', resting on British practice as determinative of our own, unpersuasive and implicitly disparaging of Australian legislative and archival practice. What relevance did British convention have, even if consistently applied by governors-general – which it clearly had not been – to Australian statutory interpretation and applications? To hear these arguments put before the Federal Court in 2017, thirty years after the passage of the *Australia Acts*, was astounding.

The claimed convention of personal ownership and confidentiality over royal correspondence was always asserted and never established; at best, it was a loosely followed practice and by no means a convention, much less a 'constitutional' one, as Professor Anne Twomey has shown.[20] Although Howe claimed that previous governors-generals had taken their letters with them after they left office, most had in fact placed their royal correspondence in the National Library, which was then the precursor to the Australian Archives, strongly suggesting their recognition of their own letters as official records.[21]

In a day of surprises, the Archives' Thomas Howe told the court that he would not be speaking to his written submissions, but to some 'supplementary submissions' that he would now put forward and that our legal team had neither seen nor prepared for. In case this sudden reliance on new material suggested some doubt about the strength of the Archives' written submissions, Howe stressed that, 'We of course fully adopt every single sentence of our written submissions. The fact that we don't necessarily reiterate them should not be taken by your Honour as some lack of pressing of them.' Instead, he insisted that it was simply because there were some 'matters of emphasis' to be made that he now introduced new material.[22]

Howe's triumphant production of a 1977 letter from prime minister Malcolm Fraser to Kerr perfectly encapsulated the Archives' approach to the legal issues involved and its attitude to the court process. I had not yet seen this letter, which had been tendered in evidence just hours before the hearing began, giving our legal team no opportunity to review it or to assess it, much less object to it, should we have wanted to, and too late even to be included in the Court Book of evidence. As Howe turned to discuss the letter, Antony Whitlam interrupted. 'We were served with a copy of it just on the eve of the case,' he said. 'We've no objection to you [Justice Griffiths] looking at it', Whitlam said, 'but it apparently wasn't included ... in the Court Book.' Even Justice Griffiths did not have a copy of the letter, so late was its inclusion, and Howe handed a copy up to the judge's bench.

The letter had apparently been located by the Archives in its files, six weeks after the due date for lodging documents. It was not yet a public document, and I did not have a copy of it; it was simply produced on the day of the hearing without our having consented to it. This was not the only instance of the Archives missing deadlines and amending documents during the course of the case, which unsettled our preparations. We took a strategic view that it was best not to disturb proceedings, or risk a prolonged hearing with additional time and possible delays, and we allowed the material to be brought in at that impossibly late stage.

Fraser's letter was written in October 1977, six years before the passage of the *Archives Act*, and it referred only to the provisions of the draft Bill – not even of the final Bill that was presented, let alone of the Act itself. The provisions of the draft *Archives Bill*, Fraser assured Kerr, 'do not apply to the records of a Governor-General'. Of course, neither Fraser nor Kerr wanted all governor-general's records – many of which concerned the dismissal of the Whitlam government and contained explosive revelations, including about justice Mason's involvement – to be made public. Fraser's letter said nothing about, and could tell us nothing about, the final terms of the *Archives Act 1983*, since it was passed six years later and by a new, Labor government. This typified the Archives' arguments about the interpretation of the *Archives Act,* focusing on the provisions of the stalled Bill and not on the legislated Act. The exclusion of the governor-general's records from the early stages of the Bill was used to read that intention into the Act, even though the Act provided no such exclusion. This reasoning had always struck me as obtuse and unconvincing.

None of this was either surprising or new. The letter hardly seemed relevant, except as a statement of what we already knew: Fraser wanted the *Archives Bill* to exclude Kerr's records, and had an obvious political interest in maintaining secrecy over them, many of which related to the dismissal. Nevertheless, Howe presented this as 'powerful evidence from the most senior Commonwealth official' that the Palace letters were Kerr's personal property: 'there is no part of this letter that hints at the notion that the Commonwealth owned these records'.

Howe also used Fraser's letter to illustrate the Archives' key argument, that Australian Archives should follow British archival practice: 'Royal household records including the Queen's correspondence with Governors-General are protected in Britain under special archives rules. I am sure you will agree there should be no less protection in Australia', Fraser told Kerr. Howe recited this section with particular emphasis, arguing that Australia should provide equivalent protection for the Palace letters, simply because this was what was done in Britain. Yet the British archival structure is nothing like our own, since it includes an entirely separate, non-public, and royally controlled Royal Archive at Windsor Castle. To claim parity between this bifurcated monarchical system and the Australian unitary system, with our single public National Archives, was entirely inappropriate.

Then came the awkward matter of David Fricker's 'respondent's submission', lodged prior to the hearing, which contained a statement that contradicted Howe's submissions to the court: 'There is persuasive evidence to the effect that Sir John Kerr, *in his personal capacity*, gave instructions to Sir [sic] David Smith, *in his personal capacity*, to facilitate an arrangement with the Archives.' [my italics] This was central to the Archives' contention that the letters were personal, that everyone involved – Kerr, Smith, the Palace, the Queen, the Archives – had understood that they were personal and had acted accordingly at all times in a personal capacity. The problem for the Archives was that Fricker's 'persuasive evidence' directly contradicted the agreed facts, confirmed by his legal team, which stated that the letters had been deposited by Smith 'in his capacity as official secretary'. On closer analysis, Archives now realised that this agreed fact supported our case, and not theirs.

Howe tried to overcome this substantial discord in his key evidence by claiming that Fricker's respondent's submission was wrong – thereby undermining the key submission of the director-general of the National Archives – and that the agreed facts were correct. Howe presented a tangle of 'personal' and/or 'official' permutations in an effort to keep some semblance of consistency in this line of argument: 'We accept that when Sir [sic] David lodged the records he was doing so in an *official capacity*, but we say as an *agent and intermediary* for Sir John Kerr, in Sir John Kerr's *personal capacity*'. [my italics] So, Smith was acting in an official capacity, and Kerr was acting in a personal capacity; Smith was acting as an 'agent and intermediary' and not an official, although he was the official secretary and acting in his official capacity at the time he lodged the records. Justice Griffiths was struggling to keep up. 'So you leave in "personal" in the first line. You replace "personal" in the second line with "official"?', he asked quizzically.[23]

As if this were not bizarre enough, a furious David Smith later publicly disputed Howe's claim. 'That suggestion is false', he told the media. 'I acted as the Governor-General's official secretary and in accordance with his instructions.' Smith insisted that, 'I had no "personal capacity", whatever those words are supposed to mean', angrily getting to the very heart of the case.[24]

For the second time that day, Howe then introduced material that had not been presented in the written submissions. This time, it was not a specific piece of evidence, but a legal argument: the 'presumption of regularity'. Like the Fraser–Kerr letter, the Archives had not raised this approach in its formal submissions. 'Do you raise the presumption of regularity in your written submissions?', asked Griffiths. 'We don't, your Honour', Howe replied. At this, Griffiths replied, 'No. I didn't think you did', and Howe continued. To me, as the anxious applicant, this pushing of the procedural boundaries was now putting us at an obvious disadvantage.

Howe proceeded with a lengthy dissertation on 'the presumption of regularity': '[U]nless it's proven otherwise, the performance of an official act is presumed to be regular in the sense that any precondition governing its exercise is taken to be satisfied.' Which seemed to be an unduly complicated way of saying that if something is required to be done in a particular way, it should be presumed, in the absence of evidence to the contrary, to have been done correctly. Griffiths professed some difficulty in discerning its relevance, and also expressed his concern that Antony Whitlam had not had any opportunity to prepare for it: 'I would certainly want to make sure that Mr Whitlam has an opportunity properly to address. He has not been put on any notice about reliance upon that presumption either … I'm a little troubled by it.'[25] Griffiths assured Whitlam that he would have the opportunity to respond to this unexpected line of argument after Howe's presentation. However, as Howe mulled the expansive presumption of regularity for the rest of the day, that time would not come for another two months.

By 4.00 pm we had gone a full day, and Thomas Howe was yet

to complete his submission. He would need, he told Justice Griffiths, another forty minutes, and so there was an unexpected additional half-day hearing to come. Tom Brennan and Antony Whitlam were pleased, a little surprised by the emphasis the Archives continued to place on earlier versions of the *Archives Bill* rather than on the actual terms of the Act, and particularly surprised by its reliance on British practice with the Royal Archives, and on the expectations of Buckingham Palace rather than on the application of our own statutory law. Whether Justice Griffiths found this approach of post-imperial legal subservience as unconvincing as we did would have to wait until much later, until at least our scheduled second day of 6 September, I thought rather bitterly, ruing Thomas Howe's time-crunching 'presumption of regularity'.

I emerged into Phillip Street to find that a cold change had blown across Sydney, and a lone photographer was waiting for a windswept photo in a sprinkle of rain. Umbrellas were up, people were scurrying, and heads were down when I found myself standing on the kerb, waiting for the traffic to clear – alongside Justice John Griffiths. I'm not sure whether it was a look of surprise or horror I glimpsed in his face, but with that flicker of recognition he sprinted across Macquarie Street, narrowly missing an oncoming taxi that slid to a halt as the rain tumbled down. It had been a long day.

Chapter Six

Fourteen minutes

David Fricker walked up the semi-circular driveway, through the heavy panelled doors and into Government House. He carried with him a National Archives of Australia records box, filled with Palace letters. It was 2013. Following repeated requests by researchers to access the letters, Fricker had taken them to Government House to discuss the possibility of their release.

The office of the governor-general, Dame Quentin Bryce, together with the National Archives, jointly sought the advice of the solicitor-general, Justin Gleeson SC, on whether the Palace letters were personal or official communications, and therefore Commonwealth records.[1] The incoming attorney-general, Labor's Mark Dreyfus QC, strongly supported the release of the letters and readily agreed that the solicitor-general should advise on their possible release. Dreyfus thought it 'ludicrous' that correspondence between the Queen and the governor-general could be labelled personal. 'They were not inviting each other to afternoon tea!', he later argued. 'We live under a passive monarchy where the rule of law and the principles of transparency and probity are not run past the Queen for her approval but established in this parliament ... and upheld in the courts of Australia.'[2]

Everything hinged on Gleeson's advice. If the solicitor-general considered the Palace letters to be official vice-regal communications and not 'personal', the prime minister, Julia Gillard, as the responsible minister, could advise the governor-general to inform the Queen that the letters were to be released under the Australian *Archives Act*. If not, the Queen's embargo would remain.

Government House was spinning with the arrival of Gleeson's advice, which could see the final severance of this vestigial colonial tie, the end of royal control over our national archives and our documentary history. And for the first few pages, it seemed that it would. Reading through Gleeson's advice as it seemed headed ineluctably towards the release of the letters, a senior government official told me he thought this was going to make history.

However, it appears that, as with most legal opinions, Gleeson also sounded a note of caution, an 'on the other hand' caveat flagging potential problems, as legal opinions must, acknowledging the difficulty posed by the current embargo over the letters being 'in accordance with the Queen's wishes'. From this, the Archives interpreted Gleeson's Opinion as meaning that it could not release the letters, and 'that it does not have the power or authority to give access other than in accordance with the instrument of deposit'. The Queen's embargo remained.[3]

In history as in politics, timing is everything. Within weeks, a leadership change and an election loss intervened. The Labor government lost office in September 2013, and for the next four years the pursuit of the Palace letters became lost to public view. The new coalition government was led by Tony Abbott, an arch conservative and ardent monarchist who quickly reintroduced knighthoods, the first of which was bestowed on the Queen's consort, the multi-titled Prince Philip, thereby transforming a blustering attempt at royal deference into international parody.[4]

Senator George Brandis, the youthful friend of Sir John Kerr turned Liberal Party grandee, was Abbott's attorney-general and also minister for the arts, a portfolio that included the National Archives of Australia.[5] Under Brandis, as the minister responsible, the solicitor-general's advice about the possible release of the Palace letters was quietly shelved and never released. Abbott was in turn replaced by Malcolm Turnbull as Liberal leader and prime minister in 2015, in a bitter party-factional dispute. The contrast between the two could not have been greater. Turnbull was a prominent republican – he had led the Australian Republican Movement in 1999 in a failed referendum to sever Australia's ties to the monarchy and establish an Australian republic.

Perhaps it was a rush of newly anointed prime ministerial excitement, or an opportunity to revisit his earlier anti-British-establishment success with his spectacular victory in the *Spycatcher* case; but, not long after his ascension as prime minister, Turnbull vowed that he would 'resolve the impasse' over the Palace letters by personally approaching the Queen and asking her to release them. Turnbull's push for their release was reportedly supported by his attorney-general, Brandis who, together with Turnbull, had 'decided that this correspondence had been falsely labelled as "private", and that the Governor-General will be advised by the responsible Ministers to request the Palace to release the correspondence'.[6] My strong and longstanding view was that asking the Queen for her permission to release our own archival records was both legally and politically wrong – it accepted the claim of royal secrecy and privilege over the governor-general's records, and sought an imperial release from it. It did nothing to resolve the fundamental question of whether the Palace letters were Commonwealth records to be dealt with under Australian law.

In advising Turnbull about the letters, whatever that advice might have been, Brandis had done the politically unthinkable and failed to consult his own solicitor-general. Even worse, he had ignored Gleeson's previous advice on this very matter, which the solicitor-general had prepared for the office of Governor-General and the Archives just three years earlier. At this point, Brandis's and the solicitor-general's already acrimonious personal and political relationship erupted spectacularly and publicly; Gleeson, describing his relationship with Brandis as 'irretrievably broken', resigned. It was the end point in a long political and personal struggle between Brandis and Gleeson, the two most senior legal figures in the country, which involved in part the Palace letters and Gleeson's still secret advice about them. Gleeson cited as one of the factors in his dramatic resignation a failure by Brandis to seek his previous advice in relation to the release of correspondence between Sir John Kerr and the Queen in 1975. It appeared, as one commentator said at the time, that Brandis 'did not want to hear what [Gleeson] had to say about the release of the letters'.[7]

Out of this political turmoil, one question was absolutely vital for the Palace letters Federal Court case that was then in progress – had prime minister Turnbull advised the Queen to release the Palace letters, as he had promised? The answer to this was critical: if the letters were suddenly to be released with the Queen's imprimatur, the case might well be redundant. James Whittaker at Corrs Chambers Westgarth wrote to the prime minister in June 2017, asking Turnbull 'to confirm whether or not you have approached Buckingham Palace and/or the Governor-General to request the release of the correspondence in question'.[8] On the eve of the second day's hearing before Justice Griffiths in the Federal Court, the prime minister replied: 'Discussions/communications between the Prime Minister and Her Majesty the Queen are confidential.'

On 6 September 2017, we gathered again in courtroom 21B in Sydney's Law Courts building, two months after the hearing had first begun. This unexpected additional half-day had been scheduled in order for Antony Whitlam QC to have the 'right of reply' promised then by Justice Griffiths, but which the lengthy submission of the Archives' barrister, Thomas Howe QC, had left no time for.

The intervening two months had been busy. The extra time had, in the end, been propitious, giving us the opportunity to gather more evidence, conduct more archival searches, and follow some leads about the new evidence introduced by Howe on the eve of the hearing – Malcolm Fraser's 1977 letter to Kerr. When Howe had triumphantly produced Fraser's letter, he had failed to include a crucial document referred to in it: cabinet submission no. 1731 of 26 October 1977. Since Antony Whitlam was yet to give his response to either the new evidence or Howe's presentation, we used this time to prepare a detailed written submission dealing with both. In all, we would present six new documents in response to the Fraser letter, including the cabinet submission, which I had readily found on open access in the Archives. Neither Fraser's letter, nor the terms of the draft Bill to which it referred, could be understood without that submission, since, as Fraser wrote, 'the detail of this [the draft Bill] is set out in Submission No. 1731'.

So, what did submission no. 1731 actually say? The most important thing was that it fully acknowledged that the Palace letters were Commonwealth records. This was a cabinet submission that dealt entirely with the 'archival control of the custody of and access to Commonwealth records', and it considered the letters one of a particular 'class of records', together with cabinet records, Executive Council records, and other unquestionably Commonwealth records, that were to be excluded from the reach of the draft *Archives Bill*. The exclusion of the records of a governor-general in the earlier versions of the Bill was in itself nothing new. What was new and, we thought, highly significant was the acknowledgement that they were nonetheless Commonwealth records.

The missing cabinet submission completely overturned Howe's interpretation of Fraser's letter, that the exclusion of a governor-general's papers from the *Archives Bill* implied 'personal' ownership. It showed, to the contrary, that the governor-general's records were excluded from the Bill as part of a particular group of Commonwealth records, not as personal records.

Beyond the documents contesting Fraser's letter, there were three historical aspects that Antony Whitlam was to emphasise in his right of reply: the appointments and backgrounds of governors-general; the different locations of their records; and the history of the Archives and of the Archives legislation. In different ways, each of these related to one of the most interesting facets of this case: its intersection of law, politics, and history. In pursuing these, Whitlam was pointing to something very familiar in interdisciplinary research and rarely acknowledged in the singular focus of the law: legal meanings are constructed through the prism of history and politics, disturbing though that might seem for legal purists. In the splendid reflection of Australia's first solicitor-general, Sir Robert Garran, 'constitutional law is not pure logic, it is logic plus politics. However shocking this thought is, we cannot get away from it'.[9]

Howe's arguments about the records of past governors-general were impossible to understand separate from their historical and political contexts, to which he had made scant reference. Howe made much of the fact that of the seven governors-general before Lord Casey, none had left their personal papers or their Palace correspondence with what is now the National Archives – 'Archives holds no records whatsoever of any of these governors-general' – and six of them had placed their records with the National Library of Australia.[10]

Howe argued that placing their papers with the National Library rather than the Archives was indicative of personal ownership, that each departing governor-general had taken their personal papers with them before deciding subsequently to lodge them with the library. The reality was more pedestrian. It took just a quick perusal of the history of the Archives, as we detailed in our 'submissions in reply', to show that from 1944 to 1961 the function of the Archives was performed by the Archives Division of the National Library. That essential historical context transformed the picture completely to now show that six governors-general before Casey had indeed placed their personal records in the Archives – by placing them in the National Library. Whitlam would bring these details, and the cabinet submission, to the attention of Justice Griffiths at this second day's hearing.

The hearing was scheduled to begin at 10.15 am and finish at 12.30 pm, providing just over two hours for verbal submissions. Since the main purpose of this short hearing was for Antony Whitlam to present our points in reply, already held over from two months earlier, I expected that he would be speaking for most of that morning. However, Thomas Howe was not yet done with his submissions from the first day, and he asked for a further forty minutes. Whitlam would then have over an hour to speak, which would give him good time to work through all the material in our submission in reply.

As the hearing resumed, Howe rose to speak with the familiar opening, 'Your Honour pleases'. He got no further before Whitlam interrupted his 'learned friend', drawing Justice Griffith's attention to the submissions in reply he intended to give, and pointing to the documents we had tendered in response to the Fraser letter, in particular the cabinet submission, which, Whitlam emphasised to Griffiths, was 'an important one'. Whitlam was determined that his intention to speak in reply was clear to the court and could not be ignored. Justice Griffiths called on Howe to 'resume your submissions in chief'.

It was 10.35 am as Howe began taking the court through the royal correspondence of every governor-general since Lord Stonehaven, ending with Lord Casey's 'immediate predecessor Lord Sydney, who left office in 1965'. Except, as Justice Griffiths pointed out, there was no governor-general Sydney. Howe should have paid more attention to the vice-regal history we had sketched in our submission. What followed was a comedic exchange marked by historical error and inadvertent parody.

'There was a *Governor* Sydney', Justice Griffiths mused, at which Whitlam corrected him: There was a Viscount Sydney, he was 'Secretary of State', not governor and not governor-general.[11] Griffiths hazarded another guess, 'Slim, is it?' Whitlam corrected him again: 'Later, Viscount Slim, but not Viscount when he was a GG', before correcting them both on the governor-general before Casey, 'It's De L'Isle', Whitlam said, sounding slightly exasperated.

> **Mr Howe:** Viscount De L'Isle.
> **His Honour:** I think it was Lord De Lisle, wasn't it?
> **Mr Whitlam:** Lord De L'Isle.
> **Mr Howe:** Lord De L'Isle.[12]

This historical lapse could not have provided a clearer example of the pitfalls of ahistoricism in this area, and it didn't end there. Howe was soon struggling with the date on which Sir John Kerr took up office as governor-general, mistaking the date of his appointment in June 1974 for the date of his taking up the office. Whitlam again corrected him, 'No, it was July … He was appointed by that instrument in June, but he didn't take office until July 11.' Justice Griffiths quipped, 'I better swear you and put you on the witness box, Mr Whitlam.'[13] It was the only faint moment of levity I felt all day.

And so it continued, through all governors-general up to and including Sir John Kerr, as Howe argued that there was 'a shared understanding' among them that the Palace letters were personal.[14] 'They might be wrong', Griffiths pointed out; after all, what the governor-general, or the Archives staff, or the prime minister, or even the Queen herself believed to be the case did not make it so. Mere assertions of their 'personal' nature did not determine the legal construction of whether they were personal or Commonwealth property – that was for Justice Griffiths to rule. 'Ultimately you would accept that I am charged with the responsibility for construing the legislation ... their views don't bind me', he said. On that, we were in complete agreement.

More than an hour had passed before Howe ended his excursus through the royal correspondence of governors-general before and after Kerr, when Griffiths expressed his concern about the time Howe was taking. 'Your estimate last time was about forty minutes. Well, it seems to have taken a bit longer than that. How long are you going to be?' Howe offered to finish at ten past twelve, which would be a further half-hour, and would leave Whitlam with just twenty minutes to present his reply.

Howe continued arguing for reciprocity between British and Australian archives, that Australian rules should mirror those in the UK, in what he called a 'regulation in favour of reciprocity'. He even argued that there could be 'shared ownership' of the letters between Kerr and the Queen, which no one had to that point suggested.

As the morning ticked away, even the 'principle of regularity' dealt with so extensively on the first day got another run, despite Justice Griffiths' view of its dubious relevance: 'To what does the principle of regularity attach in the particular circumstances of this case?', he asked. Howe pressed on, apparently heedless of time or relevance, for another thirty-five minutes. And with every one of those precious minutes being taken up, I felt our carefully prepared submissions draining out of courtroom 21 and disappearing down Phillip Street in an interminable legal filibuster.

When Justice Griffiths finally called on Antony Whitlam to speak, it was 12.13 pm, and we were due to finish at 12.30 pm. Whitlam moved 'very quickly' through the historical context, keen to get to the cabinet submission rebutting Howe's strained interpretation of Fraser's 1977 letter to Kerr, and then on to the convoluted trajectory of the *Archives Act*, in order to stress that the Act that came into force in 1983 was a different scheme altogether from that proposed in the draft Bill six years earlier. Our written submissions in reply were extensive, and there was simply no time to work through it all.

Whitlam concluded by posing a question and a corollary: the Archives contended that the Palace letters were not Commonwealth records because the correspondence was not owned by the Commonwealth. 'Who then do they say it is the property of?', Whitlam asked. According to the Archives, he continued, it was the property of Kerr's second wife's daughter, Stephanie Bashford:

The consequence of the Commonwealth's argument is this: ... these extraordinarily sensitive, very personal documents could be demanded back by Mrs Bashford tomorrow and ... returned to Mrs Bashford for her to dispose of as she wishes. ... On the Commonwealth's argument, it would be perfectly appropriate for Mrs Bashford to retrieve the documents [the Palace letters], sell them to whomever she wishes, including perhaps another nation.[15]

The implications of this disarming corollary so piqued Howe that he was up on his feet at once, wanting to counter it. And so that was the end of Antony Whitlam's right of reply that we had waited over two months to present – fourteen minutes.

***

A rare early-morning snow was drifting across Canberra, the café windows turning to mist from the people crowding around to watch snow falling in Kingston. It was shortly before the second day's hearing, and I was deep in the papers of the former Liberal senator Alan Missen, who had refused to support Malcolm Fraser's efforts to exclude governors-general's records from the *Archives Bill*.

Missen was one of the core group of dissident Liberal senators in 1975 vehemently opposed to Fraser's decision to block the Whitlam government's supply bills in the Senate – 'the nearest thing to wrecking democracy', Missen had termed it – and who were threatening to break ranks and pass supply the longer the stalemate continued.[16] I found it impossible to separate Missen's opposition to Fraser's *Archives Bill*, which would have kept all of Kerr's papers about the dismissal secret, from his determined opposition just three years earlier to the blocking of supply and the dismissal. And so, as we waited for the Federal Court judgment to be delivered, I returned to Missen's papers with its manuscript boxes bursting with draft *Archives Bills*, committee reports, draft amendments, and second-reading speeches, curious as to the strength of Missen's conviction that the governor-general's records should be in the Archives and open for public access.

Missen had always been something of a rebel in the Liberal Party, of which he was a founding member, pushing for its 'small-l' liberal side against the hard-line conservatives of the old United Australia Party. He had caused an outcry in 1951 with his strident opposition to prime minister Robert Menzies' multiple efforts to pass the *Communist Party Dissolution Bill*, and had actively campaigned against the government's unsuccessful referendum to pass it.[17] Two decades later, Missen again agonised over his party's political tactics with the Coalition's unprecedented decision to defer the government's supply bills in the Senate, deeply concerned by the breach of convention. In early October, 'I urged the party not to agree to the course proposed, which I felt was, both in principle and practice, to be deplored', Missen wrote.[18]

Throughout that vital month, Missen waged an internal campaign against this contentious tactic as rumours raged that he and other Liberal senators were on the verge of crossing the floor and allowing the budget to pass. Nevertheless, none of the doubting senators spoke out publicly, and the budget was duly deferred. Over the succeeding years, rumours that there had been a group of Liberal dissidents set to vote against their leadership resurfaced intermittently, only to be denied and advanced in turn with every posthumous confession and new revelation in the history of the dismissal.

It was while I was searching through Missen's records on the draft *Archives Bills* that I came across a document that answered these competing claims about the rogue Liberal senators. Another missing piece in the dismissal history had finally emerged.

Missen's position on supply had become a marker for the partisan claims that passed as history in the decades after the dismissal. Those who supported Fraser and Kerr's actions emphatically denied that Missen or any other Coalition senators would have crossed the floor, claiming that, 'Missen had no intention of crossing the floor and voting against the Malcolm Fraser led opposition on this issue.'[19] Others insisted that a small group of Liberal senators were set to break ranks and allow the budget to pass, and that only Kerr's actions had prevented that final capitulation.

Missen's biographer, Anton Hermann, neatly glides over the month in which supply was blocked, as though Missen had barely raised a murmur against it in the party room in early October, before accepting the party line: 'During the 1975 constitutional crisis, he opposed the Senate's withholding of supply from the government, although he reluctantly voted with the Opposition on procedural issues.'[20] Missen's close friend and colleague Peter Baume suggests otherwise: 'Of all these doubters, Missen was the one of greatest clarity of view and experience. He was a man of courage and determination and I wonder how long it would have been before he, or one of his colleagues, would have cried "enough". We will never know.'[21]

Well, we do know. Missen's papers answer the burning question of whether the rebel senators would have allowed the budget to pass. Among Missen's papers is a single typed document, a personal diary entry headed 'Confidential. Diary entries in respect to the constitutional crisis – October 1975'.[22] It begins: 'This is a record for future reminder, of events which have transpired in recent days, concerning the decision of the Opposition Parties to defeat, or delay, the Budget. It is highly confidential, and is retained for historical purposes.'

Missen's diary vindicates the view that a political solution to the crisis was at hand and that the Senate was about to 'break', and refutes the historical claims of both Fraser and Kerr that the Senate would never have passed supply. Missen recounts that he, together with four fellow dissident Liberal senators – Jessop, Bessell, Laucke, and Bonner – had made a pact, just days before the dismissal. Missen writes, in his entry for the week ending 3 November 1975, that 'a bleak position' for the opposition had developed, and if 'it was a choice between voting for or against the Budget Bills, we would all abstain and allow the Budget to pass'. The five rebels had 'quietly reached this resolution on the Tuesday' – that is, one week before the dismissal.

Hermann cites this diary in confidently asserting that Missen 'adhered to his original strategy by refusing to break ranks on the floor of the Senate'.[23] Hermann makes no reference to the wavering senators' later agreement shortly before the dismissal that, if faced with a choice of voting for or against the budget, they would abstain.[24] This selective use of entries from Missen's diary, largely ignoring the shifting positions of the five doubters, their anguish and sense of betrayal of their political principles, and their resolution, has marred our understanding of the dismissal for too long. This agreement would have had critical consequences for Whitlam's decision to call the half-Senate election, had that election been granted contingent on the passage of supply.

The unexpected detail in Missen's papers about the intentions of the rebel senators had also added, for me, to the growing questions over what Kerr was telling the Queen about these manoeuvres in the Senate and over the half-Senate election. It is generally forgotten that Fraser had already publicly stated on 22 October 1975 that he would respect whatever decision the governor-general made, later conceding that if the half-Senate election had been called he would have resigned the Liberal leadership, and the budget bills would have been passed: 'What we would have done is to let Supply through.'[25] Fraser's treasurer, Phil Lynch, had also acknowledged this in an unpublished interview with the journalist Alan Reid: 'If the GG had made a decision for a half-Senate election, yes ... there was not much we could do about it. It would have been', Lynch told Reid. Asked whether they would then have granted supply, Lynch replied, 'We would have.'[26]

What then did Kerr tell the Queen about these critical decisions by the opposition, so often lost to history, about the fragile situation in the Senate and over the half-Senate election? Did he inform the Queen of the wavering opposition senators and the uncertainty of their position? And did he tell her of Fraser's public commitment to 'respect and accept' whatever decision the governor-general made?

It was at this time, as we waited for Justice Griffiths to hand down his decision, that I was first contacted by someone inside the Archives in a 'private communication', with a dossier of Archive documents. I had often wondered whether such a contact in the Archives would come forward; now, with the evidence in the Federal Court concluded, and some clarity over the type of material that might help our case, it had happened. Although they asked that their identity not be made public, they made no effort to hide it from me or the legal team, and referred us only to open-access documents in the Archives that were already in the public domain and that might be useful.

Much of this material focused on the Archives Bills and their contested provisions, on Brandis's fracas with the solicitor-general, and on the property-based definition of 'Commonwealth record' – all of which we had already seen. I didn't know whether to be disappointed that there was nothing new in this haul, or to be pleased that our research had been so thorough. Either way, it was reassuring to know that someone in the Archives was hoping for our success and willing to help us achieve it.

The rumblings of internal dissatisfaction were growing with the Archives' mounting expenditure contesting this case. The Archives had faced a decade of budget cuts, and had shed nearly 25 per cent of its staff, and yet in just two years it had already spent $500,000 fighting my efforts to secure public access to the Palace letters.[27] As the minister responsible, George Brandis would have had final approval over this significant expenditure, and as attorney-general he could also have taken over the case and ended it, paving the way for the public release of the letters. He chose not to, and the political dimensions of the case grew as the costs escalated. With public criticisms of access delays, depleted resources, and over-stretched staff, the Archives had become, as Professor Anne Twomey described it, 'completely dysfunctional', and was fracturing.[28]

That was not the last we would hear from our contact inside the Archives.

***

Six months had passed since Justice Griffiths had reserved his judgment in September, and we had heard nothing. The average time for the delivery of Federal Court judgments was three months, and the Palace letters case was by no means a complex one – a single applicant, a sole respondent, with a central legal question over the meaning of a Commonwealth record – and the longer we waited, the more concerned we became.

Finally, on 7 March 2018, Corrs Chambers Westgarth received an email from Justice Griffiths' chambers:

> Justice Griffiths has asked me to apologise for the delay in publishing the judgment in this matter as his Honour has been preoccupied with other judicial demands. There is an existing advanced draft judgment which his Honour hopes to finalise and publish by the end of the month.

At least now we knew that there was a draft, and that we might receive the judgment by the end of the month – fully six months from the end of the already protracted hearing, and eight months since the first, substantive, full day's hearing.

Late on Friday 16 March 2018, Justice Griffiths handed down his decision. Tom Brennan and the solicitors from Corrs walked with me down Phillip Street, past the now-familiar huddle of journalists and cameras awaiting the outcome, and into the Law Courts building. Antony Whitlam was in his chambers, waiting to hear the decision and to read the judgment alone; we would join him afterwards. Would these historic letters between the Queen and the governor-general about Kerr's dismissal of the Whitlam government be recognised as Commonwealth records and opened for public access? Could we now, forty-three years later, finally know that history?

It was two years since I had first walked into Tom Brennan's office with a copy of *The Dismissal Dossier* and walked out with the idea of a court case. I took my seat behind the legal team, gripped my court notes, and tried to stay hopeful. Within minutes, Justice Griffiths had said those two devastating words: 'Application dismissed'.

Chapter Seven

'Who cares what the Queen thinks?'

Antony Whitlam's normally placid demeanour was gone; he was flushed and agitated. Justice Griffiths' judgment was still in his hand as he rose from his desk: 'I don't mind losing,' he said, waving the handful of pages towards us, 'but I do mind losing for things I didn't say!' In that rare moment of indignation, Whitlam had captured the most disheartening part of what was, for us, a lamentable judgment – its misrepresentation of the essence of our case.

Griffiths had prepared a summary document, something only done for Federal Court matters of 'public interest, importance or complexity', recognising the 'clear public interest' in the Palace letters that 'relate to one of the most controversial and tumultuous events in the modern history of the nation, namely Sir John Kerr's dismissal of Prime Minister Gough Whitlam'.[1] The judgment acknowledged that the Palace letters consisted of 'letters or telegrams between Sir John Kerr acting in his capacity as Governor-General and the Queen', that they had been deposited in the Archives by Mr David Smith, also acting 'in his capacity as Official Secretary', and that the letters addressed 'topics relating to the official duties and responsibilities of the Governor-General'.[2] Nevertheless, Griffiths found, with devastating finality, that I had 'failed to establish any reviewable error' in Archives' decision denying me access to them.[3] The Palace letters were Sir John Kerr's personal records, his personal property, and not Commonwealth records. The Queen's embargo over them therefore remained.

At 47 pages, the judgment was brief, and Griffiths' analysis, essentially the reasons for his decision, just 14 pages. In that analysis, Griffiths had miscast our 'core submission', describing it as: 'that the correspondence comprising AA1984/609 should be viewed as the property of the Commonwealth simply because its subject matter relates to the performance of the Governor General's role and function'.[4] This, as Antony Whitlam felt most keenly, was something we had never said. Our central submission had always been more precise and nuanced: the Palace letters were Commonwealth records because, first, they were between the Queen of Australia and the governor-general, written when both were acting in their official capacities; and, second, because their subject matter related to the performance of the governor-general's role and function.

In his analysis, Griffiths reduced that central submission to a crude absolutism – that *all* communications by Kerr whose 'subject matter relates to the Governor-General's role and function' were Commonwealth records *simply because of* that subject matter. This was a classic straw argument, readily refuted in the judgment that followed, since there are many aspects of a governor-general's communications that are not also Commonwealth records, despite their subject matter relating to the performance of his role and functions – Christmas cards to other dignitaries, for instance, or medical checks prior to leaving for official visits overseas, or a personal diary describing aspects of their daily work. We had argued only that documents prepared by Commonwealth office-holders, including the governor-general and the Queen, in the performance of their office *and concerning matters relating to the performance of their office*, were Commonwealth records. Those important caveats had escaped Griffiths' view as he re-presented our core submission as crude and unqualified. It was all the more egregious since Whitlam had emphasised the narrowness of our approach to the central question in several exchanges with Griffiths during the first day of hearings.[5]

Even more perplexing was that Griffiths accurately described our submission in his introductory remarks: 'The applicant's core submission was that communications by Constitutional office-holders in the performance of their office concerning the Government of the Commonwealth ... are Commonwealth property'.[6] Yet in the judgment itself he omitted the essential qualifier, 'in the performance of their office', recasting it as a blunt, catch-all concept that, just to add to the conceptual injury, he then criticised as being too broad: 'In my respectful view, that submission adopts an unduly broad-brush approach to the role and responsibilities of the Governor-General'.[7]

On reading this searing judgment, the impact of Whitlam's lost right of reply was telling. Griffiths had failed to engage with our submissions on either the care and control over the letters by David Smith, who had deposited them with the Archives, or the law of public office regarding Commonwealth ownership of them, both of which Whitlam had intended to speak to in his reply.[8] It was not that Griffiths disputed the argument about the law of public office; in this context he did not examine it at all, dismissing it in just two sentences without elaboration.[9] By contrast, two pages of his brief analysis were spent respectfully exploring the faddish 'principle of regularity' propounded by the Archives' lawyer, Thomas Howe QC, at such length on both days of the hearing, before concluding that it was irrelevant.[10]

The summary was shattering enough, and the full judgment even more so. The court accepted the Archives' submissions on almost every substantive point: on the interpretation of the *Archives Act* as meaning that the governor-general's records were excluded from it, even though the Act did not expressly exclude them; on the 'perception of ownership' of the letters by Kerr, Fraser, Buckingham Palace, and other officials as indicative of Kerr's actual personal ownership of the letters;[11] and on the unique, 'strong *sui generis* quality' of the correspondence between a governor-general and the monarch, which 'traditionally has been regarded as the personal property of the correspondents'.[12]

The notion of *sui generis* was a perfect legal cloak for claims of royal exceptionalism, effectively placing the letters outside the governor-general's official correspondence and the expectations of responsible government, and at the same time ensuring their secrecy.[13] Griffiths went further on this even than the Archives had submitted, in finding that 'both The Queen and the Governor-General have a mutual interest in the ownership and disposal' of the letters, enabling the Queen to exercise control over access to them. The notion of 'mutual interest' neatly dealt with the dubious status of the changes made to Kerr's conditions of access 'on the instruction of the Queen', by which the Queen had given herself an indefinite embargo, after Kerr's death.

In this trail of legal disappointments, it was Griffiths' deference to British law and expectation that I found most disheartening. In accepting the claimed convention of royal secrecy over the letters as 'personal' correspondence, Griffiths ruled that it would require a statement of 'clear and explicit language' to overturn it.[14] He clearly did not accept that the *Archives Act 1983*, which made no mention of any such convention or established practice, was sufficient to indicate that our own statutory regime governed the letters.[15] This finding not only recognised the convention of royal secrecy; it gave primacy to it over any Australian law that did not explicitly overturn it. Griffiths accepted the relevance of 'the position in the United

Kingdom' regarding the secrecy of royal letters, and the need to be 'broadly consistent' with the 'special archival arrangements' of the Royal Archives in Windsor Castle, in reaching his extraordinary finding that British law and practice, not Australian law, applied to the Palace letters in Australia.[16] This conclusion, which returned Australia to a subservient colonial status in its archival relationship with the United Kingdom, was particularly difficult to digest. Yet now we had to.

I faced the dreadful realisation that far from releasing the Palace letters, my failed efforts had only left them tied up even more tightly at the mercy of royal whim in a judicially conferred outsourcing of our vice-regal archives to the Royal Archives. This was not good.

There is a performative, ritualistic, aspect to the law that becomes its essential protector in the face of defeat. Court judgments are harsh, unforgiving rejections of carefully structured, meticulously evidenced, perfectly presented legal logic – after which the lawyers on both sides return to their chambers and pick up their next file. Professional survival is marked by a series of rapid emotional transitions: from disappointment to indignation, through a critique of the manifest failings of judges unable to recognise the brilliance of legal arguments; to finding 'clear errors of fact and law' in the judge's reasoning; and, finally, in the perfect denouement, to rousing cries of 'Appeal!'

With the downcast legal team still pouring over Griffiths' judgment, I left Whitlam's chambers for a long media interview at which I was no less despondent. I used the standard non-committal words, 'My lawyers are examining the judgment, and we will make a decision about any further action shortly.' In fact, after this dispiriting judgment, the question of where we might go from here had not even crossed my mind.

So, this was the end of our efforts to unlock the Palace letters: all I had achieved was to cement their unavailability, our subservience to the monarch, and the legal recognition of an absurd, insulting royal 'convention' of secrecy over our own historical archives. Abject humiliation at every level. I was certainly in no rush to return to the disconsolate dissection of the merits or otherwise of Griffiths, J. I slowly retraced my steps down the long corridor as the sound of animated voices rolled towards me, and the only word I could make out was 'appeal'. What a transformation! It was as if a legal morgue had suddenly come to life, an infectious energy was bouncing off the certainty that there were clear grounds for appeal.

Antony Whitlam never lost his focus or his perspective. Whatever he thought of the Federal Court decision – 'Of course, I disagree with it,' he said – he advised me to seek another legal opinion about it. I needed fresh eyes, a disinterested assessment of the judgment and the prospects of appeal, and, even more difficult, I needed this from someone willing to do this *pro bono*. But where could I hope to find a senior barrister with both the gravitas and the public-spiritedness for that? And one more thing, Antony said: I had just three weeks to do it.

I left Whitlam's office with the faintest glimmer of hope as darkness was closing in on an early Sydney autumn. I had no barrister, no funds, and three weeks to find both and to lodge an appeal. The case hovered in legal limbo, and the only way I could think about where it might go from there was not to think about it at all. I focused on the next step – everything beyond that was unknown – and as I did at every major point during the case, I wrote about it, in an article for John Menadue's bastion of long-form political essays, *Pearls & Irritations*. Every few months, John would prompt me to write about the case and about the letters, even when I might have baulked at the very thought of it, and those pieces became a discursive record of an uncertain process.[17]

This time, there was something else to write about, something that had been agitating me since the first day's hearing. For eight months I had stayed silent about the dramatic revelation during the court proceedings that the Archives had misled me when it had first denied my access request to the copy file, and had then overseen changes to Mrs Bashford's conditions of access during the case, once again locking the copies away from public access. I had made no comment about any part of this disturbing episode, not wanting to risk the court process or rankle Justice Griffiths, and now was the time to write about it. In a piece for *Pearls & Irritations*, I detailed the Archives' inordinate determination to keep the Palace letters secret and its denial of my request to access the copies in 2011 on the basis that the file was 'completely closed'. My summary was that, 'It took another five years and a federal court action to reveal that this was simply not true.'[18]

Under the damning headline, 'Palace letters: historian claims National Archives misled her over copies', *The Guardian UK* then brought these disturbing actions to broad public knowledge for the first time, sparking a rare reaction from the Archives. Christopher Knaus from *The Guardian's* transparency project began, 'A leading historian has accused Australia's National Archives of misleading her when it barred her access to duplicates of [the Palace letters].'[19] For David Fricker, who had previously declined to comment on his contentious *post facto* change to the conditions of access over the copies, the ventilation of these 'serious allegations' stung, and he launched into a defensive denial:

There is no grand conspiracy. It's not because I'm obsessed about keeping secrets; it's what I have to do to preserve the integrity of the institution and maintain the trust of our depositors, who have deposited these very, very important documents.[20]

The changes to the Instrument of Deposit, Fricker insisted, were merely 'clarifying' the conditions of access.[21]

The day after this public excoriation of the Archives' constructed closure of 'these very, very important documents', the Palace letters case, which had seemed all but finished, rose again. Bret Walker SC agreed to advise on the prospects of an appeal against the Federal Court decision, and to appear in such an appeal, if it proceeded, and he would do so on a *pro bono* basis, along with the rest of the legal team. This was an extraordinary decision by Walker, one of Australia's top barristers and fast becoming *the* top barrister. I knew little about him other than that he was a former Independent National Security Legislation Monitor, that he had represented the major tobacco companies in their unsuccessful fight against the Gillard government's plain-paper-packaging legislation, and that he was currently representing Cardinal George Pell in his appeal against child sex-abuse convictions. It all made an interesting mix with the Palace letters case.[22] It was strangely comforting to think that the deep pockets of big tobacco and the Catholic Church might in some small way cross-subsidise my crowd-funded, *pro bono* case to unlock our royal dismissal correspondence.

Walker agreed with Antony Whitlam and Tom Brennan's advice that we had strong grounds for appeal. The remaining question was one that only I could answer: would there even be an appeal? At every stage in this legal process, I confronted the pressing issue of costs – both the non-legal costs and the far more significant prospect of adverse costs, the risk of an order to pay the National Archives' immense legal costs if I lost. I decided to relaunch the crowd-funding campaign as '*Release the Palace letters: the appeal*', and began the fund-raising process again.

Costs were becoming a major issue for the National Archives as well, raising questions about its priorities and whether it should be fighting attempts to access its most significant historical records in this way. Parliamentary questions on notice to the Liberal federal attorney-general, Christian Porter, revealed that the Archives had already spent half a million dollars of its stretched budget in contesting the case at the Federal Court, and they would face a significant amount at the appeal.[23] If I lost, I could face an order to pay the Archives' legal costs in full, close to $700,000.

At this point, the legal team all agreed that I should request an agreement with the Archives that would effectively cap the amount of costs I might face, should I lose the appeal. It was a huge step in my consideration of whether to continue with the case. There was, however, one very big catch: the Archives was unlikely to consider any cost arrangement unless I had actually filed the appeal. I could hardly expect my adversary to help salve my financial concerns and enable me to go ahead with the appeal by locking in a cost arrangement in advance.

Here was my essential dilemma: I could not get a cost agreement without appealing; I could not risk appealing without a cost agreement; and if I appealed without a cost agreement and then requested one, the Archives still might not agree to it. This was all bluff and pressure tactics, an interlude in which the Archives was waiting to see if I went ahead with the appeal, or abandoned it in the face of the daunting prospect of costs. Who would blink first?

The tension over those weeks was immense, and it was the closest I came to admitting defeat. Appeal first, the lawyers calmly advised, seek the cost agreement, and if Archives refuses it, then make a decision about continuing. Here was a strategy I recognised: basically, keep going, and put off the final decision until later. Perfect.

On 9 April 2018, I filed a Notice of Appeal in the Federal Court, appealing against 'the whole of the judgment and all of the orders' handed down by Justice Griffiths.[24] There were two main grounds for appeal: Griffiths' finding that the letters were the property of Sir John Kerr and not Commonwealth records, even though it was agreed that they were created and received by Kerr in the performance of his office; and, second, that Griffiths had wrongly inferred from the subjective 'perceptions of ownership' of the letters – by Kerr, Fraser, the Palace, who all claimed to believe that Kerr owned the records – that Kerr did in fact own them.

With the appeal filed, I requested a party/party cost agreement from the Archives. As a statutory body, the National Archives is bound to act as a 'model litigant', particularly in public-interest cases, and I hoped they would agree to party/party costs as a way of minimising my prospective costs and in order to move forward with the appeal. Two days later, the Australian Government Solicitors responded, 'We are instructed not to agree to your client's Appeal Costs Agreement.'[25]

A chance meeting with Jacob Varghese from Maurice Blackburn lawyers in Melbourne convinced me to reconsider one final avenue for financial protection: a Protective Cost Order from the Federal Court itself, which would cap the costs I could face. In this, Justice Griffiths had done me a great favour by acknowledging the 'clear public interest' in the letters and that they related 'to one of the most controversial and tumultuous events in the modern history of the nation'; not only did this highlight the public interest and significance of the letters, but it also opened the door to a protective cost order. The Federal Court is one of the few jurisdictions in Australia that provides such protection, even for vital public-interest cases, minimising the financial barriers to access to the courts that skews the legal system so profoundly. With the Archives refusing a cost agreement, a protective cost order from the Federal Court was my last hope for continuing the appeal without facing the risk of adverse costs. If this did not succeed, I would have no option but to withdraw.

At this critical time, the case was supported by the legal and advocacy organisation Grata, which helps secure the essential financial protection required for people to take public-interest cases to court. Named in honour of Grata Flos Matilda Greig, who in 1905 became the first woman admitted to practise law in Australia, Grata provided much-needed assistance with fund-raising to secure some protection against the risk of adverse costs. The great difficulty was that protective cost orders are rarely granted for public-interest cases, and usually only for matters of environmental, land rights, refugee, and anti-discrimination law. This case concerned a different type of public interest – to do with open access, transparency, and the right to know. If I secured this order, the Palace letters case would mark a new element in that public-interest pantheon. Importantly, and in line with their model-litigant responsibilities, the Archives did not contest my application, and on 22 June 2018 the Federal Court granted me a protective cost order, capping my costs exposure at $30,000.

With the appeal already scheduled to be heard by the Full Federal Court on 28 November 2018, it felt like a very big win.

On 21 August 1975, the governor-general, Sir John Kerr, addressed a private dinner for Sydney's cardinal, Sir Norman Gilroy, on a favoured theme, 'the Monarchy in this modern world and the Governor-Generalship today'.[26] It was an imagined monarchist idyll in which Kerr cast himself a central role. In this rambling, cloying exposition of royal idolatry, Kerr's errant view of his role as being to protect the Queen was on full display. Kerr was first and foremost a monarchist, 'otherwise I would not have taken this position', he confided to this high-conservative audience, which included the New South Wales Liberal premier, Tom Lewis, the governor of New South Wales, Sir Roden Cutler, and two visiting lords. Proudly describing himself as 'the Queen's only personal representative in Australia with direct access to her', Kerr revelled in his imagined personal proximity: 'I am in constant communication with her on a wide variety of matters, on most of which I am communicating directly to her.'

Forty-three years later, I was about to find out just how constant that communication had been. I had begun the case knowing little about the Palace letters, other than the evidence we had put to the court. We did not even know how many letters there were. As the case progressed, however, compelling new details emerged about them. One of the most important of these was their number: there were literally hundreds of Palace letters – 212 of them, to be precise – which was something I had never imagined. At most, I had expected there might be 40 or 50 letters in total, since previous governors-general had commonly reported to the Queen on a quarterly basis; but 212 letters sent between the Queen and the governor-general over a three-year period, with the great bulk of them written in the months before and after the dismissal, was a staggering number.

It was becoming increasingly difficult to claim that the Palace letters were nothing unusual, no more than conventional exchanges between a governor-general and the monarch. Hundreds of letters written during 'one of the most controversial and tumultuous events in the modern history of the nation' was hardly conventional. Just as important as the number of letters was a critical revelation during the case, that the Queen's letters to Kerr 'convey the thoughts of The Queen to the Governor-General'. This particularly significant detail is crucial to understanding the historic implications of the letters.

Since the case began, I had faced the incandescence of a dwindling band of Kerr supporters, monarchists, and the odd News Corp employee determined to present my legal pursuit of the letters as in itself a 'conspiracy', rather than as the kind of unexceptional archival research done by historians the world over. Every article referred reflexively to a wild 'conspiracy theory', using an unrecognisable refraction of my words – 'a pastiche of phrases, stripped of their context', as the *Justinian* termed it in a coruscating critique of their 'apoplectic' commentaries – to construct and denounce claims I had never made. The 'conspiracy' was of their own creation.[27] These base attempts to denigrate me and my work had begun years earlier, from the first of the revelations from Kerr's papers of Mason's role, which had turned the previous dismissal history on its head. It ran like a cantankerous ripple behind the latest revelations, despite the claims of 'exclusive' regularly attaching to their stories, and always ready to dismiss my research and my unpalatable conclusions as 'invented', based on 'no evidence', and even 'garbage'.[28] That 'garbage' now filled the Appeal Book with documentary evidence from years of archival research, making its way to the Full Federal Court for the appeal hearing on 28 November 2018.

The day began with a deluge. A month's worth of rain thundered across Sydney in less than two hours, flooding the city streets, turning roads to chaos, and making rivers from footpaths. The stairways in the rock face under Kings Cross were transformed into waterfalls, cascading all the way down to Woolloomooloo, along what had once been natural waterways.

In the middle of this biblical torrent, the Federal Court appeal was due to begin in an hour, and I had no hope of getting a bus, a train, or a taxi – all delayed for at least ninety minutes – and I stood in the rain with water filling my shoes, waiting for a taxi that never came and an Uber that eventually did. I finally arrived with minutes to spare, and joined the surprisingly large crowd snaking through the scanner and up to courtroom no. 23. James Whittaker, senior partner at Corrs Chambers Westgarth, had come to hear the morning session, a large number of journalists drifted in whom I recognised as having followed the case from the beginning, and

David Fricker arrived with a quietly confident nod of recognition towards them before taking his favoured position at the back of the court. Some supporters of the crowd-funding campaign gave me a thumbs-up – this was their case as well, and they were following every move and riding every bump along the way.

This was the first time I had met Bret Walker SC, on the day he appeared for me before the three Federal Court judges making up the Full Federal Court of Appeal: Chief Justice Allsop, and Justices Robertson and Flick. Walker was sharp, incisive, compact, and slightly owlish behind his round gold-rimmed glasses, and very different from his 'learned friend', Tom Brennan, with whom he was appearing at the appeal. With the case now on appeal, the Archives had gone right to the top: the solicitor-general of Australia, Stephen Donaghue QC, was appearing before the Full Federal Court with Craig Lenehan.

In our written submissions, Bret Walker had synthesised the original grounds for appeal into just one: Griffiths' finding that the Palace letters were the property of Sir John Kerr and not the Commonwealth.[29] This single ground, effectively challenging the entirety of Griffiths' judgment, took two forms: the first, legal, dealt with the law of public office, the claimed 'constitutional convention' of royal secrecy, the constitutional relationship between Australia and the United Kingdom, and the statutory interpretation of the *Archives Act*, on each part of which we argued that the Federal Court had erred. The second aspect was broadly evidentiary, on the historical facts, covering the inferences of personal ownership drawn by Griffiths from the archival documents that we had presented, and the custody of and control over the letters by the official secretary, David Smith. All of which, we argued, supported the inference that the letters were the property of the Commonwealth.[30]

Walker immediately undercut the reasoning at the heart of Griffiths' judgment regarding the unique nature, or what the judge

ABOVE: The long and the short of it. Jenny Hocking, Tim Bunker of Corrs Chambers Westgarth, Tom Brennan, and Antony Whitlam QC, ready for the Federal Court of Australia hearing, 31 July 2017. *(Daryl Dellora)*

RIGHT: The view from Buckingham Palace as the case begins, confirming the Palace letters must remain strictly confidential. *(FOI 131, National Archives of Australia)*

BUCKINGHAM PALACE

2nd February, 2017.

Dear Mark,

Thank you for your letter and enclosures of 1st February in which you give notice of the commencement of legal proceedings in the Federal Court of Australia to examine whether records held by the National Archives of Australia, including correspondence between The Queen and former Governor-General Sir John Kerr, ought to be defined as official Commonwealth Records under the Archives Act 1983.

Your letter seeks to establish, as a matter of public record, the terms of the understanding between our respective offices under which the records of Governors-General are deposited in the National Archives of Australia. I can confirm that, as the previous correspondence highlighted in your letter indicates, it is the firm view of this office that there is a strong public interest for communications between the Sovereign and her Governors-General to be subject to a strict convention of confidentiality.

The Royal Household agrees with the assessment outlined in your predecessor's letter of 7th April 2011 that correspondence between the Sovereign and her Governors-General and their respective offices are made in confidence. These are essentially private communications which are inherently sensitive. It has therefore been my understanding, and that of my predecessors, that the records in question are not caught by the Archives Act 1983, but are instead retained on the advice of the Royal Household for a minimum period of 50 years to reflect the uniqueness of the length of a reign. For the avoidance of doubt, I can confirm that the embargo period of 50 years applies in each of

LEFT: Sir Martin Charteris, private secretary to the Queen.

LEFT LOWER: 'The task is done'. The official secretary, David Smith, prepares a duplicate set of Palace letters for the former governor-general, Sir John Kerr, central to the success of the Palace letters case. *(National Archives of Australia)*

GOVERNMENT HOUSE

CANBERRA

3 June 1978

Dear Sir John,

The task is done, and with these papers come my apologies for taking so long. I am afraid that I badly under-estimated the number of hours needed to do the job, as well as the number of free hours I could have at the copying machine when no-one else was about, and when I was in Canberra. Just dismantling the files, removing the staples, unfolding the large press clippings and adjusting the reduction mechanism to copy the larger papers took even

ABOVE: Media interest in the case grew as it progressed to the High Court of Australia. Jenny Hocking speaks after being granted leave to appeal to the High Court, 16 August 2019. *(Grata)*

ABOVE: Queen Elizabeth II farewells the prime minister, Gough Whitlam, and Margaret Whitlam at the end of the royal tour, 25 October 1973. *(National Archives of Australia)*

Government House,
Canberra. 2600.

22 October 1975.

My dear Private Secretary,

      I shall get this letter into Friday's bag.
It is the first to go.

      May I say first of all that Her Royal
Highness The Princess Margaret arrived this morning
after a tiring journey. We have not yet had a real
conversation but I hope she is comfortable. We shall
be seeing more of her later in the day and especially
at dinner and are looking forward to this.

      I may have to add to the constitutional
story in the couple of days between now and the
dispatch of this letter, but it seems sensible to
summarise the happenings since I last wrote.

      The amount of Press coverage is now enormous
and it is very difficult to add to the clippings in
any useful way. However, I enclose some recent
clippings.

      Yesterday, (Tuesday, 21 October) I carefully
considered the Ellicott memorandum and decided to ask
the Prime Minister to obtain for me an opinion of the
law officers of the Crown on the propositions set out
in it. He agreed to do this and has asked for the
opinion on his own behalf with the intention of passing
it on to me. I realise of course that the law officers
will profoundly disagree with what Mr Ellicott said and
may go so far as to say that there is nothing left of
any substance in the reserve powers of the Crown. But
it does not follow that in an extreme constitutional
crisis I would accept that. I have of course, on any
view, little room to move contrary to the Prime Minister's
advice.

      I am under very great pressure, through the
Press, to act. Sir Robert Menzies issued a statement
about the crisis which was published in this morning's
Press. I send the full text.

      Yesterday I swore in a new Minister for
Agriculture, Mr Keating, who took the portfolio for
Northern Australia from which Mr Patterson had resigned
in order to take over Senator Wreidt's previous
appointment as Minister for Agriculture.

.../2

ABOVE: Sir John Kerr to Sir Martin Charteris, 22 October 1975, indicating that he may not 'in an extreme constitutional crisis' accept the advice of the Australian law officers. *(National Archives of Australia)*

BUCKINGHAM PALACE

PERSONAL AND
CONFIDENTIAL

4th November, 1975.

My dear Governor General

This is to thank you warmly for your letter
which began on 22nd October and was completed the next
day. The Queen has read it with much interest and also
with much concern for the pressures to which you are
being subjected by the crisis. I will make this a
brief reply as your letter of 27th October, which arrived
this morning demands a more detailed answer. I shall
hope to send this off within a day or two. I hope you
will forgive me, therefore, if in this letter I restrict
myself to one or two comments which may sound very
ingenuous to you who are in the thick of the conflict.

When the reserve powers, or the prerogative,
of the Crown, to dissolve Parliament (or to refuse to
give a dissolution) have not been used for many years,
it is often argued that such powers no longer exist.
I do not believe this to be true. I think those powers
do exist, and the fact that they do, even if they are not
used, affects the situation and the way people think and
act. This is the value of them. But to use them is a
heavy responsibility and it is only at the very end when
there is demonstrably no other course that they should be
used.

With the greatest respect, I am sure you are
right in taking the line that your crisis has not yet
crossed the threshold from the political into the
constitutional arena. Mr. Fraser wants to believe it is
already a "constitutional" crisis because he wants you to
bring about an election which he thinks he can win. If
the tide of public opinion continues to flood against him he
may well modify his view, and look for a way of retreat.

Again, with great respect, I think you are playing
the "Vice-Regal" hand with skill and wisdom. Your interest
in the situation has been demonstrated, and so has your
impartiality. The fact that you have powers is recognized,
but it is also clear that you will only use them in the
last resort and then only for constitutional and not for
political reasons.

Your very sincerely

Martin Charteris

His Excellency the Governor-General
of Australia.

ABOVE: Sir Martin Charteris to Sir John Kerr, 4 November 1975, on the reserve powers: 'those
powers do exist'. *(National Archives of Australia)*

ABOVE: The governor-general, Sir John Kerr, with Frank Crean, minister for overseas trade (left), Prime Minister Gough Whitlam, and Jim Cairns, deputy prime minister and treasurer (right), 11 December 1974. Whitlam considered Kerr's appointment 'a triumph'. *(The Canberra Times)*

LEFT: Prime Minister Gough Whitlam's letter to the governor-general, Sir John Kerr, 11 November 1975, advising a half-Senate election to be held on 13 December 1975. *(National Archives of Australia)*

ABOVE: Sir John Kerr, flanked by Prime Minister Malcolm Fraser (left) and Deputy Prime Minister Doug Anthony (right), after swearing in the Fraser government ministry, 12 November 1975. *(National Archives of Australia)*

RIGHT: Prime Minister Malcolm Fraser, Queen Elizabeth II, Prince Philip, and the governor-general, Sir John Kerr, during the Queen's visit, 1977. *(Newspix)*

RIGHT LOWER: Sir John Kerr, former Canadian senator Eugene Forsey, Lady Anne (Nancy) Kerr, St Mary's Church, Stoke D'Abernon, England, 27 June 1982. *(Library and Archives Canada)*

ABOVE: At the High Court of Australia: Jenny Hocking, Bret Walker SC, and Tom Brennan, 4 February 2020. *(Grata)*

LEFT: 'Guaranteeing supply' – 45 years later. Matt Golding on the release of the Palace letters. *(Matt Golding, The Age)*

had called the 'strong *sui generis* quality', of the Palace letters: that they were unlike any other records because the relationship between the Queen and the governor-general was itself *sui generis*. Therefore, Griffiths had found, the letters contained and entailed their own *sui generis* rules. This essential aspect of *sui generis* was central to Griffiths' judgment; it was a handy means of lifting the letters into a realm of their own, vested with a royal 'uniqueness' that cast other arguments and even statute law aside, and enabled Kerr and the Queen effectively to form their own rules, to place their own conditions, and thereby to secure the secrecy of their letters. Griffiths had accepted the *sui generis* argument, and it was at the heart of his ruling in favour of the Archives. Walker took this and turned it around, arguing that there was indeed a *sui generis* aspect to this case, and that was to the case itself – not the letters, not even the relationship between the Queen and the governor-general, but *this case*, 'most aspects of which have not been considered by the court except … in these proceedings'.[31]

It turned the notion of *sui generis* around to highlight the significance of our legal action, rather than the rarity of the vice-regal relationship, disarming the Archives' elevation of *sui generis* as a concept deserving of its own rules and controls, and undercutting its force. What really concerned Kerr, Smith, the Palace, and Fraser in their discussions about the letters, and what made the letters unique, Walker argued, was not the claimed *sui generis* nature of the relationship between those writing them, but what they were writing about – the dismissal of the elected government.

The key participants in those discussions about the dismissal were determined that the discussions would never be released: 'What is significant is the high political importance with resultant possibilities concerning access or publication of those communications. Nothing really to do with property and paper; but to do with content'. It was the content of the letters that was significant, and because of which their continued secrecy as 'personal' was being pressed, and that content was the pending dismissal of the Whitlam government.[32] As Chief Justice Allsop drily observed, 'You would think that Sir John would think that if he was about to dismiss an elected Prime Minister, he might like to tell the Palace.'

This time, the court was not so readily persuaded either by the royal interest in the letters or claims of their reflecting a unique 'personal' relationship with the governor-general. Justice Flick was particularly engaged on this point. 'There's no suggestion that he was writing, to use that word loosely, in his personal, private, individual capacity as a friend of the monarch?', he asked. 'No, no, no', Walker replied. 'It's because she was the Queen, not because she's a person who – happening to be Queen – he has come to know and wanted to draw her attention to a particularly good Australian novel that she might enjoy.'[33]

Although we had been forced to drop the parallel case for access to the copy file from our claim, the copies came up repeatedly during the hearing, largely because of the striking evidence provided by David Smith's correspondence with Kerr about his late-night photocopying of them. It provided a rare diverting moment 'in an otherwise fairly bloodless case', as Walker reprised this now slightly comical series of letters from which Griffiths had inferred Kerr's personal ownership of the Palace letters:

> Your Honours may have noticed a reference to the then Mr Smith burning the midnight oil, performing a task for Sir John in London, but not during his daylight work hours. And the onerous photocopying including of awkward attached newspaper pages. His Honour describes that as being, 'also consistent with Sir John's ownership'. ... To call it equivocal is understatement ... [it] is neither here nor there concerning property.[34]

If the Palace letters were, in fact, Kerr's property, why had he not simply taken them with him? As Kerr's personal property, there would have been no need for the dutiful David Smith to spend months diligently copying the letters in order to send the copies and not the originals to Kerr, leaving the originals safely in the Government House 'strong-room'.

There was a discernible pattern in Griffiths' reasoning, particularly in the inferences he drew, highlighted by his treatment of Smith's letters – the tendency to give unambiguous meanings to ambiguous words, and even to reinterpret everyday English, in inferring Kerr's personal ownership from them. For example, the simple reference to 'our letters' in an exchange between Kerr and Charteris was taken by Griffiths as indicative of Kerr's ownership of them, rather than as an unexceptional use of the possessive adjective to mean simply 'the letters between us'. Walker described these inferences as 'nothing other than assumptions' and 'merely self-serving'. Similarly, Walker dismissed the letters between Fraser and Kerr in 1977 discussing the intended secrecy over the letters, and their desired exclusion from the *Archives Bill*, as 'self-interested assertions ... concerning ... the political nature of these documents ... That doesn't speak to property'.[35] It was precisely because of their historical significance, the context of the dismissal of the government, that Kerr and Fraser wanted the letters kept secret. This, Chief Justice Allsop observed archly, 'not to put too fine a point on it, [is] what might have been expected to be at the front of the minds of these two gentlemen'.[36]

The shift in emphasis to the historical significance of the content and context of the letters, to their *sui generis* political nature, exposed the political question at the heart of the legal question about their ownership. Justice Flick, in particular, was clearly troubled by this:

> **Justice Flick:** The Commonwealth is saying that the communication between the Governor-General in his capacity as Governor-General to the Monarch in her capacity as Queen of Australia ... concerning something fundamental to the democratic process of this country, according to the Commonwealth, is his personal property. I have difficulty with that, I must say, but I don't know why. Instinctively it sounds wrong, but I just try to search for what is [sic] the criteria.
> **Mr Walker:** I'm going to try and deepen your Honour's feeling ...
> **Justice Flick:** I'm sure you are, Mr Walker.[37]

One thing that above all else stood out was Walker's refusal to pay homage to the position of the Queen, the monarchy, or even the views of the Queen about the letters in determining the central question of property and ownership: 'Whatever respect is due to the Queen's personal opinion, that is a matter about which she can say nothing.'[38] The views of the monarch had been central for Griffiths: he had referred to the 'reciprocal interests of the Queen' and 'the ascertainment of the Queen's wishes with respect to the Palace correspondence' in accepting the convention of royal secrecy and the tortuous interpretation of the *Archives Act* as excluding the governor-general's records.[39] The royal 'convention', Walker argued, was at best 'patchy practice', there being many instances in which governors-general had not retained their letters, and had instead lodged them with the National Library, as we had argued at the Federal Court.

We strongly rejected any suggestion that the Queen might still exercise power and control over the historical records of our archives, questioning whether the Queen could have any legal right to decide on Australian ownership and control of its archives. When the *Archives Act* was passed in 1983 it was never suggested that Australia should simply 'tuck in behind the mother country' and follow British archival practice regardless.[40]

The Archives' legal argument rested for the most part on the core submissions it had successfully run in the lower court. Why change a winning formula? However, there was one notable shift in its argument, in an effort to deal with the difficulty presented to its case by the 'agreed fact' that the letters were written by the governor-general and the Queen in the performance of their respective offices. Archives argued that the constitutional positions and powers of the Queen and the governor-general meant that each had no part in the discharge of the duties of the other, and that 'the Monarch has "no part in the decisions which the Governor-General must take in accordance with the Constitution"'.[41] In writing the letters, Archives argued, Kerr was exercising his own discretionary power and not 'the executive power of the Commonwealth', unbounded by the need for the advice of his elected ministers and therefore, perversely, beyond governmental accountability.[42]

Walker's strongest submission was directed towards the solicitor-general's efforts to construct an analogy between the British Royal Archives, accessible only at royal discretion and held in the 'Round Tower' at Windsor Castle separate from the British National Archives, and our own unitary public National Archives in Canberra. The view that there ought to be consistency of treatment between the Royal Archives and our own national archives was, 'with respect, misguided'. In particular, the Archives' claim that there should be concord between the practice in the UK and in Australia regarding the letters, such that the Australian archival practice is, in effect, subservient to British practice and wishes, 'involves an unsafe intellectual bias ... What we have is a Constitution which gives to our Parliament and our courts a determination of property rights, relevantly, and determination of the political science relevant to it.[43]

It was not only that our laws were of course different and a matter for our own courts, not British law, to determine. Our political systems were fundamentally different: 'a hereditary office with this notion of royalty of the blood with a panoply of castles has no application' to Australia, with its tradition of democratic parliamentary governance. Most importantly, and unlike the Royal Archives, the Australian Archives was not designed to protect and maintain hidden histories:[44]

> We do not have a bifurcated archive structured to provide separate, secure and secret Royal archives alongside a public archive for everyone else; the role taken in the home of the hereditary Monarch historically, with respect to records ... is far too obscure to lend itself to some arcane and selective adaptation in the Antipodes.[45]

The argument put by the Archives and accepted by Griffiths, that there ought to be parity or 'symmetry' between these two different systems of archives, that British law and practice might have any input into the interpretation of Australian law by an Australian court, would be expected to rankle the three senior judges on the Federal Court as usurping their own capacity to interpret Australian law and practice.[46] This is precisely what it did when Stephen Donaghue raised it, noting that the Queen considered the 'royal convention' of secrecy as applying in the UK and therefore of relevance here. Justice Flick shot back, 'But who cares what she thinks ... who cares what Sir John thinks!'

This, neatly if rather irreverently, summed up the legal irrelevance of the views of the Queen in interpreting the *Archives Act*, or indeed any Australian law. Justice Flick asked Donaghue, almost in disbelief: 'So, because the Queen thinks that these documents should be treated in a particular way, that should dictate to an Australian court a conclusion?'[47]

At this point, just as it seemed that we were heading for an outbreak of republicanism from the bench, I felt real hope that this case might succeed and that the Palace letters would finally be released.

Chapter Eight

A royal whitewash of history

The legal new year had barely begun when the Federal Court announced that the decision on my appeal would be handed down on 8 February 2019. It was just eight working weeks since the hearing, and such a marked contrast to the eight months taken by Justice Griffiths that the hope we had all felt at the appeal hearing now grew even stronger.

Over the next few days some distracting judicial arithmetic became a constant preoccupation: three judges had heard the appeal, and we had needed to persuade two of them. Which two? Justice Flick, so clearly perturbed at the notion of any sort of royal control over our laws and archival practices, seemed the judge most likely. On the other side of this crude ledger, the 'ever austere' Justice Robertson, who said very little during the hearing, had appeared entirely unmoved.[1] That left Chief Justice Allsop, the cautious and questioning waverer, who had engaged vigorously with both barristers as if wanting to be persuaded one way or another; it was impossible to tell which. I spent a sleepless night re-reading the transcript, and was even more convinced that the outcome would depend on the chief justice.

The now familiar courtroom 23 was packed: journalists had

picked up the optimism of a positive result, and were there in force. From the presence of James Whittaker, partner at Corrs Chambers Westgarth, I knew that he was nervously hopeful; so, too, was Tom Brennan, who was there to receive the decision while Bret Walker was appearing elsewhere. Our case was one of three decisions to be handed down that morning, and the crush for seats was intense. David Fricker found the last remaining place in the back row as people milled loudly around the door until the tipstaff entered to immediate silence: 'All stand. This court is now in session!'

Chief Justice Allsop sat alone, dwarfed by the wide expanse of empty bench around him. The decision was brief and brutal: 'In the matter of Jennifer Hocking v Director-General National Archives of Australia, Chief Justice Allsop and Justice Robertson find for the respondent'. Our appeal had been dismissed, with Justice Flick dissenting. Justice Griffiths' judgment stood. The letters were personal, not Commonwealth records, and the Queen's embargo remained. Allsop's words as he read the final order really stung: 'the appellant pay the respondent's costs in the sum of $30,000'.[2] The silence cracked as the public gallery, the lawyers, and counsel stood up as one and headed for the door, journalists jostling with questions and microphones outside the courtroom as I tried to speak to James Whittaker and Tom Brennan about the decision and what our next steps might be. The disappointment was palpable.

It was tense, excitable, and noisy, and the chief justice despatched his associate to chastise us about the noise and to convey his grave displeasure at the indignity of having been left facing an empty bar table, since none of the other cases had sent a barrister. 'There must always be someone at the bar table', the associate chided firmly. Caught between the banality of overlooked legal status and the weight of defeat, I laughed.

In dismissing my appeal, the critical finding was this: the *Archives Act* did not include 'as the property of the Commonwealth what may be referred to, somewhat loosely, as the private or personal records of the Governor-General'.[3] 'Somewhat loosely' was a surprisingly imprecise and non-legalistic descriptor of the central legal question. It was immensely disappointing to see reiterated in the majority judgment Justice Griffiths' misstatement of our core submission, that the letters were Commonwealth records 'simply because their subject matter related to the Governor-General's role and function'. Despite Bret Walker's repeated reminders to the Full Court that this was not our contention, the Archives' mischaracterisation of it had taken hold, bizarrely supplanting what we had actually said. We had become locked into an alternative construction of our own argument, a form of legal gaslighting, and the easy repudiation of a position we had never put which then followed.

On almost every substantive point, the majority judgment concurred with the reasoning and decision of Justice Griffiths: the relationship between the Queen and the governor-general was in a category of its own, *sui generis,* and the Palace letters 'arose from the unique representative character of the relationship between the Monarch and the Governor-General'; and the *Archives Act* should be read as excluding the governor-general's records, even though the Act itself did not state this. Finally, the court found that the perception, the subjective belief, of others 'at the time' that Kerr owned the letters reflected Kerr's actual ownership of them and was 'a clear statutory premise of the *Archives Act*', even though the Act was not passed until eight years later.

There was one significant point on which we had cut through: the argument put by the Archives, Government House, and Buckingham Palace that there must be Australian 'conformity' with the position of the Royal Archives on royal secrecy and in relation to the private property of the monarch. On this important point, the majority agreed with our position that the claimed convention of royal secrecy, the wishes and expectations of the monarch, should have no bearing on the interpretation of Australian law: 'We see no utility in such a comparative exercise', the majority found. 'The answer to the present question is to be found in Australian law.'[4] On that much, at least, we could fully agree.

Most alarming was the Full Court's amplification of Griffiths' finding that the letters 'arose from the unique representative character of the relationship between The Monarch and the Governor-General where there was no capacity on the part of The Monarch to act or to direct the Governor-General'.[5] The court held that the fact that the Queen could not direct the governor-general on how to exercise his powers meant that the governor-general was corresponding with the Queen in his personal rather than official capacity. Therefore, it rather tortuously concluded, the letters were written in a personal capacity and not on the basis of the advice of executive government, since there could be no power relationship or direction involved in writing them.[6] Aside from the uncertain relevance of this, since the relationship between the Queen and the governor-general exists regardless of the particular exercise of it, it also gave rise to a 'perverse' and even dangerous outcome, as legal commentator Richard Ackland quickly identified.[7]

Many of the Palace letters, the court had already found, were concerned with Kerr's 'personal' exercise of the contentious reserve powers, an extreme action taken at the governor-general's own personal determination without ministerial advice or even knowledge; specifically, the removal of a prime minister and his government. By the Full Court's reasoning, *any* use of the reserve powers could be discussed with the monarch and acted upon in complete secrecy, as an unaccountable 'personal' exercise of power, unknown to the prime minister and subsequently to history, with that secrecy maintained indefinitely.

In this legal cycle of vice-regal secrecy, power, and unaccountability, the court had determined that these crucial exchanges between the governor-general and the Queen relating to Kerr's unprecedented use of the reserve powers to dismiss the government would remain insulated from public view and from political critique or reflection even decades later. Yet an exercise of these reserve powers is precisely the type of vice-regal action that demands greater, not less, accountability and transparency. In this respect, the majority judgment painted a truly dark scenario, establishing a secrecy regime around this most controversial use of the reserve powers by a governor-general. As Richard Ackland described it, 'the exercise in question was ... a potent personal deployment of power to destroy the elected government'.[8]

In this desolate legal landscape, there was one bright, restorative light – the blistering dissent of Justice Flick. In his trenchant judgment, just fourteen emphatic paragraphs, Flick found that the Palace letters were 'documents going to the very heart of the Constitutional system of government', and expressed his disbelief that they could be seen as anything but Commonwealth records:

> It is, with respect, difficult to conceive of documents which are more clearly *'Commonwealth records'* and documents which are not *'personal'* property. The documents include correspondence between a former Governor-General of this country, written in his capacity as Governor-General, to the Queen of Australia in her capacity as Queen of Australia, concerning *'political happenings'* going to the very core of the democratic processes of this country.[9]

Flick rejected the majority's finding that in writing the letters the governor-general and the Queen had been acting 'personally and not officially', a view that he archly noted 'seems to deny the very positions each occupied', particularly since there was no evidence to suggest that Kerr and the Queen had any relationship other than their formal constitutional one.[10] Justice Flick accepted, as we had always argued, that the *Archives Act* did not exclude the records of the governor-general and could not be read as excluding them on the basis of proposed wording years earlier during the drafting of the *Archives Bill*: 'any consideration of historical context ... may be interesting but is ultimately not decisive'.[11]

Although we had lost again, some pin-pricks of light had emerged in this split decision, especially with Flick's searing dissent. We had moved crab-like in the majority judgment towards the recognition of the primacy of Australian law over the need for conformity with the treatment of the private property of the monarch and the position of the UK Royal Archives on royal correspondence. Most importantly, Justice Flick's powerful dissent showed that it was possible to persuade at least one judge to overturn decades of established practice and legal presumption. And if one judge could be persuaded, why not more?

However, there was no spinning the fact that, with this decision, a rare opportunity had been lost. The greatest disappointment was the continued closure of our history: the secrecy and speculation that had been the hallmarks of the dismissal and its history would continue with the Queen's embargo over the Palace letters. The vestigial subservience to the Queen on matters of access to our own archival records had now been judicially cemented. I vented my dismay in an article for *Pearls & Irritations*: 'The fact that we still require the Monarch's permission to know our own history is surely a national humiliation':

> Those at the apex of our Constitutional monarchy – the Queen and the Governor-General – could therefore discuss matters, including even the removal of an elected government, in absolute secrecy from the Prime Minister, government, parliament and the Australian people. This was the great, and alarming, import of the Full Federal Court's decision.[12]

***

'If ever a case cried out for appeal to the High Court, it's this one!', Bret Walker had said on reading the Full Court's judgment. Tom Brennan was still chuckling at the recollection when we met in his chambers with solicitors from Corrs Chambers Westgarth soon after the Federal Court's decision. We were there to discuss the prospects for an appeal to the High Court of Australia, and I was not at all convinced that any of them would want to continue. The Full Federal Court majority decision seemed definitive – it was spearheaded by the chief justice, and both of those justices were expert in this field of administrative law, so it would be difficult to overturn. If the legal team felt there was no reasonable avenue for further appeal to the High Court of Australia, the case would end right there.

The most striking thing about an appeal to the High Court is the staggeringly low success rate – before you even walk in the door. It begins with an application for Special Leave to Appeal: just 10 per cent of those will succeed and go forward as an appeal to the High Court itself.[13] Of those who apply for leave to appeal, around 40 per cent are called to a hearing before two or three of the High Court justices, and only 25 per cent of those heard are then granted leave to appeal.[14] If our application was among the 40 per cent to be granted a special-leave hearing, each side would have twenty minutes to present its case for and against leave to appeal, with Bret Walker SC as my lead barrister given ten minutes additional time in reply. The justices would decide there and then whether leave was granted. It sounded mercifully quick and clean.

As to our prospects, Tom felt there was a strong chance that leave to appeal would be granted; the appeal itself, however, was more difficult to assess. The case addressed significant matters of public interest about the interpretation and operation of the *Archives*

Act that are fundamental to the workings of government, as well as access issues central to the transparency and accountability of those in public office. The Full Court's interpretation of the *Archives Act* as carving out the records of the governor-general, when the text did not exclude them, provided further grounds. The legal view was clear: there were strong grounds for appeal, and, if I decided to go ahead with the appeal, they would all continue to work on the case on a *pro bono* basis. The apparent 'convention of royal secrecy' had shielded the activities of the monarch and the monarchy across the Commonwealth nations for decades. It was impenetrable, and almost impossible to overcome. Few cases offered the possibility that we were now on the cusp of achieving – to challenge the Queen's embargo over royal correspondence in Australia's highest court. If there was any way I could continue, I would.

I had thirty days from the Full Court's decision to make a decision on whether to appeal. I held to the line I had taken previously – if the legal advice was solid and the legal team was willing to continue on a *pro bono* basis, I would work through the risks, and the case would continue. Besides, Justice Flick's incisive, excoriating dissent had presented such clear points for appeal that it seemed almost impolite to refuse.

On 8 March 2019, I filed an application for Special Leave to Appeal to the High Court of Australia.

It was cold, mid-winter in Canberra, when I returned to the National Archives searching for more documents, scouring through the accession records for Sir John Kerr's papers, where, I told myself, even the most obscure files might turn up something important, something I had never imagined. And then, quite suddenly, one of them did. As I waited for the High Court to consider my application for special leave, a file containing letters between Kerr and the

Queen's private secretary after Kerr had left office landed in my in-box. I had requested this file, with the arresting title 'Buckingham Palace', eight years earlier, after which it had disappeared into the archival limbo of 'with-held pending advice'. It suddenly reappeared in a 'decision on access' email, with no explanation for the eight-year delay, with its cache of letters providing a jaw-dropping account of royal intervention in Kerr's autobiography, *Matters for Judgment*, which was soon to be released.

The supportive exchanges between Kerr, Prince Charles, and the Queen and Charteris, which had been so welcome before the dismissal, soon became a major concern for the Palace, which feared losing control of both the increasingly erratic Kerr and their letters. As the outcry over the dismissal showed no sign of abating even twelve months later, including demonstrations and angry placards, and paint thrown at the vice-regal Rolls-Royce, pressure was building on Kerr to resign. Under siege, he began to agitate for the release of the Palace letters, which he felt would bolster support for his actions. This began with careless comments about the letters and about 'the attitude of the Palace' at the time of the dismissal to friends and colleagues.[15]

Word of Kerr's indiscretion, his boasting of the Queen's approval of 'the way that I am going about things', soon reached the Palace itself, to great alarm. It grew to a crescendo soon after Kerr's resignation as governor-general took effect in December 1977, with his visit to the Queen's new private secretary, Sir Philip Moore, to plead his case for the release of the letters. Kerr was intent on using the letters to garner support for his action in dismissing Whitlam if he possibly could – and what better place to do it than in his autobiography, which he was finalising in self-imposed exile in England? His book was being eagerly, and in some quarters nervously, awaited, since Kerr was loudly proclaiming that he would now report 'the facts of the happenings of 1975 ... in the interests of truth'.[16]

With publication looming, and with it the prospect that Kerr might reveal their secret discussions, the Queen's private secretary contacted Kerr directly and asked for a copy of his draft manuscript. 'Buckingham Palace has evinced an interest in the manuscript and all parts of it which touch directly upon the Queen's position and the Palace's position will need to be thought about', Kerr wrote to his lawyers in Sydney.[17] Kerr dutifully sent his manuscript to the Queen's private secretary, and it was soon 'in safe keeping now at Buckingham Palace'.[18] 'It will make fascinating reading', Moore assured him, 'I will get into [sic] touch with you again as soon as I have finished it.'[19]

Moore's brief comment on the book arrived three weeks later, and if you thought the historical dissembling about the dismissal must eventually reach a natural end, think again. The Queen's private secretary thanked Kerr for excising any references to his discussions with Sir Martin Charteris about 'the controversy': 'I am grateful to you for being so scrupulous in omitting any reference to the informal exchanges which you had with Martin Charteris. I know that you have throughout been anxious to keep The Queen out of the controversy and I much appreciate the way in which you have achieved this in the book'. Which shows Kerr to be as unreliable in print as he was in office.

Kerr could scarcely hide his delight at this royal approbation of his expurgated history: 'I did my very best of course to omit any reference to the exchanges between Martin Charteris and myself. It is particularly gratifying to me to know that the result is satisfactory'.[20] These letters not only confirm that Kerr was in contact with the Queen's private secretary, Sir Martin Charteris, regarding the dismissal, but they also reveal that the Palace and Kerr then agreed to keep these 'exchanges' hidden by omitting any mention of them in Kerr's 'autobiography'. *Matters for Judgment* duly contained no mention of his 'informal exchanges' with Charteris, nor any details of Charteris's 'illuminating observations' and 'advice to me on dismissal' that Kerr had noted in his *Journal*.[21] Despite Kerr's claims that his book would present 'the truth' and the 'facts' about the events of November 1975, it was a tawdry exercise in historical distortion, by omission – a royal whitewash of history.

Most shocking in this latest revelation of ongoing royal intrigue was the clear example it provided of the mechanism through which the secrecy that drove the dismissal – the collusion of Kerr with others, and his deception of the prime minister – continued in the construction of its history. It shows the involvement of the Palace in the construction of a flawed and filtered history about one of the most contentious episodes in Australia's history. It was a shameful episode in that shared history, the details of which were still emerging.

My application for special leave to appeal to the High Court had just jumped the first hurdle. A special leave hearing had been scheduled before the court on 16 August 2019 in Sydney. From this point on, it was like a knock-out round: if we succeeded, we would be in the High Court of Australia; if not, the case was over.

For the last time, we filed into the Law Courts building in Phillip Street, past a bank of cameras and up to the crowded courtroom. We had lost at every point in this legal journey so far, and yet I was quietly hopeful.

The application was heard by Chief Justice Susan Kiefel and Justice Stephen Gageler. Bret Walker SC appeared again with Tom Brennan, and, for the Archives, Thomas Howe QC with Craig Lenehan. Walker emphatically took the court through the Full Federal Court's 'incorrect understanding' of our core submission, that the letters were central to how Kerr discharged his role as governor-general and were written 'in the performance of his duties', stressing 'the very great importance' of the correct classification of archival records to 'the integrity of the Commonwealth and its history'. This was a question of statutory interpretation of the *Archives Act* – in particular, the meaning of 'Commonwealth record', which had never been challenged in this way before. If leave to appeal was granted, the High Court could now set that interpretation.

Although the hearing was brief, the interventions of Justices Kiefel and Gageler were sharp and testing. As Howe reiterated the Archives' argument that Kerr, the Queen, and David Smith all believed that the letters were personal, and they had followed an 'absolutely invariable practice' and understanding that the letters would be embargoed, Chief Justice Kiefel sharply asked the fundamental question, 'What is the relevance of this understanding to statutory construction?'. I silently exclaimed, *Yes!* What *is* the relevance of a personal 'understanding' of ownership for the correct interpretation of the *Archives Act*? Howe must have forgotten that Government House and Buckingham Palace had released two of the Palace letters from the 'absolutely invariable practice' of royal embargo, in order to bolster the Archives' case at the Federal Court.

Bret Walker had scarcely begun his 10-minute submission in reply, despatching the Archives' arguments as 'absurd', 'nonsense', and 'a confusion of concept', and was just moving on to the 'travesty of the way we seek to put the argument', when the chief justice quietly and almost imperceptibly leant across and conferred for a moment with Justice Gageler. 'There will be a grant of leave in this matter', Chief Justice Kiefel announced. We were in the High Court!

I floated out into the sunshine of the Law Court building forecourt, oblivious to the lonely figure of an ashen-faced David Fricker standing alongside the crush of journalists wanting a statement, which I happily gave: 'I'm absolutely delighted that this case can continue. At stake is knowledge of our own history. It is entirely fitting that whether we can see these historic letters between the Queen and the governor-general at the time of the dismissal of the Whitlam government will be a decision of Australia's highest court, and not the Queen.'[22]

Fricker looked shocked, and he was. 'It was completely unexpected, [I was] absolutely shocked', he told me when I visited the Archives again the following month. His greatest concern was the mounting cost that the Archives was facing. 'It's really eating into my budget', he said, and yet the Archives would continue to contest the case and fight access all the way to the High Court. With all the legal and financial resources of the Commonwealth behind it, the Archives had now spent over $700,000 fighting the case, and that was before we got to the High Court, where the costs would take this figure closer to $1 million.[23] I was struck again by the vast imbalance in our respective resources and level of institutional support, and that imbalance was about to get a lot bigger.

The federal coalition government of Scott Morrison was clearly determined to fight our efforts to gain access to the Palace letters, and to assist the Archives in doing so. With the case now moving to the High Court, the Commonwealth intervened on behalf of the Archives, and the federal attorney-general, Christian Porter, joined the Archives against me at the High Court appeal. The attorney-general's department also agreed to meet 25 per cent of the Archives' costs from that point on. We had faced a formidable institutional force in seeking access to the Palace letters from the Archives in the first instance, and now this would be even more so with the intervention of the attorney-general.

And so it was with some trepidation that I again approached the Archives for a costs agreement, trying to minimise my potential exposure should I lose at the High Court. After several rounds of discussions, the Archives ultimately offered to cap my prospective costs exposure to them, should I lose the appeal, at $60,000. It was clear that the financial thumbscrews were being applied more firmly this time. I had no bargaining chip to play with other than to plead public interest and the Archives' requirement to act as a model litigant, and a $60,000 cap was immeasurably better than facing the potential black hole of having to pay the Archives' entire legal fees for the Full Federal Court appeal, the special leave hearing, and the High Court appeal. I accepted the cost-cap offer.

James Whittaker had always said that this was a case that would end up at the High Court, one way or another. On 4 February 2020, we were there.

The High Court soars above its institutional neighbours along Lake Burley Griffin, in every way a reflection of the authoritarian aesthetic of the chief justice most closely associated with its construction, the conservative curmudgeon Sir Garfield Barwick. As chief justice, Barwick had overseen every facet of the building, even down to the colour of the tiles – white, gleaming, dominating – so much so that it was dubbed 'Gar's Mahal'.[24] Everywhere speaks of that legal hierarchy and venerability. From the dramatic water-featured pathway rising up to the court, to the elevated judicial bench from where the justices look down upon the lawyers appearing before them, to the wooden barrier between the practitioners and the public, it seems distinctly ecclesiastic.

All seven justices of the High Court heard the appeal, reflecting its constitutional and broader legal significance. Our appeal was again led by Bret Walker SC with Tom Brennan, and with Corrs Chambers Westgarth instructing. The solicitor-general, Stephen Donaghue QC, appeared for the Archives, with Thomas Howe QC and the newly elevated Craig Lenehan SC, with the Australian

Government Solicitors Office instructing. The wealth of knowledge, intricate detail, and conceptual finesse on display was formidable. The central question for the court was, as it had been from the outset, whether the Palace letters were personal and therefore the property of Sir John Kerr, or were Commonwealth property and therefore Commonwealth records under the provisions of the *Archives Act*.

Bret Walker opened by excoriating the Full Court's 'incorrect understanding' of our core submission, the crude 'straw man' argument propounded by the Archives that 'everything that a person who holds office does is done by that person officially. We did not, and do not say that'.[25] The Palace letters were Commonwealth records because they were 'correspondence constituting and produced for the purposes of discharging the functions and the duties of the Governor-General', and were therefore the property of the Commonwealth. It was also an agreed fact of the case established at the Federal Court that the letters addressed 'topics relating to the official duties and responsibilities of the Governor-General', which, we argued, strongly supported the view that they were not personal records.

Walker took the justices to what was always an obstacle in the Archives' case: Kerr's claimed 'personal' conditions of access to the Palace letters, which were not in fact Kerr's conditions at all. The original version of those conditions had been drawn up by the governor-general's official secretary, David Smith, *after* Kerr had left office, and they had then been changed by the Queen *after* Kerr's death. The access conditions were no longer, if they ever were, Kerr's own personal conditions of access, and the letters were now embargoed expressly 'on the instructions of the Queen', with the Queen's private secretary having an effective final veto over their release. All of this suggested that they were official Commonwealth records not under Kerr's personal control. Kerr himself believed that, given its 'archival importance', his correspondence with the Queen 'would be preserved and would be part of the archives later available for historians', and yet the conditions placed over the letters by the Queen could prevent Kerr's wishes from being met.

The Full Federal Court's key finding that the letters were personal because they reflected an aspect of the governor-general's vice-regal relationship over which the Queen had no power and no direction, which Walker termed the 'powerlessness paradigm', was 'a most extraordinary and fundamentally self-destructive argument about a constitutional monarchy ... It is of the essence that the Queen will not be acting in an uncontrolled fashion regardless of, let alone contrary to, the advice of her relevant ministers, which ... means the advice of her Australian ministers'. It was not the case that the Queen is powerless, Walker argued, but that her power is of a particular kind, a power in which the advice of elected government is central.

Arguments about the interpretation of the *Archives Act* were reprised by the Archives' legal team with little change. The solicitor-general urged the court to accept that the early drafting of the *Archives Bill* to exclude the governor-general's records should bear on its understanding of the wording of the Act. We argued that the final wording reflected the intention of the new Labor government and the wishes of the parliament, and nothing more. Put simply, the 'proposed exemption' of the records of the governor-general had been considered and 'plainly rejected', Bret Walker said. In reality, the careful choice of wording in the *Archives Act* was far more than that, as we were about to find out.

I had heard nothing from our contact in the Archives since the Federal Court hearing, after which they had provided me with a range of documents relating to the *Archives Bill*, most of which we were already familiar with. On the eve of the High Court hearing, however, they contacted me again, this time with something really significant. The *Archives Bill* and subsequently the Act had been recast in 1982 with the inclusion of the nebulous term the 'official establishment of the Governor-General', precisely in order to ensure the secrecy of the Palace letters. Letters between the Australian Archives, the attorney-general's department, the official secretary, David Smith, and the Department of Prime Minister and Cabinet in September–October 1982 showed how this legislative artifice had been achieved.

'They are of course official, but if the Governor-General chooses to treat them as personal (ie by not giving them to the Official Secretary) there is little we can do,' Mr S.A. Hamilton from the prime minister's department told his deputy secretary.[26] 'If we, rightfully in my view, wish to encourage all future Governors-General to treat such reports to the Queen as official papers ... they would be subject to the 30 year rule. This seems to me to be appropriate – despite UK attitudes.'[27]

David Smith was closely involved in the redrafting of the *Archives Bill*, insisting that the Queen's letters remain closed.[28] The problem this created for the departmental heads was that, '[I]f the Palace reports are to be treated as official records ... a lengthy and cumbersome provision to exclude Palace reports explicitly is needed. As we have previously discussed, this would draw attention to the exclusion.' This, the Senate would not support.[29]

The solution proposed was to include the ill-defined 'official establishment of the Governor-General as a Commonwealth institution'. The benefit of this uncertain term was that it would 'leave some room for flexibility in dealing with communications between the Governor-General and the Palace' – even though, as the deputy secretary of the prime minister's department continued, 'We may see these as official, and I would personally argue this very strongly.' This was how the Bill was then constructed: it was not from any unqualified belief that the letters were personal – in fact, quite the contrary – but as a sophistry designed to ensure the Queen's embargo over the letters as 'personal' documents.

Although within the department it was thought 'odd' that reports to the Queen would be regarded as personal', the head of the department, Geoffrey Yeend, recognised that this was the only way to 'protect' the letters from public access, even though he, too, acknowledged they were official records:

> The only way to protect Governors-General's reports to the Queen is to regard them as personal papers and not put them into Archives. This is precisely the opposite outcome to what I intended when I persuaded Sir John Kerr to put his papers in Archives in the first place ... Governor-General's reports to the Queen on specific issues are also very much part of Australian history and should be in our official records.[30]

The letters were 'regarded' as personal only in order 'to protect them from public access'. Here it was, in clear departmental memos, just as we were about to enter the High Court – and we could not use them. If we had received these documents earlier, we would have sought to table them as evidence, and they would undoubtedly have been significant. As it was, we could do nothing but read them with some astonishment, and wish that we had been sent them sooner. 'They are', said Bret Walker on reading them, 'rather piquant'.

In asserting the personal nature of these letters and allowing Kerr's own personal conditions of access to prevail, rather than the provisions of the *Archives Act*, the National Archives was forced to concede some startling yet unavoidable corollaries. As personal property, this 'volatile' correspondence, as the solicitor-general, Stephen Donaghue QC, described it, could be removed from the Archives, sold, or even destroyed, despite their acknowledged historic significance. Walker, arguing against this appalling prospect that governors-general might keep for themselves the product of their duties of office – in this instance, the Palace letters – for their later private sale, or for auction at Sotheby's, described it as 'an absurd proposition'.

If the letters were personal, the chief justice asked Donaghue, why did Kerr leave them with the official secretary and not just take them with him when he left office? 'He didn't', Donaghue replied. 'He left them in Smith's storage room.' Justice Gordon leant forward, staring intently, and corrected him: 'When you say storage room, you mean strong room, don't you?' It was an excellent pick-up, of two similar words with two very different meanings. Smith's 'storage room' suggested his private space, perhaps even at his home, but the official secretary's 'strong room' indicated that the letters were being cared for in the official establishment.

The Archives pursued an unfortunate analogy to the ownership of ministerial documents, leading down a rabbit hole of which a modern-day *Alice in Wonderland* would be proud, before emerging with the remarkably broad proposition that drafts and copies of ministerial documents could belong to the minister personally. If so, they could likewise be removed, shredded, sold, or redacted, and never made available for public access. Historians and national-security advisors alike might have something to say about that broad brush.

The damage to our national archival heritage and to our history from this alarming rendition of the Palace letters as Kerr's personal property is obvious. If accepted, it would place a wide range of government documents outside the Archives and potentially available for private sale.[31] It was a most unusual and disconcerting position for the National Archives of Australia, whose core function includes the 'preservation' of our national archival heritage, to argue so strongly and with such expansive financial commitment that part of the historical heritage of the nation must be considered 'personal' and therefore open for removal or even destruction.

Finally, Walker dismissed the Archives' renewed focus on the argued 'convention' of royal secrecy over the Palace letters, based on British practice in its Royal Archives at Windsor, as 'an antipodean non-parallel' that would 'tie us to the mother country' over access to our archival records. The Archives' continued deference to the Queen's embargo meant that those ties over our history and our archives remained firmly in place, unless the court found otherwise.

This remnant of colonialism is untenable for Australia as an independent nation, and has denied us access to an extraordinarily significant part of our archival heritage for decades. The High Court appeal had provided a rare challenge to royal secrecy, an opportunity to cut the residual colonial ties and to open the Palace letters, against the wishes of the Queen but in the interests of our own history, and to fill the most important gap remaining in the history of the dismissal of the Whitlam government.

Chapter Nine

'Constitutionally unthinkable'

In just three months, everything had changed. Days before the High Court hearing in February, the first case of COVID-19 in Australia had been confirmed, and within weeks no state or territory was untouched.[1] By late March our cities were in lockdown, state borders closed, and airports deserted. Even the legal system had abruptly stopped, leaving cases frozen in mid-hearing to be picked up again when the infections slowed and the responses thawed. The High Court stopped sitting in March, and only special-leave applications and judgments were being delivered, all of them 'virtually'.[2] The Palace letters case was one of the last to be heard by the full bench before the High Court closed its doors.

Restrictions were just beginning to be lifted when I heard from Chris Marshall at Corrs Chambers Westgarth that the court would hand down its decision at 9.30 am on Friday 29 May. The court was technically 'sitting' in Brisbane that day, and its decisions were being streamed into the High Court in Canberra, where the courtroom was open to a small number of people watching the large screen as Chief Justice Kiefel read the decisions and orders on video-link. I was in Melbourne, agitatedly alternating between the High Court Twitter feed and emails.

And then, from Terri King, came a text message with a single word: 'YES!!!!!!' An ABC journalist who was in the High Court in Canberra to hear the decision had sent it to Terri the moment it was delivered. How very appropriate it was to share that extraordinary moment with Terri King, who had been with the case in such a profoundly important way from the start. We barely had time to talk before Chris Marshall rang, still working his way through the several judgments – there were four separate judgments, three of them in our favour – and to see how many of the justices had found for me. 'It's five,' he said, still reading. 'No, no – it's six!! It's six to one!' *The appeal must be allowed.* What a wonderful decision for our history.

In that emphatic 6:1 decision, the High Court ruled that the Palace letters were Commonwealth records and not 'personal communications' as the Archives had been claiming for decades. The court ordered the director-general of the Archives to 'reconsider' my original request for access to the letters with the letters now recognised as Commonwealth records. The decision ended the Queen's embargo, paving the way for their release under the *Archives Act*. Several High Court orders then stemmed from the central decision that the letters constituted 'Commonwealth records within the meaning of the *Archives Act 1983*'.

The most important order in terms of the release of the letters followed: that a 'writ of mandamus issue to compel the Director-General of the National Archives to reconsider' my original request for access to the letters. The High Court then issued three separate orders relating to costs, with the National Archives ordered to pay my costs at all three stages of this legal action: at the Federal Court, at the Full Federal Court on appeal, and at my appeal to the High Court of Australia. It could not have been a more complete vindication.

The National Archives' significant expenditure on contesting the case had suddenly doubled: they now faced a total cost of close to $2 million, to come out of their already strained budget.

The six justices who found in our favour were Chief Justice Kiefel and Justices Bell, Gageler, and Keane, with a joint judgment; and Justices Gordon and Edelman, who had each written a single judgment. Only Justice Nettle found for the National Archives that the Palace letters were personal communications between Kerr and the Queen, and not Commonwealth records. This was, as I wrote soon after:

> an immensely significant decision for our history, for transparency, and for accountability including of those at the highest levels of governance in a constitutional monarchy. And, where it all began, this land-mark decision has now ended decades of secrecy over a key aspect of the dismissal of the Whitlam government – the Queen's correspondence with the Governor-General, Sir John Kerr.[3]

The court's ruling was a stark rejection of the National Archives' denial of access to the Palace letters on the grounds that they were 'personal' – always an absurd description for letters written by two people at the apex of a constitutional monarchy, during our greatest political crisis. The majority found that 'Communications between the Queen and the Governor-General are inherently communications of the Commonwealth as a body politic', describing it as 'constitutionally unthinkable' for them to be considered 'personal to the individuals involved'.[4]

The High Court's rejection of the Full Federal Court's judgment was explicit, with the plurality despatching the appeal court's central finding: 'We cannot see how the correspondence could appropriately be described, however "loosely", as "private or personal records of the Governor General"'.[5] In reaching its decision, the High Court had followed its own path along the 'two limbs' of the 'elaborate statutory definition' of the term 'Commonwealth record'.[6] Whereas we had argued that the letters were Commonwealth records because they were the 'property of the Commonwealth', the High Court focused instead on the 'second limb', that the letters were the property of 'a Commonwealth institution' and were therefore Commonwealth records. The Commonwealth institution in question was the 'official establishment of the Governor-General' in the person of the loyal official secretary, David Smith. This focus on the second part of the definition of Commonwealth record brought to the fore the role of Smith, both in helping to write the letters and in their subsequent preservation and control.

In the end, it all came down to the fastidious control of the letters by Smith in his 'strong room' at Yarralumla and his lodgement of them with the Archives in his capacity as official secretary. The plurality found it 'compelling' that Smith had the 'lawful power to control the physical custody' of the letters. A key piece of evidence the judges relied on in reaching this conclusion were the letters from Smith to Kerr, which I had viewed in the National Archives shortly before the case began, that described in painstaking detail Smith's 'laborious copying' of the Palace letters after hours at Yarralumla. It was here that archival research and legal reasoning intersected most clearly in what was, to me, a fascinating judgment.

Not only did those letters point to Smith's control over the letters, but they also revealed that he had helped Kerr write them. The court saw this as further evidence that the Palace letters had been constructed in the course of the official secretary performing his official functions.[7] Justice Edelman found that, '[T]he exchange of correspondence was treated by Sir John Kerr as an official issue. Sir John was assisted by Mr Smith in the preparation of correspondence sent to the Queen and in discussing the correspondence received from the Queen'. The letters, Edelman found, were written 'with the assistance of an officer of the public service who formed part of the official establishment of the Governor-General'.[8]

Justice Gordon, also in agreement with the majority, found even more strongly that Sir John Kerr had relinquished any potential property interest by agreeing that his official secretary should retain custody of the documents and then deposit them with the Archives.[9] Justice Edelman saw Kerr's 'desire to preserve the documents given their historical import' as 'militat[ing] powerfully' against their being his personal records.[10]

On every one of the three key aspects of our arguments that had been rejected in the lower courts, the High Court found for us: Kerr's 'personal ownership' of the letters could not be inferred from the assertions of Kerr, prime minister Fraser, the official secretary, and the private secretary that they were 'personal'; the *Archives Act* did not expressly exclude the governor-general's correspondence with the monarch, and could not be read as having done so on the basis of earlier versions of the Bill; and the claimed 'convention' of royal secrecy was not proven.

On the Archives' contention that Kerr's property right in the letters could be assumed from the belief or assertions of others that the letters were 'personal', Justice Edelman bluntly identified the obvious legal flaw: 'A person does not obtain a property right by thinking they have a property right.'[11]

The majority acknowledged, as we had submitted at every stage, the 'unusually long' parliamentary process in the passage of the *Archives Act*, in which the change of government to the Hawke Labor government was critical. Following the new government's amendments to the previous Bill, the *Archives Act 1983* did not exclude the governor-general's records.[12] The justices observed that the amendments took quite a different approach from earlier iterations of the Bill: first in removing the proposed blanket exclusion of the records of the governor-general, and second by including the 'official establishment of the Governor-General' in its definition of 'a Commonwealth institution'.[13]

The majority found, as we had also contended, that the Queen's change to the terms of Kerr's original Instrument of Deposit was 'noteworthy' and indicative of the official nature of the letters, since 'Sir John Kerr was not consulted ... indeed Sir John had died'.[14] This was an inescapable evidentiary point of mortality! The posthumous change to Kerr's access conditions, at 'the Queen's instructions', had critically undermined the claim that the letters were his personal property. Justice Edelman concurred: 'The role of London in amending rules of access is ... in tension with an understanding that the originals of the correspondence are the personal property of Sir John Kerr.'

Beyond the central findings relating to the Palace letters, the court's ruling on the claimed 'convention' of royal secrecy was no less dramatic. In a final coda, 'for completeness', the majority judgment turned to this second area of significance. In the immediate wake of the High Court's ruling, this aspect of the judgment was almost entirely overlooked by media and legal commentators. And yet it is this element of the court's decision that will have the greatest impact on other royal holdings across the Commonwealth, on royal secrecy, and on the traditional lack of transparency over communications between the monarch and the governors or governors-general of former dominions. Fifteen other Commonwealth nations routinely apply this same 'royal convention' to their archival records, which the High Court had now explicitly overturned.

The majority emphasised that, to the extent that their conclusion that the letters were Commonwealth records 'might run counter to the current understanding of the Private Secretary and to the present expectations of Her Majesty', this conclusion was 'the product of the application of the *Archives Act*, properly interpreted, and 'the product of legislative choices ... which resulted in enactment of the *Archives Act*.[15] This was a direct statement of the primacy of Australian law over the express wishes of the Queen.

It might have been thought that, in the year 2020, such a statement of Australian legal autonomy no longer needed to be made; but it did, and its implications are significant. The High Court's ruling has brought the Palace letters firmly under Australian law, ending the quasi-imperial imposition of the Queen's embargo over our archival records and over our knowledge of our own history. Its implications will be felt most strongly over the embargoed Palace letters of other governors-general, and in the state archives holding state governors' royal correspondence. More broadly, the decision provides a precedent for access decisions in other Commonwealth nations, and potentially even in the United Kingdom, where public access to the Royal Archives is denied, except with the permission of the monarch.

On this point, Justice Edelman was emphatic. In a section headed 'There was no convention that the correspondence was not official or institutional', Edelman firmly refuted the existence of this royal convention, describing the supposed precedents argued by the Archives as evidence of it as 'at best, "thin"'.[16] Here, the document from the UK Archives that I had sent to Corrs soon after the case began, and that had been submitted in evidence at the Federal Court, had proved important. Edelman referred to the 'labelling convention' that this document revealed: state governors used the label 'personal and confidential' to describe their correspondence with the monarch, even though they were part of 'official despatches'. This UK document had exposed the bureaucratic sophistry at the heart of the labelling convention perfectly, and it was particularly satisfying to see its significance recognised at the highest judicial level.

With its landmark decision, the High Court had overturned decades of archival practice that had determinedly yet inconsistently locked royal records away from public view on the grounds that they were 'personal'. Its impact was keenly felt in Buckingham Palace, and with some trepidation, since the decision paved the way for the letters to be released, against the wishes and expectations of the Queen, as the judgments made clear.

When the case began, the Queen's private secretary had argued strongly against the release of the letters, even claiming that their continued secrecy was essential 'to preserve the constitutional position' of the monarchy. In rejecting this presumption of royal secrecy and an apparent fear of imminent monarchical collapse, the High Court had enforced a measure of transparency and accountability over a monarch and a monarchy once seen as untouchable.[17]

Nowhere has this insistence on open access to our own archives been more important than where this case began: the incomplete history of the dismissal of the Whitlam government. What made this case so important was the significance of original documents to the evolving historical understanding of the dismissal. As a highly contested and polarised episode, having access to original contemporaneous records – as opposed to subsequent interpretations – was imperative. There could be no more significant records than these letters between the governor-general and the Queen regarding what Justice Griffiths had described as 'one of the most controversial and tumultuous events in the modern history of the nation'. And now, after a four-year legal battle, we were just a step away from seeing them.

We had won, but the letters had not been released, and for the next three weeks it looked as if they might not be. The National Archives responded to the High Court's decision in a media release later the same day. 'The National Archives is a pro-disclosure organisation', it read, without a hint of irony, which operated on the basis of making records publicly available 'unless there is a specific and compelling need to withhold it'. The director-general then stated in several interviews that, under the terms of the *Archives Act*, he had ninety working days within which to make his decision on access to the letters and that he was examining them for possible redactions. After the elation of the High Court decision, this was crushing, suggesting as it did that the Palace letters might not be released in full, and even then, not for several months. We firmly believed that the Archives' interpretation of the High Court decision and its order was incorrect.

It was widely and mistakenly assumed, including by the Archives, that this order required them to consider my request to access the letters as a new request, under section 31 of the Act, which deals with general-access requests, for which the statutory time is ninety working days.[18] This was not the case. I immediately issued a statement that a 'reconsideration' is dealt with under section 42, 'Internal reconsideration of decisions', which is required to be done 'as soon as practicable, and within *30 business days*' [my emphasis]. In which case, the letters had to be released by mid-July, not late October.

The second common assumption in interpreting the decision, again driven by the Archives' public statements, was the expectation that there could be redactions made to the letters if there was a 'compelling need', potentially limiting their release dramatically. In a second statement on 2 June, the Archives announced: 'We set out to release all Commonwealth records that are in the open access period however [sic] exemptions under section 33 of the Act may apply.'[19] The key question was whether the Archives would claim that any of the letters comprised 'exempt records', and redact them in part or in full. After such a long legal struggle, this was devastating; again, we believed it was wrong.

Although the *Archives Act* allows for exemptions to be made on specified grounds, the suggestion that these provisions applied equally in this case failed to take into account the strong comments in the High Court judgments, which bore directly on the question of possible exemptions. Correctly interpreted, we argued, in a strongly worded letter to the Archives' legal team, those judgments precluded the reasonable possibility of redactions. In short, we were again in dispute with the Archives, this time over the meaning of the High Court decision itself and its central order.

Rarely, if ever, is a writ of mandamus actually issued, since a High Court order is usually complied with immediately. (The last time a writ of mandamus was served by the High Court was in 2014 against the minister for immigration and border protection, Peter Dutton.)[20] Three weeks after the High Court decision, David Fricker stated that he was 'not working to any legislative deadline' and that it might take even longer than ninety working days to prepare the letters for release: 'I'm not spending time reading the legislation, I'm spending time reading the Palace Letters.'[21]

As the immediate release of the letters seemed to be slipping away from us, Corrs Chambers Westgarth contacted the registrar of the High Court to begin the process of issuing the writ of mandamus. Serving the writ would oblige the Archives to comply within two weeks, and that would in turn meet the thirty working days since the High Court decision which, we insisted, was required for it to reconsider my application. In early July 2020, Corrs Chambers Westgarth sent the Archives' solicitors a final request that the Archives provide a date for complying with the High Court order. We requested a response by Thursday 9 July, with the intention that if a schedule for release had not been agreed to by then, the writ of mandamus would be served the following day.

As I waited for the Archives' response, Nick Bonyhady from *The Age* rang to ask how I felt about the Archives' announcement that the Palace letters would be released in four days' time. The

Archives had just released a media statement that the letters would be released, in full, on Tuesday 14 July – exactly thirty working days after the High Court decision, just as we had argued.

It was nearly ten years since I had first sought access to the letters, five years since I'd lodged a freedom-of-information request, and four years since I'd commenced action in the Federal Court against the National Archives, later joined by the federal attorney-general. The Archives, Government House, and Buckingham Palace had all argued fervently against their release; and even then, the Archives had prevaricated in complying with the High Court order.

To say that there had been major institutional resistance to the complete and unexpurgated release of the Palace letters would be a spectacular understatement. And yet here we were, with the Palace letters now set to be released in full, following a decision of Australia's highest court and not at the whim of the Queen. So, how did I feel? Absolutely stoked!

Chapter Ten

'My continued loyalty and humble duty'

The release of the Palace letters was pure theatre. Every element was meticulously stage-managed: the set, the props, the narrative. The director-general of the National Archives, David Fricker, who had spent four years and nearly $2 million arguing against their release, and had supplied a secret submission to the court in doing so, now proclaimed the Archives to be a 'pro-disclosure organisation' as he presented and interpreted the letters to the public for the first time. The sheer audacity of it turned a bizarre occasion into the surreal.

In a carefully curated selection, Fricker worked his way through just nine of the 212 letters, which told a particular story – as such a limited interpretive frame must. While professing merely to be giving 'a bit of a preview', a gentle and benign positioning was clear. 'I'm not a historian ... archivists should not be historians,' Fricker insisted, before proceeding as archivist *qua* historian to explore the handful of letters.[1] For, at this unprecedented release of letters between a governor-general and the reigning monarch, against her express wishes and of unparalleled significance to our history, there was no historian present. It was a glaring, conspicuous exclusion.

One letter in particular, from Kerr to Charteris on 11 November 1975, after the dismissal, was highlighted as 'an important document' in terms of the role of the monarch at the time and whether, as Fricker termed it, 'interventions were happening'. With Kerr's key sentence displayed on screen, Fricker read: 'I decided to take the step I took without informing the Palace in advance', and noted how this critical phrase was repeated with emphasis by Charteris in his reply of 17 November 1975: 'In NOT informing the Queen what you intended to do before doing it'. Fricker posited these *post hoc* assertions as central to considerations of the role of the Queen, which, in this ahistorical schema, lay in what Kerr and Charteris wrote to each other *after* the dismissal, rather than what was said before it.

This was performance masquerading as history, a crude exercise in setting the narrative. Even as Fricker was speaking, and forty minutes before the letters were publicly released, a News Corp journalist duly made an early call, based on that single letter from Kerr after the dismissal: 'It was better for her Majesty NOT to know.' It was soon followed by another hastily tweeted verdict, this time drawing on Charteris's reply and with an accompanying image of the original letter, 'the Queen was "NOT" informed'.[2] News Corp's London establishment newspaper, *The Times*, chimed in under the heading 'Letters prove Queen had no part in Australia PM Gough Whitlam's sacking'. The *Daily Mail* agreed: 'The Queen DIDN'T order the Governor-General to dismiss Australian prime minister Gough Whitlam' – as if anyone thought that she had.[3] As tabloid journalism, it was entirely predictable; as historical analysis, it was risible.

The great disappointment in this callow charade was that after such a titanic team effort to release the letters, which were of unparalleled significance, they could be so easily reduced to the equivalent of a 'gotcha' moment, a headline in search of a story. It was as if the entire cache of the Palace letters, a vast and complex window on the vice-regal relationship at an unprecedented time of crisis in our history, could be read from just one letter written by the key protagonist, Sir John Kerr, *after* the event. The words of Chief Justice Kiefel on the limited evidentiary value of mutual assurances between Government House and Buckingham Palace that the letters were personal, written 'conveniently after the litigation was commenced … confirming each other's understanding', seemed particularly apt.[4]

Buckingham Palace soon joined the rush to its defence, issuing a rare public statement proclaiming that the letters confirmed that 'neither Her Majesty nor the Royal Household had any part to play in Kerr's decision'. The royal statement did not acknowledge the High Court's landmark decision that the Palace letters were not 'personal' records, and instead reasserted its belief in 'the longstanding convention that all conversations between … Governor-Generals [sic] and The Queen are private', completely disregarding the fact that our High Court had just ruled otherwise. It was as if the Palace letters case had never happened.

The instantaneous verdict, 'The Queen in the clear!', could not withstand even the most cursory examination. It told us nothing about the nature of the letters, the process through which Kerr had reached his decision to dismiss the government, and, most importantly, the part played by his correspondence with the Queen in that decision. More sophisticated analyses, based on all the letters and not just one, took slightly longer to emerge, since there were 1,200 pages to work through. *The Guardian*'s Katharine Murphy reflected that amplifying what came after, rather than before, the dismissal, as the rush to 'clear' the Queen had, 'misses the larger truth of what this profoundly important cache of correspondence lays bare … only a handful of days before the dismissal, Charteris did, in substance, intervene'.[5]

Professor Chris Wallace concluded that the letters showed the Queen 'providing not just comfort but actual encouragement to the governor-general in his sacking of the government'.[6] Michael Pelly, legal editor at the *Australian Financial Review*, was left in no doubt that 'the Palace gave Kerr a green light to sack Whitlam'.[7] It is simply impossible to read these letters, with their consideration of intensely political matters, Kerr's repeated undermining of the government, and their discussion of the use of the reserve powers to dismiss the elected government, and conclude otherwise. In Nick Feik's blunt assessment in *The Monthly*, 'No respectable historian' could accept that the Queen played 'no role' in Kerr's decision to dismiss Whitlam.[8]

The Palace letters are the most significant historical records about the dismissal, and the only ones to explore the real-time communications between the governor-general and the Queen over the critical months during which Kerr reached his decision to dismiss the government and appoint the opposition in its place. They provide a remarkable insight into Kerr's views of the unfolding political situation, his fear of his own recall, his frailties, his need for royal approbation, and his planning for and eventual decision to dismiss the government. In doing so, Kerr acted unilaterally, in a vice-regal capacity as the Queen's representative in Australia, using the contentious 'reserve powers of the Crown' to dismiss an elected government in a raw display of residual quasi-imperial power.

In this post-colonial penumbra of unregulated vice-regal action, it was inevitable that the lingering question would be whether the Queen had played any role in Kerr's decision to dismiss the Whitlam government. The Palace letters were finally about to answer that critical question.

As a physical archive, the Palace letters reveal much that is lost in their homogenous representation in digital form. Immediately notable is their asymmetry: in the paper on which they are written, in their length, their frequency, and, overwhelmingly, their tone. Kerr writes more letters than Charteris, more often and in greater detail – the most being four letters in a single day and the longest single letter being eleven pages, with one nine-page letter containing forty-three pages of attachments.[9] Although voluminous, as contemporaneous copies of his original typed letters, Kerr's letters appear slight, almost ephemeral, on thin carbon-copy paper. They stand in sharp contrast to the wealth and ritual behind the Queen's letters, and reinforce the particular relationship at play – a monarch writing to her representative, the centre dealing with the periphery. The thick, white paper with its deeply embossed blood-red Buckingham Palace or Balmoral Castle crowned letterhead is still gleaming, decades later.

There is an unmistakeable hierarchy at work here, in which the governor-general is in every way the junior to the Queen's amanuensis, her private secretary, Sir Martin Charteris. Kerr is ingratiating, repeatedly apologetic, and in need of affirmation, which Charteris unfailingly gives in a detached, formulaic, slightly mocking tone. The Queen, he writes, has read Kerr's letters 'with much interest', she is 'deriving pleasure and interest from them', and is reading them 'with close attention'.[10] The Queen's letters to Kerr all come through her private secretary – a formal nexus in keeping with the role of the private secretary as the official channel of communication with the monarch. Charteris writes for and as the Queen. His words are her words.

It is farcical to seek to distance the Queen from her own letters on the basis that they were written by Charteris, much less to claim that this constitutes a royal form of 'plausible deniability', neatly releasing the Queen from responsibility for whatever troubling interactions they reveal.[11]

From his very first letter of 15 August 1974, an eleven-page missive that is in every way a marker of what is to come, a constant theme is Kerr's disparagement of the government and of Whitlam. Kerr is obstreperous, querulous, and disruptive as he quibbles with, queries, and disputes government decisions and advice, even seeking to evade Whitlam's advice to him on the new honours system. In this first letter, Kerr raises a matter that is already of great concern for the Palace: the prospect of the Queen receiving conflicting advice, and her possible embarrassment, over state appeals to the Privy Council and the new royal title. The Queensland premier, Joh Bjelke-Petersen, affronted by Whitlam's change to the royal title, was petitioning for the Queen to be known as the 'Queen of Queensland'.[12]

This first exchange sets the bounds for what is to come. Just one month into the job, Kerr cavils against the wording of the proclamation calling the joint sitting of parliament following Labor's victory in the May 1974 double-dissolution election. This was an historic moment for the government, for Whitlam, and for Australia. With the government's return at the 1974 election, Whitlam had become the first Labor leader to win two consecutive elections, and the government had gained three Senate places in that rare victory. It was also the first and only time that the full provisions of the double-dissolution mechanism of section 57 of the Constitution had been used, calling together both houses of parliament. Six of the government's most important bills were eventually passed at the joint sitting, enabling the introduction of Medibank; electoral equity, or 'one vote one value'; Senate representation for the Northern Territory and the Australian Capital Territory; and the establishment of the Petroleum and Minerals Authority (PMA).[13]

Kerr's gaze is neither to history nor to the legal advice he has received regarding the proclamation, but to his own contrary view that presenting all six Bills to the joint sitting could be unconstitutional. In fact, the terms of the proclamation calling the joint sitting were not only a formality, but the proclamation itself was not for Kerr to review, since the six 'trigger bills' for the 1974 double dissolution had been signed off by his predecessor governor-general, Sir Paul Hasluck, and therefore had to be recited into the proclamation under the section 57 mechanism.[14] Nevertheless, in this, his first official function as governor-general, Kerr disputes the advice of the solicitor-general, Sir Maurice Byers, the head of the attorney-general's department, Sir Clarrie Harders, and attorney-general Lionel Murphy that all six bills could be put before the joint sitting, albeit that one of them was under High Court challenge.

While acknowledging that it is perhaps inappropriate for him as governor-general to, 'be my own lawyer, and make my mind up about what the law permitted me to do', Kerr proceeds to do just that. 'I was in fact highly doubtful', he tells Charteris, that the government's legal advice regarding the joint sitting was correct. The High Court soon found otherwise.[15]

Kerr's reluctance to accept the government's, and the legal officers', advice to him on the joint sitting is just the first of a litany of depredations in what can only be seen as the most extraordinary vice-regal undermining of an elected government. Kerr rails against policy decisions, queries the merits of appointments, and reveals details of Executive Council meetings, the most important and highly confidential meetings of executive government. And yet, while the increasingly truculent governor-general conveys all this to the Queen, he communicates none of it to his prime minister. In these letters, ranging from the deferential to the obsequious, Kerr is revealed as insecure, indiscreet, easily led by flattery, and expertly played by the supercilious, seasoned Palace courtier, Sir Martin Charteris. Never was a man less suited to the position of governor-general than Sir John Kerr.[16]

Kerr writes in great detail about very little, for this is a highly selective record of political events that at times reads more like reports from an informant than from the head of Australia's executive government. Invariably, his letters focus on the minutiae of perceived governmental wrongs, and scarcely a letter passes that fails to present the government as unstable, facing 'continued uncertainty and speculation', and always with the threat of 'another election' or the possible 'denial of Supply' just around the corner.[17]

This is the case from Kerr's first letter, containing his reflections on the political situation following the government's re-election. The Labor Party had gained three Senate seats at the 1974 election, and the Democratic Labor Party had been wiped out, losing all five of its senators; the government and the opposition held equal numbers in the Senate, and there were two Independents. While one of the Independents re-joined the Liberal Party, the South Australian senator Steele Hall confirmed his support for the government on matters of supply, leaving the Senate numbers on the vital question of supply evenly split. Kerr nevertheless tells Charteris that 'the Opposition remains firmly in control of the Senate' and that 'things remain very fluid and unpredictable'. It is not only in hindsight that such comments raise serious questions about the reliability of the political assessments that Kerr was presenting to the Palace.

As this opening salvo depicts, the Palace letters highlight Kerr's peculiar conception of his role as governor-general. It does not hold up well. In a major speech to the Indian Law Institute in February 1975, Kerr presented himself as 'a Head of State making a State visit' to India, with full 'Head of State' status, in the absence of Australia's actual Head of State, the Queen. Kerr articulated a view of the governor-general as no 'mere figurehead', as someone with a 'significant role to play', ever watchful for signs of a government acting against the Constitution and the 'public interest' – however he might define that quintessentially subjective term. In this role, Kerr said, the governor-general had to remain apolitical at all times: 'He must not get into political controversy, be partisan or try to act politically himself. He must not try to manipulate the political process.'[18] Yet throughout these extraordinary Palace letters, this is precisely what Kerr is doing.

The fundamental 'constitutional principle' that the monarch and the dominion governors act on the advice of responsible ministers had been confirmed at imperial conferences nearly fifty years earlier. Just months before the dismissal, Kerr acknowledged this defining principle of the vice-regal relationship: 'Everyone knows that the Governor-General must act on the advice of his ministers – his constitutional advisers', he told an audience at the Union Club in Sydney.[19] Yet in his first letter to the Queen, he disputes that advice and the constitutional principle underpinning it, as he does in subsequent letters of far greater significance.

Kerr's reflection on being 'my own lawyer' is an opportunity for Charteris to remind the governor-general of this defining principle – neither to gainsay the legal advice of the law officers, nor to dispute the prime minister's advice on matters of policy and governmental decisions. Instead, Charteris acknowledges the inappropriateness, and at the same time encourages it: 'Even if, as you say, a Governor-General should not be his own lawyer, I can see that there is much advantage in his having a mind trained in the law.' Kerr's predecessor governor-general, Sir Paul Hasluck, had reflected on this very question in his 1973 Queale lecture, an exceptional exposition of the role of the governor-general in a constitutional monarchy. Never one to see the office of governor-general as a vehicle for personal power, Hasluck was insistent that a governor-general will not 'make any personal pretension to be an expert himself'.[20]

Kerr's questioning of his legal and ministerial advisors during his first weeks of office had caused considerable consternation at the highest levels of governance, as confidential documents from within Department of Prime Minister and Cabinet reveal. Just weeks after his appointment, Kerr sought a meeting with Sir John Bunting, the head of the department, the law officers, and the head of the attorney-general's department, Sir Clarrie Harders, to discuss 'the Joint Sitting matter'.[21] From his first weeks in office, Kerr was willing to consider the role of the governor-general as an active and political one, in which he was open to seeking other avenues of advice and even to formulating his own legal advice, above the advice of the government and the law officers.

If ever there was an opportunity for the Palace to place appropriate bounds around the vice-regal correspondence, this first exchange was it. The governor-general must remain strictly neutral. As Kerr himself acknowledged, he must maintain 'the neutral position of representative of the Crown in Australia'.[22] By venturing into the political space with his adverse commentaries to the Palace, expressing his denigration of government decisions and his disagreements with his legal advisors, Kerr had breached this fundamental role from the outset. It was for Charteris to pull their communications back to the appropriate level of political neutrality, to pay heed to the defining feature of a constitutional monarchy that the Queen must remain 'politically neutral', and to remind Kerr of his core responsibility to act on the advice of responsible ministers, or at the very least, to speak to them.

Kerr himself provides the opening for Charteris to do this in his first letter, and again in his second letter, in which he specifically asks for Charteris's feedback on his letters. It is surely humiliating for the governor-general, an immediate past chief justice of New South Wales, to seek royal approval, even for how he is to write his own letters: 'Perhaps you could let me have an indication as to whether or not there is too much or too little detail in the kind of communication that I have been sending to you.' And just as humiliating is Charteris's condescending reply, reassuring Kerr that, 'I have no hesitation in saying that they seem to me to be just about right.'

Kerr's errant perception of his role as governor-general extended to his relationship with the leader of the opposition – by imagining that he had one. The governor-general has no constitutional relationship with the leader of the opposition, who is merely the leader of the party that has lost the previous election. His constitutional relationship is with his chief advisor, the prime minister. In a highly relevant parallel, Kerr sought advice at this same time on whether he should 'grant an audience' to the leader of the opposition, Billy Snedden, to discuss a political matter of government policy.

The advice from the attorney-general's department was emphatic: absolutely not. The internal advice was given on 9 August 1974, and concluded: 'To agree to such a thing would be contrary to existing constitutional conventions and could seriously weaken the constitutional role of the Governor-General in the Australian constitutional framework.' The advice was that 'the appropriate channel for communication ... is either the Prime Minister or the appropriate Minister of State'. The department firmly advised that even if the leader of the opposition tried to address Kerr on political matters, for example at a social function, 'the Governor-General could either (a) inform the Leader of the Opposition that he must not, because of constitutional convention, discuss such matters or (b) undertake to report the Leader of the Opposition's views to the Prime Minister'. The department's view was clear: the governor-general must not engage in political discussions, and the prime minister must be informed if any attempted engagement arose.[23]

This departmental advice had established clear boundaries around Kerr's behaviour domestically, as Charteris should have also in relation to his politically charged vice-regal communications. Instead, when there was an opportunity for appropriate parameters to be established in their earliest letters, Charteris engaged with Kerr on the contentious questions he was raising. It has been said that Charteris's letters to Kerr are not at all unusual, that they are 'mostly just grateful for the information and concern for Kerr's wellbeing'.[24] This is simply not correct. Not a single letter from Charteris can be characterised in this way, and it is baffling how such a striking representation of them can be made.

The Archives' lists of key points from the Palace letters, prepared for the public presentation of them, show just some of the topics covered by Charteris in his early letters: Sir John Bunting's appointment as Australian high commissioner; Commonwealth/ State relations; Government use of personal advisors; concerns of the senior ranks of the public service; Royal Commission into the Australian Public Service; Labor caucus; Miss Morosi in press in UK; the Queen's interest in Mr Fraser's attempt to supplant Mr Snedden; Senate casual vacancy; Mr Fraser leader of the opposition; political developments and top public servants; comment on decision re dismissal of Mr Cameron; political situation and similarity in UK; the Australian political situation and the Executive Council meeting of 14 December 1974.[25]

The contents of these hundreds of pages of Palace letters make it impossible to accept the claim of their politically disinterested nature. Kerr reported on conversations, meetings, and events to Buckingham Palace in the context of a highly intense party-political conflict unfolding in Australia. The frequency alone is extreme. The governor of South Australia, Sir Mark Oliphant, reported annually *after* the events, not with contemporaneous political commentaries on them.

What was pivotal throughout was that the Queen engaged with Kerr on these inherently political matters, including on government policy decisions, and, even worse, on the existence and possible use of the reserve powers against the government. It is difficult to imagine a greater level of political involvement than this. The foundations for the dismissal – Kerr's demonstration of his willingness to challenge the advice of elected ministers, his and Charteris's shared abrogation of their essential political neutrality, and Kerr's determination to keep his thoughts secret from the prime minister – had been laid in their first exchange.

Over the following weeks, Kerr stepped directly into the political arena, positioning himself between the senior public servants and the government, reporting on 'a feeling of malaise' that had been 'quite specifically reported to me' by the powerful public service 'mandarins' in his private conversations with them over drinks at the Commonwealth Club in Canberra. It was hardly surprising that among the senior levels, and in particular among the few remaining departmental secretaries who had dominated the upper echelons of the public service since Sir Robert Menzies' time, tensions had arisen at the end of twenty-three years of conservative government, and with the appointment of some new heads of department and the reshuffling of others.

In his letter of 6 September 1974, Kerr reveals to Charteris that he has been having 'private talks' with these disgruntled heads of department, unknown to the prime minister, and is taking personal action in response: 'I have made it my business to see most of the Permanent Heads of the public service and especially the most senior ones.' Kerr writes that there is 'an uneasy feeling' among the mandarins he has spoken to and that, 'I have been asked, as head of the Executive in Australia under The Queen, whether I would be prepared to interest myself in the welfare of the Public Service.'

Whitlam had recently appointed Sir John Bunting, Menzies' long-term secretary of the Department of Prime Minister and current head of the Department of Prime Minister and Cabinet, as Australia's high commissioner to the United Kingdom. Bunting was a 'personal friend' of Charteris, and Kerr writes that Bunting's presence in London will be 'important to the Palace'. Continuing in the vein established in his first letter, Kerr disparages Whitlam's choice of Bunting's replacement, John Menadue: 'It was not so much the decision to offer London to Sir John that was disturbing in the top levels of the Public Service, but rather the introduction of someone who, though originally a public servant, had been in private industry for a number of years ... Sir John [Bunting] ... when he came to realise how his replacement would be selected was naturally concerned.'

Three months later, Kerr makes similar criticisms of what he calls 'another controversial appointment', the new head of the Department of Immigration and Labour, Dr Peter Wilenski, a former private secretary to Whitlam.[26] Kerr puts to Charteris the opposition's view that these were 'political appointees'. Kerr's now-revealed adverse reflections on government decisions, and his acceptance of views held by displaced and disgruntled senior public servants and the opposition, was not only beyond the role of the governor-general; it was clearly 'improper'.[27]

Equally concerning for the asserted political neutrality of the monarch is that Charteris gently encourages Kerr down this politicised path, both in the content of the letters and specifically regarding his intervention with the heads of department. In his reply of 14 September 1974, in which he describes the Labor Party as a 'radical party', Charteris points to 'a great many problems in the next year or two between the National Government and the States in which The Queen will inevitably be involved', and encourages Kerr to use his 'beneficial influence' over the senior public servants. Neither Kerr nor Charteris ever suggest that these 'private discussions' with the public service heads, or simply their concerns, ought to be brought to the attention of the prime minister or to John Menadue, the incoming head of his department. Menadue has recently described Kerr's actions in speaking 'privately' to the heads of department about their 'malaise' with the government as 'completely improper'. Speaking to me soon after the release of the letters, Menadue said, 'A governor-general should never do a thing like that. He should be above politics and distinct from it.'[28]

Kerr's repeated speculations throughout his letters about potential problems and disasters awaiting the government convey an overarching sense of a government beset by instability and marked by impermanence. In some instances, such as with the heads of departments, Kerr amplifies an existing area of dissatisfaction; at times, he circulates acknowledged 'rumours and gossip'; and at other times, he passes on little more than a baseless claim.[29] On 8 November 1974, Kerr raises again the possibility of supply being blocked by the opposition in the Senate, and the timing he suggests is quite specific: 'This will inevitably raise the question, around the middle of next year, of another precipitated election which would have to be based on denial of Supply by the Senate ... The question will be whether the Leader of the Opposition feels ready to force another election somewhere about August by denying supply in late June.'

In this same letter, Kerr speculates further on 'serious difficulties' for the government, suggesting to Charteris another problem: the treasurer, Frank Crean, will soon be leaving politics, and his seat could be at risk, to the extent that 'a serious protest against the Government ... [could] possibly [lead to] the defeat of the Labor candidate'.[30] Kerr's speculation about Crean was completely wrong. First, Melbourne Ports was then one of the Labor Party's safest seats, won on primary votes alone by more than 10 per cent; second, Frank Crean did not leave politics for another three years.[31]

Kerr's unfounded speculation about the treasurer and the resultant 'serious protest' against the government exemplifies the reason for the putative convention of the political neutrality of the

Crown. The monarch ought not to engage in politically charged discussions with a governor-general that are untested, unverified, and unknown to the prime minister. At any stage, the prime minister's advice and views on such subjects may be more reliable and entirely different, and it is this advice that the governor-general and the monarch are obliged to act upon. The political neutrality of the Crown is not only an asserted protocol; it is a protocol on which the credibility and survival of a constitutional monarchy within a parliamentary framework depends. The betrayal of this defining principle is indefensible. Kerr was conveying an incomplete, partisan, and at times false version of Australian political events, which the government and the prime minister had no opportunity to counter.

The letters take a disturbing turn towards the end of 1974 over the government's introduction of the new Australian system of honours and the 'table of precedence' in which royal and Australian honours were to be recognised. Kerr was peculiarly agitated by what he saw as an inappropriate placement for existing holders of royal honours, below the highest level of the new Australian honours. *Quelle horreur*!

Furious that Whitlam has not accepted his view on this, on 19 December 1974 Kerr sends the prime minister, who is then in London and due to visit the Queen the following day, a sharply worded, inflammatory, and highly inappropriate confidential cablegram: 'Still disappointed that proposed table of precedence makes no provision for those who have been or may be honoured by The Queen. However, as this view has been put to you and you have decided to exclude it I have felt impelled to put the proposed table to the Queen, on your advice, with my support. Palace will no doubt note the omissions ...' As if it actually mattered.

In his final letter for the year, Kerr's duplicity is explicit. Kerr has told Whitlam that he has dutifully conveyed the prime minister's formal advice to the Queen 'with my support'. He had, and he hadn't. On 19 December 1974, Kerr also cables Charteris that he is sending him 'formal advice of my support for proposed new Australian table of precedence which the Prime Minister will submit to the Queen tomorrow'. At the same time, Kerr sends Charteris a copy of his confidential cablegram to the prime minister, together with a coded telegram expounding his disagreement with that advice. Kerr tells Charteris that he had tried to persuade Whitlam to change this policy and had been 'unable to obtain agreement of Prime Minister', and had therefore 'felt impelled to support table in the form in which he finally advised me'. Kerr then sends the advice by telegram to the private secretary: 'Please advise The Queen that the new table has my support stop Governor General',[32] having already told Charteris that he does not in fact support it.

By 1975, Kerr has moved from doubting the government, defying policy decisions, and querying advice to openly disputing the prime minister's formal advice to him as governor-general to relay to the Queen, and finally to seeking ways to evade it. Still bristling over the advice he had been bound to give the Queen regarding the table of precedence, Kerr's letter of 4 January 1975 shows that being 'impelled', as he sees it, to convey Whitlam's advice had embarrassed and humiliated him. Nothing reveals Kerr's misconception of his role as one of real power, and of protecting the Queen rather than of upholding the constitutional practice of acting on the advice of responsible ministers, more than these letters laying bare his anguish at having to convey Whitlam's advice to the Queen on matters so dear to Kerr's heart – the Royal Anthem, the Royal Honours, and the order of precedence.

That Kerr, a loyal and committed monarchist, had been required to state his 'support' for Whitlam's advice to end these 'colonial relics', as Whitlam had described them, strained Kerr's capacity to function as governor-general at the most fundamental level. His hands have been tied, he complains to Charteris, by the pesky core requirement of a constitutional monarchy that he follow the prime minister's advice: 'I had firm advice from the Prime Minister ... it is extremely difficult for me if I have firm and official advice from the Prime Minister.'

At this point, Kerr should simply have resigned as governor-general. He had shown himself unable to perform the most fundamental requirement of that high office – to convey the prime minister's advice to the Queen – without seeing this core constitutional relationship as politically distasteful and personally humiliating. In fact, as Kerr later wrote in his autobiography, he had decided since August 1975 to 'remain silent' to the prime minister, a constitutionally preposterous position for any governor-general to take and for any prime minister to be placed in.[33] As Hasluck describes in his Queale lecture, communication and openness is at the heart of the proper relationship between the governor-general and the prime minister, his chief advisor: 'With the Prime Minister the Governor-General can be expected to talk with frankness and friendliness, to question, discuss, suggest and counsel.'[34] Without this openness, with only 'silence' towards the prime minister, what role can a governor-general play other than one of his own making?

What followed in Kerr's letter of 4 January was remarkable and utterly improper. Kerr seeks Charteris's assistance in finding a way of 'handling' Whitlam and his unwanted advice in the future: 'I mention this matter in some detail because you may feel disposed to suggest to me improved ways of handling the matter such as this.' Kerr suggests that the best way to do this would be for Charteris to raise any such policy matter with the Queen first, and for Kerr then to be able to present his own wishes to Whitlam as having the Queen's approval, which Whitlam would find difficult to act against: 'It would be a very great assistance to me … to be able to say that the matter has been discussed with the Queen and that what I'm doing has her approval.'

It was not only Charteris with whom Kerr was secretly discussing ways of 'handling' Whitlam's advice on royal matters. Previously unpublished documents from the UK Archives, released to the British journalist Christopher Hastings under Freedom of Information on the same day that the Palace letters were made available, reveal that Kerr had also raised this subject with the British high commissioner, Sir Morrice James, undermining the prime minister, Gough Whitlam, and government policy in the process. In a letter to the Foreign and Commonwealth Office in London, James describes his 'private talk' with Kerr in October 1974 about the 'difficulty' the governor-general was facing:

> I went over this ground with Sir John Kerr in a private talk … He told me that he was trying to think of a way around the difficulty of the pattern contemplated by Mr Whitlam for the playing of the National Anthem: the trouble was, however, that Mr Whitlam by his incautious handling of the whole issue had caused it to become irretrievably a political one, and highly charged with partisan feelings.[35]

Neither Sir Morrice James nor Charteris appears to have questioned the nature or reliability of Kerr's political commentaries, or wondered at his partisan interpretations, as he sought their advice on 'a way around' the prime minister's decision on playing the new National Anthem at vice-regal events.

There is a touch of the absurd and arcane in Kerr's simpering concern over the pattern for the playing of the new National Anthem and whether there should be four or six bars in the vice-regal salute; the fast-receding Royal Honours; the order of precedence for dignitaries; whether he ought to wear 'full morning dress and decorations' at his swearing in (Whitlam had suggested a lounge suit; Charteris assures him that he is 'right to wear morning dress' in defiance of Whitlam's suggestion); and whether 'the curtsey by ladies' should continue in his presence. Kerr raises these matters with Charteris in a letter from Yarralumla on 9 September 1974, the day of his first wife's, Lady Alison Kerr's, death.[36]

Far more serious are the discussions between Kerr and Charteris about the existence and possible use of the reserve powers, and it is in these letters that the more extreme political dimension of the Palace letters is laid bare. Letter by letter, from as early as July 1975, months before supply is blocked in the Senate, Kerr draws the Queen into his planning for the unfolding political situation, his concern for his own position as governor-general, and the possible use of the reserve powers of the Crown to dismiss the government.[37] On 3 July 1975, Kerr tells Charteris that the leader of the opposition, Malcolm Fraser, may now have his 'extraordinary circumstances', and attaches a *Canberra Times* editorial referring to his 'powers and duty'. And on 20 September 1975, raising the prospect of a forced election, Kerr tells Charteris that 'if Mr Whitlam will not advise one I may have to find someone who will'.

From these discussions, Professor David Lee concludes that, 'The correspondence on various occasions shows Charteris encouraging Kerr that it was sound of him to think that use of the reserve powers was one of his options.'[38]

The first indication that the Palace was aware that Kerr was actively considering the use of the reserve powers comes in a crucial letter from Charteris on 2 October 1975 (two weeks before the opposition deferred a vote on supply in the Senate). When the Palace letters were released, this was the first letter I looked for. It is pivotal in unravelling the prior knowledge of the Palace of the prospect of the dismissal. It confirms, first, that the Palace was aware from September 1975 of Kerr's concern for his own position, in the context of his possible dismissal of the government. The letter further confirms the details about Kerr's conversation with Prince Charles in Port Moresby, in which Kerr had indicated that he was 'considering having to dismiss the government', recounted by Kerr in his *Journal* entry, as I had revealed some years earlier.

In his letter of 2 October 1975, Charteris relays to Kerr a conversation he has just had with Prince Charles about Kerr's conversation with the prince during the Independence Day celebrations in Port Moresby the previous month, and Kerr's concern that Whitlam might recall him as governor-general:

> Prince Charles told me a good deal of his conversation with you and in particular that you had spoken of the possibility of the Prime Minister advising The Queen to terminate your Commission with the object, presumably, of replacing you with someone more amenable to his wishes. If such an approach was made you may be sure that The Queen would take most unkindly to it. There would be considerable comings and goings, but I think it is right that I should make the point that at the end of the road The Queen, as a Constitutional Sovereign, would have no option but to follow the advice of her Prime Minister.

These are powerful words to a governor-general who is considering the possible use of the reserve powers. There is nothing neutral in Charteris's adoption of Kerr's assertion that Whitlam might seek his recall 'with the object, presumably, of replacing you with someone more amenable to his wishes', nor in the Queen's expression of displeasure and that 'she would take most unkindly to it' at the prospect of advice from Whitlam to recall Kerr, which is a matter solely for the prime minister to determine. And, as *Justinian* noted, 'there is nothing in the letters indicating the same attitude if

Kerr dismissed Whitlam'.[39] The involvement of the Queen in any discussion with Kerr about his tenure as governor-general, unknown to the prime minister, was manifestly improper.

The appointment and recall of a governor-general is clearly and unquestionably a decision for the Australian prime minister alone, and has been since Labor prime minister James Scullin's testy and firm advice to King George V in 1930 on the appointment of Sir Isaac Isaacs as governor-general. The sole channel of advice was specified and agreed at the 1930 Imperial Conference, which reported specifically on the appointment and recall of a governor-general that:

> (1) The parties interested in the appointment of a Governor General of a Dominion are His Majesty the King ... and the Dominion concerned. (2) The constitutional practice that His Majesty acts on the advice of responsible Ministers applies also in this instance.

The only two people who should have had a discussion about the tenure of the governor-general were the prime minister, Gough Whitlam, as the responsible minister, and the Queen. For the Queen to discuss the question of the governor-general's tenure with Kerr himself, much less express a political view that 'she would take most unkindly to it' should the prime minister decide to do so, was an appalling breach of that elemental relationship. The affirmation that this gave Kerr while he was 'considering having to dismiss the government', as Prince Charles put it, is stark.

However, Charteris's statement points to a more disturbing level of involvement. Professor Paul Rodan concluded, 'Only the most obtuse of governors-general could fail to interpret this as a favourable sign; the Palace seems encouraging rather than neutral ... The references to "comings and goings" and "at the end of the road" speak volumes: any such recommendation from Whitlam would only be implemented after some delay.[40] The nature of this exchange leaves moot the reflex qualifier that 'at the end of the road she would have no option but to follow the advice of her Prime Minister', since, in the context of the dismissal of one prime minister and the installation of another, the obvious question is *Which prime minister would that be?*

The entry from Kerr's *Journal* about this crucial conversation with Prince Charles, and the subsequent exchange with Charteris, had formed part of our evidence submitted to the Federal Court on the nature of Kerr's correspondence with the Queen. The *Journal* entry provides the backstory to Charteris's guarded description, giving Kerr's end of his conversation with Prince Charles, and greatly adding to the significance of Charteris's letter, which has now confirmed it.

Kerr writes that he had confided to Prince Charles that he was considering dismissing the government and that he feared therefore that Whitlam might recall him as governor-general if he found out about it. Kerr records Prince Charles's solicitous response: 'But surely Sir John, the Queen should not have to accept advice that you should be recalled ... should this happen when you were considering having to dismiss the government.' Prince Charles relayed this dramatic conversation to Charteris, who reassures Kerr that if Whitlam sought to recall him, the Palace would, as Kerr described it, 'try to delay things'.

When I revealed this critical exchange between Kerr, Prince Charles, and Charteris from Kerr's *Journal* in 2012, it was dismissed by some who were still clinging to the view that the Queen had played no role in Kerr's decision to dismiss the government.[41] *The Australian* denounced my recitation of Kerr's *Journal* entry, describing the exchange it details with Prince Charles and Charteris as 'unsubstantiated', a mere 'conspiracy', and as 'a direct assault on the integrity of the Queen and Governor-General', for which, it claimed, there was no evidence. 'The Charteris letter to Kerr has never been sighted or produced', it proclaimed. With the release of the Palace letters, it has been.

Turning to Kerr's handwritten notes, which I had also described, it continued: 'While other handwritten notes refer to "Charteris' advice to me", there is no evidence it concerns Kerr signalling to Charteris his intention to dismiss Whitlam.' This is a misrepresentation of a key document in an already fractured history, relying entirely on the omission of two key words that follow. The actual statement among Kerr's papers reads: 'Charteris' advice to me *on dismissal*'. [my italics] With those words in place, and Kerr's note correctly described, the connection between the Palace and Kerr's planning for the dismissal is impossible to avoid.

In his *Journal*, Kerr had interpreted this conversation with Prince Charles and the subsequent letter from Charteris – now confirmed with the release of the Palace letters – as ensuring a period of 'delay' if Whitlam sought his recall. The Queen's assistant private secretary at the time, Sir William Heseltine, has gone further, confirming Kerr's interpretation and acknowledging the 'political' dimension to it. In an interview for the ABC documentary *The Crown and Us* in 2018, Heseltine confirmed that if Whitlam had sought Kerr's recall, the Queen would not have simply acted on the prime minister's advice, and would have adopted what Heseltine described as a 'policy of political delay'. A more profound breach of the defining relationship between the monarch and the prime minister in a constitutional monarchy can scarcely be imagined.

It is impossible to overstate the significance and the impropriety of this exchange between the governor-general, Prince Charles, and the Queen through Charteris, back to Kerr. It shows the Palace to have been in a deep intrigue with Kerr over his tenure as governor-general, in the context of his possible dismissal of the government – all of it unknown to Whitlam. This politically and constitutionally shocking exchange is a profound rupture of the vice-regal relationship, at the heart of which is the requirement that the appointment of the governor-general is made by the Queen on the advice of the Australian prime minister alone.

This critical letter has also confirmed that the Queen, Prince Charles, and Charteris were all aware, by September 1975, that Kerr was 'considering having to dismiss the government' and was keeping this possibility secret from the prime minister. Charteris's failure to remind Kerr of his responsibility to speak to the prime minister, to seek his advice, and, both constitutionally and morally, that he not deceive him, could only have been taken by Kerr as support, if not encouragement, for the deceptive path he was taking. After all, the Palace was now a part of that deception.

From this point on, knowing that Kerr was considering dismissing Whitlam, and having agreed to a course of action should Whitlam seek his recall, the Palace was *already* involved.

Chapter Eleven

'You will do it good'

In October 1975, Sir Martin Charteris was worried. The 'very serious danger' of the Queen receiving conflicting advice from her Australian ministers, which he had raised with Kerr in his first letter, was playing heavily on his mind. In September 1975, Charteris had approached the UK Foreign and Commonwealth Office (FCO) and asked them to report any matters that might lead to the Queen receiving conflicting advice.[1] The FCO reported just one: the prospect of a half-Senate election.

Although the FCO's fear was entirely speculative, it had kept their South West Pacific Department thoroughly occupied for weeks. At heart, it was a purely political matter, generated by the opposition's threat that its conservative state premiers would advise their governors not to issue the writs for the half-Senate election. According to this fevered speculation, Whitlam might then advise the governor-general to advise the Queen to advise the governors to issue the writs. It was this triple-step hypothetical that the FCO feared could lead the Queen to be given conflicting advice from the prime minister and the state governors.[2] 'If this is right, we would expect that the Governor-General would decline to act on Mr Whitlam's advice', the British High Commission told the FCO confidently.[3]

The continuing British ignorance of the interstices of Australian political structures was stark. The constitutional framers had allowed for exactly this state-based electoral disruption under the remarkably prescient section 11, 'Failure to choose Senators', which exposed the coalition's threat as baseless and self-defeating. The effect of section 11 was that the Senate could be constituted even if some states failed to provide representation to it.[4] If the opposition were to put its threat into practice, it would have left the Coalition without their usual quota of Senate representation, and the Whitlam government in command of the Senate. Nevertheless, the FCO, Charteris, and the British High Commission all saw this threat stemming from the half-Senate election as real, and the hypothetical involvement of the Queen as 'one we would wish if at all possible to avoid'.[5]

The FCO's desire to avoid the half-Senate election, as if our electoral process was its to determine, was directly linked to the Palace through Charteris. In fact, it was Charteris who had initiated these discussions in September 1975 when he asked the FCO to report on any matters on which the Queen could be given conflicting advice and, critically, 'whether anything could be done to avoid them'.[6] With Charteris's direct involvement in these extraordinary discussions, it is clear that this ominous British concern went right to the Queen herself. The desire to 'avoid' the Queen's possible 'embarrassment' was at the heart of these concerns about the pending half-Senate election.

As these discussions continued, the most senior bureaucrat in the FCO, the permanent under-secretary, Sir Michael Palliser, cancelled a planned tour of eastern Europe and made a whirlwind two-day trip to Australia.[7] On 16 October 1975, as the Senate was debating its unprecedented motion to defer the government's supply bills, Palliser arrived at Yarralumla for a meeting with the governor-general and the British high commissioner, Sir Morrice James. The next day, Palliser met the governor of New South Wales, Sir Roden Cutler, in Sydney. Barely 48 hours after he arrived, Palliser left Australia, taking with him the 'comforting confirmation' that 'the Governor-General could be relied upon' to protect the Queen in any action he might take regarding the supply crisis.[8]

As these details continued to emerge in recent years, News Corp columnist Gerard Henderson joined his stablemates' evidentiary disdain to claim bizarrely that the meeting with Palliser never happened. 'There was no evidence', he declared; 'almost certainly, the event never took place'.[9] And yet Palliser's briefing papers and his itinerary from the FCO detail his rushed visit and full schedule, and the vice-regal notices in the *Canberra Times* announced his meeting with Kerr: 'Sir John received the following callers: Sir Morrice James, British High Commissioner; Sir Michael Palliser, permanent under-secretary-designate, Foreign and Commonwealth Office'.[10] Henderson dismissed it all as 'conspiracy theory', a pattern that would be repeated in News Corp's peculiar representation of these events and the Palace letters.

Palliser's visit exposes a recurrent curiosity in the Palace letters: the identifiable gaps, of which this is one. This meeting was as important to Charteris as it was to Kerr. Charteris was being kept informed by the FCO of its investigation into possible areas of 'conflicting advice' to the Queen, and in particular the 'problem' of the half-Senate election; and yet, in the Palace letters, neither he nor Kerr mentions this critical meeting with those at the highest levels of the FCO and the British High Commission. Another notable absence is any reference to Kerr's secret meetings and conversations with the High Court justice Sir Anthony Mason that were taking place over these critical months. These gaps and partialities in the letters are reinforced by Kerr's use of attachments as a form of selective corroboration, rather than as a representation of the range of deeply polarised views in Australia at that time. The various attachments form part of a particular version of events, one in which Kerr's role is central, and whose resolution without his intervention is impossible. They are fundamental to his construction of a case for the inevitability of dismissal.

The treatment of the central issue of the half-Senate election is emblematic of this tendentious approach. The letters give scant consideration to the one option proposed by and finally acted on by the prime minister in relation to the blocking of supply – the half-Senate election.

On 12 September 1975, Kerr speculates to Charteris on what Whitlam might do if supply is blocked in the Senate. In this letter, Kerr canvasses only two possibilities: a dissolution of the House of Representatives, or a double dissolution. As an indication of the prime minister's options, this is incomplete and disingenuous. In his politically charged description of Whitlam as possibly 'toughing it out' and 'refusing to recommend a dissolution', Kerr fails to mention as an option the one election that Whitlam had indicated he would call if supply were blocked.

Kerr raises the prospect of a half-Senate election in a later letter, two weeks before supply is blocked, dismissing it as 'another tactic' that Whitlam 'is trying out publicly'.[11] The language is intemperate and telling, since the timing of the half-Senate election is constitutionally determined under section 13, and it was due at that time.[12] Nevertheless, Kerr sees this not as a possible solution to the blocking of supply, but only as a problematic tactic. In his reply of 8 October 1975, Charteris adopts this politicised terminology, describing it as a 'tactic' that, while constitutionally proper for Whitlam to call and for Kerr to 'agree to', nevertheless could raise 'considerable problems … in which you would be involved.'

The government's intention to call that election was formulated at a late-night caucus meeting on 16 October 1975, the day supply was blocked. This was widely reported at the time, as was the acknowledgement that the governor-general would have no option but to act on that advice: 'The Prime Minister is making preparations to hold the half-Senate election … He is likely to see the Governor-General, Sir John Kerr, in the next few days.'[13] Yet, in a confusing and contradictory letter to Charteris the following day, Kerr still presents the half-Senate election as a 'tactic', a 'possibility' beset by hypothetical difficulties, even suggesting that Labor ministers are concerned about 'violence in the streets', before conceding that the 'Prime Minister's tactics' are to continue to seek supply and to call the half-Senate election 'in due course'.[14]

Yet after the government's intention to call the half-Senate election has been announced, Kerr tells Charteris that Whitlam has decided 'that the Senate must reject supply outright *before he will call an election of any kind'*.[15] [my italics] This was simply untrue. Even the FCO knew that the half-Senate election was the government's intention, as a telex from the British high commissioner on 15 October informed them: 'Mr Whitlam has indicated that he will not request dissolution of House of Representatives but will seek to hold half-Senate elections due before 1st of July 1976.'[16] Kerr backed up his view of the problematic half-Senate election with a series of attachments.

The half-Senate election was the only election that would have addressed the critical factor in the blocking of supply – the political make-up of the Senate. The coalition had been able to defer supply, rather than vote to accept or reject it, because it had engineered a temporary majority in the Senate due to the replacement of two Labor senators with non-Labor appointees. The Senate that had been elected in May 1974 had been substantively recast with the replacement of New South Wales Labor senator Lionel Murphy in February 1975, and Queensland Labor senator Bert Milliner in July, by non-Labor appointees by their conservative state governments. The resultant 'tainted' Senate, as Liberal member Jim Killen described it, would be corrected at the half-Senate election with the election of two replacement senators who would take their places immediately, together with two new senators for each of the mainland territories – the Australian Capital Territory and the Northern Territory.[17]

It was this complicated Senate algebra that meant the ALP could potentially gain control of the Senate for six months following the half-Senate election.[18] The half-Senate election was therefore the one election that the coalition feared most, since it held out the possibility that the government would have a temporary majority in the Senate. Although many commentators remarked on this at the time – including Alan Reid, who described the coalition as being in a state of 'panic' about the Senate election – Kerr conveyed little of this deeply party-political concern in his extensive newspaper clippings to the Queen.[19] In his despatches, the mooted speculative 'problems' with that election erased it as a viable option for the government, obscuring the determination of both the opposition and the FCO to avoid it. It was as if the prime minister's decision to call an election was subject to a vice-regal veto depending on its possible outcome.

Kerr's desultory consideration of the government's intended response to the deferral of supply – a course of action on which he knew he would be bound to accept the prime minister's advice – reflects the selective nature of his correspondence with the Queen. The lack of consideration of the Senate election is in marked contrast to their pointed discussion about the existence and use of the reserve powers, which emerges at this same time. This is the Palace letters at their most political, establishing a pathway to dismissal that unfolds from September 1975, when the possibility of the reserve powers enters their view and the half-Senate election slides briefly into frame, only to slide out again just as quickly, leaving barely a trace.[20] In all the Palace letters, it is those discussing the reserve powers that are the most significant, and through which Kerr moved inexorably towards dismissal.

'It was all Canada's fault', Guy Rundle wrote soon after the release of the Palace letters, and, in a sense, it was.[21] Like so much else in this tortured history, the role played by the Canadian senator Eugene Forsey was greater than we had ever known or understood before.

It begins with the Queen's letter of 24 September 1975, in which Charteris raises the possible use of the reserve powers. The most important part of this short letter is Charteris's hand-written addendum, casually pointing Kerr to the work of Eugene Forsey, a Canadian senator and expert on the reserve powers in the former dominions:

P.S. I suppose you know Eugene Forsey's book 'The Prerogative of the Dissolution'? [sic] I believe he lays it down as a principal [sic] that if Supply is refused this always makes it constitutionally proper to grant a dissolution.

Although Charteris refers to supply being 'refused', it is notable that at this point supply had not yet been deferred, and it never was refused.

What is most remarkable about this recommendation from Charteris, who was not a lawyer, was his choice of Forsey as an appropriate expert on a uniquely Australian parliamentary situation before it had even happened. Kerr hardly needed Charteris to tell him about the work of Eugene Forsey; like all Australian constitutional lawyers, he knew Forsey's work, just as he knew the work of the Australian expert on the question of the reserve powers in Australia, Dr H.V. Evatt. Evatt's definitive text, *The King and his Dominion Governors*, sat alongside Forsey's *The Royal Power of*

Dissolution of Parliament in the British Commonwealth on every legal bookshelf as the work of the two great scholars in this field.

Charteris's reference was not a collegial recommendation of a theorist of whom Kerr might not have been aware, but to a particular theorist in a contested field – whose knowledge of the Australian constitutional structures was, at best, limited. Forsey thought there was no such thing as a half-Senate election – an extraordinary failing, given the political impasse in late 1975 and the possible resolution to it. 'He could find no mention of such an election in the Australian Constitution', the Canadian under-secretary of state for external affairs reported.[22] The wording of section 13 of the Constitution, 'Rotation of Senators', had apparently eluded Forsey, yet this is the expert whom Charteris urged upon Kerr.

Charteris's recommendation of Forsey was not only inappropriate, given his ignorance of the Australian circumstance; it was clearly directive. Forsey was a constitutional conservative, a 'royalist radical' with 'a profound reverence for British Tory constitutionalism', and a strong proponent of the existence and use of the reserve powers.[23] In Charteris's own words in a later letter to Kerr, Forsey was a 'stalwart upholder of the prerogative of the Crown' – and although he had not told Kerr this previously, Forsey was also Charteris's friend.[24]

Most critical is that Forsey and Evatt drew 'opposite conclusions as to the constitutionality and propriety of the [Canadian] Governor-General's 1926 dissolution of the Canadian House of Commons', the Canadian constitutional crisis seen as most comparable to the situation in Australia in 1975.[25]

This was the 'King–Byng affair' of 1926, in which the Canadian Liberal prime minister, William Mackenzie King, had sought to have parliament dissolved and an election called, which the governor-general, the British Lord Byng, refused. Byng called on the conservative leader of the opposition, Arthur Meighen, to form government, despite Meighen's lack of a majority in the House of

Commons. When Meighen lost a vote in the House, Byng granted him the dissolution he had denied prime minister King. Forsey was well known for his fierce support of Lord Byng's decision, which he prosecuted throughout his major works over several decades.[26] Evatt's view was that 'Lord Byng should have refused Mr Meighen's request for a dissolution and recommissioned Mr King as Prime Minister', and granted King the dissolution he had requested.[27]

The 'King–Byng affair' had led to the key changes at the 1926 and 1930 Imperial Conferences to the appointment of a governor-general solely on the advice of the Dominion ministers and the specification of the 'Constitutional practice' that the Crown must act on the advice of responsible ministers. In other words, the 'precedent' of Lord Byng was, even by 1926, no precedent at all, since the Imperial Conference later that year made a clear statement of the primacy of responsible government over vice-regal discretion.

In his brief personal aside to Kerr, Charteris had pointed Kerr in the direction of someone with a very particular conception of the reserve powers as both extant and relevant – a view not shared by Kerr's constitutional advisors, the Australian law officers, or the prime minister – and whose work provided a theoretical validation for dismissal.

It is now commonly said that the reserve powers clearly do exist, a fact cemented by Kerr's actions in exercising them; however, prior to the dismissal, their existence was highly contested, if not denied. Many believed that, with the passage of time, and the infusion of the sentiments of responsible government through the parliament as the embodiment of the popular will, the notion of the Crown's reserve powers – a residue of the doctrine of the divine right of kings – was antithetical to democratic governance and had long since fallen into desuetude. With his dismissal of Whitlam, Kerr breathed substance into a largely ceremonial role, providing the necessary precedent for their present revivification. What matters in examining the Palace letters is the view held of the reserve powers *before* the dismissal, not after.

In 1973, for instance, Professor Markesinis argued that, 'the right to dissolve and to time dissolution is nowadays a prime ministerial prerogative'.[28] In 1965, Professor Crisp wrote that the decisions of the 1926 and 1930 Imperial Conferences, and the passage of the Statute of Westminster, 'have converged to strip away most of the substance of his [the Governor-General's] prerogative and discretionary powers, in practice almost to vanishing point. Today his principal powers are exercised and functions performed, probably without exception, on the advice of his Ministers'.[29]

The Commonwealth solicitor-general, Sir Maurice Byers, was later even more emphatic: 'The reserve powers are a fiction. They don't exist. You can't have an autocratic power which is destructive of the granted authority to the people. They just can't coexist. Therefore you can't have a reserve power because you are saying the Governor-General can override the people's choice ... and that's a nonsense.'[30]

On 21 October 1975, with supply now blocked in the Senate for nearly a week, Whitlam asked the law officers – Byers and the attorney-general, Kep Enderby – to prepare a joint opinion for Kerr on the reserve powers, their existence, and whether they could be used in the current situation.[31] This was in response to a provocative public statement by the shadow attorney-general, Robert Ellicott, released as soon as supply was blocked, that not only did the reserve powers exist, but that the governor-general should immediately invoke them to dismiss the government and hold a general election. The Palace letters show that at Kerr's dinner for the visiting Malaysian prime minister, Tun Razak, on 16 October, the leader of the opposition, Malcolm Fraser, had impressed Ellicott's statement on Kerr and had arranged to leave a copy for David Smith to collect at the Commonwealth Club.[32]

In a key letter, while the legal advisors' joint opinion is being prepared for him, Kerr tells Charteris that he expects them to advise him that the reserve powers do not exist.[33] One of the most important statements in the Palace letters then follows. Kerr writes that he would not necessarily accept the advice of his constitutional advisors: 'it does not follow that in an extreme Constitutional crisis I would accept that'. In this declaration, three weeks before the dismissal, Kerr has let the Queen know that he is prepared to act against the advice of his advisors *before* he has even received it. And at no stage after this statement of vice-regal discretionary abrogation does Charteris express concern that Kerr is contemplating such a breach of his constitutional relationship, remind him to speak to his prime minister, or ask him what the advice of the law officers actually was.

There is no letter from Kerr prior to the dismissal telling Charteris of the joint opinion that he received from the law officers on 6 November 1975, advising that the reserve powers had most likely fallen into desuetude as relics of a sovereign power not used for nearly two centuries, and that there was no basis for their use in the current parliamentary stalemate. As he delivered Kerr the joint opinion, the attorney-general, Kep Enderby, told him in even stronger terms that, in his opinion, the reserve powers did not exist.[34] The joint opinion noted that 'no Government has been dismissed by the Sovereign since 1783', and that 'their very rarity and the long years since their exercise cast the gravest doubt upon the present existence of that prerogative'. It concluded that, 'The mere threat of or indeed the actual rejection of Supply neither calls for the ministry to resign nor compels the Crown's representative thereupon to intervene.'[35]

Despite this clear advice from the government's legal advisors, Kerr did as he had told Charteris he might do, and refused to accept it. Instead, he turned to one of his other secret advisors, the High Court justice Sir Anthony Mason, sending him, without the government's permission, the joint opinion. Mason read it, disputed it, and told Kerr, 'I don't agree with it', thereby abetting the governor-general's refusal to act on the advice of his responsible ministers.[36] The longstanding New South Wales solicitor-general Michael Sexton QC has described Mason's interventions as 'extraordinary' and 'a clear abuse'.[37]

Mason, having provided Kerr with a legal view of his own, then helped him secure the written advice of the chief justice, Sir Garfield Barwick.[38] Kerr met with Barwick, against the prime minister's explicit advice, on the day before the dismissal. Whitlam had advised Kerr against speaking to Barwick because the governor-general's appropriate legal advisors were the solicitor-general and the attorney-general; because the High Court had determined in 1921 that it cannot give advisory opinions; and finally, because in the recent tightly split High Court decisions on challenges to Whitlam government legislation, Barwick had consistently found against the government.[39] Through this subterfuge, unknown to Whitlam, the legal advice of the solicitor-general and attorney-general was secretly dispensed with by Kerr in concert with a High Court justice, and countermanded in writing by the chief justice. There could be no greater abrogation of the separation of powers, let alone of professional and personal propriety, than this.

The nub of the problem in this miscast political narrative can be seen in Kerr's acknowledgement that he has not spoken to, and will not speak to, the prime minister about the most pressing constitutional and political matter in our history. What is absent throughout these letters is any recognition by either Charteris or Kerr of the governor-general's most fundamental duty – to act on the advice of his constitutional advisors, specifically the prime minister. Instead, the government is simply side-stepped as Kerr asks for and is given advice by the Queen's private secretary, at times contrary to Whitlam's advice and the law officers' advice, including on the existence and use of the reserve powers. At the same time, the leader of the opposition, Malcolm Fraser, is placing the most extreme, and improper, pressure on Kerr to act. Fraser himself later acknowledged that in the week before the dismissal he had spoken in the strongest terms to Kerr, threatening to 'denounce him as a "Labor stooge" if he did not act against the government.[40]

With the prospect of vice-regal action now apparent, Kerr tells Charteris on 27 October that he is concerned that any decision he makes could 'affect the Monarchy in Australia'. In obvious contrast to his refusal to accept the advice of his constitutional advisors, Kerr asks Charteris for 'any observations' that Charteris thinks 'should be taken into account in the interests of the Monarchy in Australia' in any action that Kerr might take about the supply crisis. Let's unpack this a bit further, because it is striking. Kerr has already told Charteris that he may not accept the advice of his legal advisors in relation to the situation in the Senate, and he now asks Charteris to provide him with advice about 'the interests of the Monarchy' to assist him in reaching his decision. With this, Kerr invites the Palace to contribute directly to whatever action he is to make. Far from the Palace having no involvement in Kerr's decision, Kerr has ensured that it does.

Whereas Kerr has decried Whitlam's expectation that he would always act on the prime minister's advice as the humiliating suggestion that he is a 'compliant' governor-general, rather than as the simple expression of their conventional constitutional relationship, he has no such concerns about receiving Charteris's advice – indeed, he welcomes it. The Queen's private secretary has now usurped Kerr's Australian constitutional advisors, confirming and giving substance to Kerr's reference elsewhere in his private papers to 'Charteris's advice to me on dismissal'.[41] Move over responsible government, right there.

These letters from Kerr provide the essential context for two pivotal letters from Charteris that follow, and which push Kerr most strongly toward the use of the reserve powers. On 4 November, the non-lawyer Charteris tells Kerr definitively that the contested and controversial reserve powers do exist: 'those powers do exist ... but to use them is a heavy responsibility'. In a mix of overweening flattery, patronising hyperbole, and legal direction, Charteris continues, 'I think you are playing the "Vice-Regal" hand with skill and wisdom. Your interest in the situation has been demonstrated, and so has your impartiality. The fact that you have the powers is recognized, but it is also clear that you will only use them in the last resort and then only for constitutional and not for political reasons.'

While some commentators have described Charteris as here advising Kerr to be cautious, this is completely untenable. Charteris has advised Kerr explicitly on the existence and use of the contentious reserve powers, against the advice of his advisors, and kept secret from them. The *Washington Post* was unequivocal: 'Queen Elizabeth II's office assured her representative in Australia he had the power to bring down the Australian government a week before he took the extraordinary move in 1975.'[42] When Kerr might choose to use those powers is hardly the point.

Having established for Kerr the Palace's advice that the contested reserve powers do exist, Charteris moves, in a letter the following day, to the more fractious political question of using those powers to dismiss the elected government. Most importantly for Kerr, Charteris specifically assuages Kerr's concern, which he had raised the previous week, that any decision he makes 'could indirectly affect the Monarchy in Australia'. This 'is, of course true', Charteris writes. 'This places you in what is, perhaps, an unenviable, but is certainly a very honourable position. If you do, as you will, what the Constitution dictates, you cannot possible [sic] do the Monarchy any avoidable harm. The chances are you will do it good.' These letters are the ballast that Kerr needs, giving him, as Professor David Lee described, 'the confidence that his dismissal of the Prime Minister would not be disavowed by the Palace'.[43]

This final letter from the Queen's private secretary, just days before Kerr dismissed the government, ends with a lengthy quotation from former Canadian prime minister Arthur Meighen, the conservative recipient of the Canadian governor-general's largesse in 1926, when Lord Byng granted him the dissolution he had denied former prime minister King. It is hardly surprising that Meighen held an extremely positive view of an interventionist governor-general with discretionary reserve powers, to be used even against the advice of his ministers. Charteris points Kerr to Meighen's 'splendid phrase about the role of the Crown/Governor-General in the Canadian Constitution', and just in case the inference is not sufficiently clear, Charteris adds, 'I think it is good stuff'. The quotation from Meighen begins:

> The sphere of discretion left to a Governor-General under our constitution and under our practice is a limited sphere indeed, but it is a sphere of dignity and great responsibility. Within the ambit of discretion residing still in the Crown in England, and residing in the Governor-General in the Dominions, there is a responsibility as great as falls to any estate of the realm or to any House of Parliament.

Six days later, on 11 November 1975, the governor-general exercised that 'sphere of dignity' and discretion, and dismissed the Whitlam government without warning, just as the prime minister was advising the half-Senate election.

***

Gough Whitlam shook Kerr's hand 'from ordinary habit and simple courtesy', walked down the long Yarralumla corridor and left, unaware that Malcolm Fraser was already there, secreted in an anteroom with David Smith at the other end of the corridor, to be sworn in by Kerr as prime minister. In his letter to Charteris describing these events, Kerr writes that Whitlam said, 'I shall have to get in touch with the Palace immediately', frantically looking for a telephone in order to do so. Kerr's claim was always absurd, since there was no shortage of telephones at the Lodge, where Whitlam went directly from Yarralumla and from where he rang his key advisors and his wife, Margaret, who was then in Sydney. Whitlam could have 'got in touch with the Palace immediately' had he wanted to, and he did not. This was Kerr's crude *post hoc* validation for his deception of the prime minister over the half-Senate election, and for his failure to 'advise and warn' him of the possibility of dismissal. His insistent claim that Whitlam would immediately seek his recall as governor-general never transpired.

In fact, the first person to contact Buckingham Palace was the official secretary, Mr David Smith, more than an hour after the dismissal – Kerr being incapacitated by his post-dismissal lunch.[44] Whitlam contacted Charteris three hours later, introducing himself as 'a private citizen', as Charteris describes in his letter to Kerr of 17 November 1975. Charteris reports that Whitlam 'spoke calmly' and that he 'did not ask me to make any approach to The Queen, or indeed to do anything other than the suggestion I should speak to you [Kerr] to find out what was going on'. This comment, remarkably, has been interpreted as Whitlam having 'wanted the Palace to pressure Kerr to reinstate him as prime minister'.[45] It is an impossible inference to draw.

Whitlam's strategy as he left Yarralumla, having suffered what he described to me as 'the greatest shock I had ever experienced', was entirely institutional. He believed, remarkably enough, that the parliamentary processes would see him back in office by the end of the day, and indeed they should have. Parliament was set to resume at 2.00 pm, and Whitlam's intention was for the Senate to pass supply and the House of Representatives to pass a motion of confidence in him and in a government led by him. That motion, worked up over lunch at the Lodge, can be found in the national archives.[46] It was never used, as events soon overtook it. Whitlam had to frame a new motion from the floor of the House as details gradually emerged. In formulating his approach, Whitlam suffered from the irredeemable disadvantage of ignorance born of deception, unaware that Fraser was already prime minister, and never anticipating that Kerr would, on the advice of his longstanding confidant and 'guide', High Court justice Anthony Mason, ignore the defining confidence motion of the House of Representatives.

The House of Representatives reconvened at 2.00 pm, in an electrifying session in which the fate of two governments hung in the balance – the evicted elected government of Gough Whitlam and the appointed government of Malcolm Fraser. At 2.34 pm, Fraser rose to announce that the governor-general had already appointed him prime minister, and the House erupted. The crowded public gallery strained under the weight of angry onlookers leaning perilously over the balcony, hurling insults at the equally agitated members below. The *Hansard* reporters struggled to hear over the deafening noises of distress and disbelief. At 3.03 pm, Fraser lost the critical motion of confidence in the House of Representatives by 10 votes. The same motion called on the governor-general to recommission the government led by the member for Werriwa, Gough Whitlam.

Whitlam fully expected that, with these requisite elements of government in place, he would be returned to office that afternoon. supply had been passed, and he had the confidence of the House of Representatives on the core question of the formation of government.

He rang Margaret again and told her not to return to Canberra, as he would be back in office by the end of the day.[47] Whitlam had not reckoned on Kerr's 'second dismissal', the pre-emptive closure of the parliament itself in order to avoid receiving notification of the House of Representatives' vote of no confidence in the Fraser government. Kerr, now belatedly concerned that the motion of the House might need to be addressed, rang Sir Anthony Mason. Mason was emphatic: the no-confidence motion, he told Kerr, was 'irrelevant'. This statement from a High Court justice to the governor-general, repudiating the definitional motion of the House of Representatives on the formation of government – a denial of the very essence of responsible parliamentary government – was a staggering breach of the separation of powers that Mason determinedly kept secret for the next thirty-seven years.

Following the want-of-confidence motion against Fraser, the Speaker of the House, Gordon Scholes, left immediately to contact the governor-general: 'As Speaker I was going to personally deliver to the Governor-General the opinion of the House'.[48] The official secretary, David Smith, refused him an appointment, and it was only when Scholes told Smith that he intended to recall the House if Kerr refused to see him that an appointment was made for 4.25 pm. Scholes waited for over an hour, believing that Kerr had agreed to see him to receive the no-confidence motion: 'We were acting on the assumption that the Governor-General would do what was right.' Scholes then arrived at Yarralumla at 4.25 pm to find the gates locked, until David Smith drove out – unknown to Scholes, headed for Parliament House. When Scholes handed Kerr the motion of the House, Kerr told him he had already dissolved parliament. Armed with Mason's advice, Kerr had refused to see the Speaker and had dissolved both houses, leaving Fraser in office as prime minister.

As Scholes recalled: 'The Governor-General refused to accept the last resolution passed by the parliament, which was a confidence vote.'[49] Malcolm Fraser consequently bore the ignominy of being the only prime minister in Australian history to have refused to resign after losing a motion of no confidence in the House of Representatives.[50] Kerr later wrote to his longstanding friend and ardent supporter J.B. Paul that if he had reinstated Whitlam following the passage of supply in the Senate, and the vote of no confidence in Fraser, 'the whole exercise would have been aborted'.[51] What exactly was 'the exercise', if not to secure the passage of supply and ensure responsible government, as he had claimed?

It is a quirk of history that with all his Labor colleagues dismissed from their ministerial positions, Scholes retained his parliamentary position as Speaker. The tenure of Speaker is determined by parliament and cannot be countermanded, even at the whim of an activist governor-general.[52] Scholes retained his office, his title, and his influence, and he used them as best he could 'in defence of the rights of the House'. Scholes' view was that to appoint a prime minister expressly lacking the confidence of the House was 'quite out of line with the role of a Governor-General or the Crown', and the following day he wrote to the Queen, pointing to 'the danger to parliamentary democracy' of a prime minister 'imposed on the nation by Royal prerogative rather than through parliamentary endorsement'. Kerr's refusal to see him as Speaker was, he told the Queen, 'an act of contempt for the House of Representatives', and as Speaker he called on her to restore the Whitlam government 'in accordance with the expressed resolution of the House'.[53]

Kerr's actions on 11 November 1975 were unprecedented. He had removed from office, without providing any warning and any options, a government that retained its majority in the House of Representatives. He had placed in office, on his own nomination, a party led by the leader of the opposition that had lost the previous two elections, which did not have the confidence of the House, and whose actions had caused the breakdown over supply in the Senate. In doing so, Kerr had averted the greatest fear of the opposition, the half-Senate election that he and Whitlam had discussed over the previous five days and that Whitlam was to announce in the House of Representatives that afternoon. In their devastating partisan effects, Kerr's actions were not only unprecedented, but they were also transparently political.

Kerr had given Whitlam no indication of any of his concerns about the half-Senate election, nor made any suggestion that he would not accept his advice, and had given him no warning of the possibility of dismissal – as Charteris was well aware. Kerr reminded Charteris after the dismissal: 'It is true that I did not tell Mr Whitlam that I intended to dismiss his government until the point of time came when I was about to do it. You know the reason.'[54] This was Kerr's greatest moral failing, his refusal to warn his prime minister. Even Sir Anthony Mason, Kerr's secret confidant and guide, later insisted he told Kerr that he must warn Whitlam and, 'as a matter of fairness', that he must give Whitlam the opportunity as the incumbent prime minister to go to an election: 'I told him that, if he did not warn the prime minister, he would run the risk that people would accuse him of being deceptive.'[55] In his failure to warn the prime minister, Kerr had put himself and his concern for his own position ahead of his constitutional responsibilities to the head of elected government.

In his 'Statement of Reasons' published the day of the dismissal, Kerr made no mention of Whitlam's advice to call the half-Senate election on 11 November 1975, nor the agreed wording for the announcement in the House that he had finalised with Whitlam that morning. Kerr told Charteris: 'I knew from him by telephone that that was his advice.'[56] In his statement, Kerr described the half-Senate election disingenuously as a discussion of 'a possibility' that 'might be held', a passive construction in which Whitlam's advice to call it did not feature. However, the amended draft of Kerr's statement told a different story. In Kerr's original version, he stated that Whitlam, 'advised a half-Senate election. I felt constrained to reject this advice'. This was then amended to its final form: 'There has been discussion of the possibility that a half-Senate election might be held under circumstances in which the government has not obtained supply. If such advice were given to me I should feel constrained to reject it'.[57] The falsification of history had begun.

The official secretary, David Smith, later acknowledged that Whitlam had indeed 'called on the Governor-General [on 11 November 1975] to advise a half-Senate election to be held on the 13th December'. This, Smith describes as the reason for the dismissal: 'Had Whitlam not decided to go to Government House on that day to ask the Governor-General for a half-Senate election, the events of 11th November simply would not have occurred.'[58]

A critical element in the dismissal not mentioned by Kerr or Charteris in these letters, nor in much of the history since, is the precedent set by Kerr's predecessor governor-general, Sir Paul Hasluck, the previous year when supply had been threatened by the opposition in the Senate. Hasluck's constructive, appropriate, and proper conversations with Whitlam over that time served as a model for what Whitlam expected Kerr to do, and for what Kerr should have done, in November 1975.

Despite Kerr's repeated claims to the contrary, Whitlam was not 'intent on governing without supply'; after all, it was his government that had three times tried to get the Senate to pass supply, and the opposition that had three times refused to do so. Indeed, prior to supply being blocked, Kerr had discussed with Whitlam the question of securing temporary supply through the Senate should he advise the half-Senate election, as Kerr described to Charteris on 30 September 1975.

Whitlam expected that, following his advice to call the half-Senate election, Kerr would do what Hasluck had done in 1974, and grant the half-Senate election, conditional on supply being passed by the Senate.[59] Kerr never gave Whitlam, or the Senate, that opportunity. A parliamentary paper setting out the series of events that had been arranged with governor-general Hasluck in 1974 was due to be tabled in the House on the afternoon of 11 November 1975, to demonstrate both precedent and continuity. In the aftermath of the dismissal, it was never tabled.

On 17 November 1975, Charteris replied to the Speaker, Gordon Scholes: 'The Queen has *no part* in the decisions which the Governor-General must take in accordance with the Constitution.'[60] [my italics] The Palace letters have demolished that claim, making a mockery of the vaunted 'political neutrality of the Crown'. They reveal the Queen, through Charteris, to have engaged with Kerr in consideration of the most controversial and quintessential political matters, kept secret from the Australian prime minister, including the refusal of the governor-general to follow the advice of his responsible ministers, the use of the reserve powers against that advice, and the possible dismissal without warning of the government that retained its majority in the House of Representatives. They show that the Queen knew as early as September 1975 that Kerr was considering dismissing the government and, worse, knew of his failure to warn the prime minister about the possibility of his dismissal. For a constitutional monarch who must remain politically neutral at all times, this was unconscionable.[61]

On 13 December 1975, the Fraser government was returned to office in a landslide victory. The Labor Party was decimated, losing thirty seats, in its worst result in decades.

***

Six weeks after his dismissal of the Whitlam government, Kerr flew to England and visited the Queen. He and Lady Kerr spent a weekend as guests of the Queen at her private country estate at Sandringham, and met with senior Conservative minister Lord Carrington and key members of what Charteris called 'the Establishment'.[62] Charteris was closely involved in Kerr's itinerary during this six-week official visit, organising his engagements with the Queen, his lunch with Carrington and Lord Blake, and his meetings with 'the Establishment'.[63]

It was all a resounding success. Charteris told Kerr that his visit had ensured that this important elite now understood his reasons for his dismissal of the government: 'your visit to London was very valuable because the Establishment here now has a much clearer idea of what happened in your constitutional crisis. ... most people think that what you did was right'.[64] Dining in London shortly before the New Year, Charteris and Kerr looked back on those tumultuous events. 'Your discrimination is not limited to Constitutional issues', Charteris observed of Kerr's new wife, Lady Anne Kerr, in a handwritten note on Buckingham Palace letter-paper. 'I bet Eugene Forsey would have liked to be a fly on the wall!', he added.[65]

Soon after their return to Sydney, Lady Kerr was appointed a Commander Sister of the Order of St John, a royal order of chivalry granted at the 'absolute discretion' of the Queen.[66] The announcement was made by the Prior of the Order of St John in Australia, the governor-general, Sir John Kerr.[67] On the copy of the official announcement in the archives, a handwritten note reads, 'Was this deliberate to counter reports that GG's action had shocked the Royals?'

Lady Kerr's royal honour was followed by a visit from the Queen's second cousin and Prince Philip's beloved uncle, Lord Louis Mountbatten, who had 'much admired' Kerr's 'controversial action' in dismissing Whitlam. Mountbatten had written to

Kerr immediately after the dismissal to let him know of his great admiration for him and for his 'courageous and constitutionally correct' action. In February 1976, Mountbatten stayed with prime minister Malcolm Fraser at Kirribilli House, visiting Kerr at Admiralty House to convey his respects and admiration in person.[68] Kerr had no doubt that Mountbatten's views 'on the matters relating to our crisis' were shared by the Palace, telling Sir Garfield Barwick that this had been made clear to him in the Queen's letters after the dismissal.[69]

Charteris's own view was clear. He could see no option but dismissal, telling Kerr that 'no other course was open to you' and that he had 'found no one who has been able to tell me what you ought to have done instead'.[70] Following the prime minister's formal advice to the governor-general to call the half-Senate election was, to Charteris, not a course that was open to Kerr. On the occasion of Kerr's award of the Knight Grand Cross of the Order of St Michael and St George in April 1976, Charteris wrote to congratulate him: 'Many Governors-General get this award before they have had a chance to earn it in that office: no one can say that about you!'[71]

There was no pretence at neutrality in Charteris's comments on Whitlam's public statements about the dismissal, in particular on Whitlam's insistence that since supply had been passed and he had the confidence of the House, he ought to have been recommissioned as prime minister. And yet this was a firm view among those concerned by Kerr's refusal to see the Speaker and to acknowledge the motion of the House; it was shared by legal academics Leslie Katz and Professor Colin Howard, and was hardly an outlier position.[72] 'Mr Whitlam could perfectly well have continued to govern and Mr Fraser should certainly have resigned', Professor Howard wrote in a letter to *The Times*.[73] Nevertheless, Charteris described his 'aggravation and amazement' upon reading Whitlam's remarks which, he told Kerr, were 'to put it mildly, "a bit over the odds"!'[74]

Kerr's priority was always to protect the Queen and the monarchy. The notion of the governor-general as the Queen's 'personal representative' was, to Kerr, a literal one. In a handwritten letter to Charteris shortly before his weekend with the Queen, Kerr outlined his particular understanding of his role in relation to November 1975: 'Many of the ... decisions I had to make were specifically made in order to protect the Crown and the Monarchy in the future.'[75] He had not warned Whitlam, Kerr told Charteris, because he feared Whitlam might then have recalled him, and he could not 'risk the outcome for the sake of the Monarchy'.[76] With that decision made, they would all have to deal with the increasingly fractious consequences.

Although Charteris had reassured Kerr just days before the dismissal that whatever decision he made could only do the monarchy good, this had been unduly hopeful. Demonstrations and angry protests followed Kerr at every public engagement, and intense debate over the dismissal continued. Kerr told Charteris, more in hope than in fact, that the demonstrators were merely 'a rent a crowd' and that the furore would soon abate.[77] It did not. As the protests continued into 1976, the ever-needy Kerr sought royal reassurance with a feigned suggestion of resigning, not for the first time. Charteris was insistent: resignation would be seen as 'an admission of error', and in the interests of the monarchy, he should not do so.

Kerr had first raised the prospect of his resignation soon after the dismissal. The Palace's view was emphatic: Kerr must not do anything that might suggest he had 'acted incorrectly' in dismissing Whitlam, or that he doubted his decision.[78] Kerr had never intended to go, he later told Sir Robert Menzies, and nor did the Palace want him to go. As Charteris wrote, there was 'relief here' at Buckingham Palace that Kerr had not resigned.[79] Despite the expression of 'relief' and his entreaty to Kerr that he not resign, Charteris told

Kerr somewhat superfluously, 'you must of course make your own decision'. The construction was pure artifice, since Kerr had already told Charteris that, 'I shall put the Monarchy and the Governor-Generalship first' – and their view was that he must not resign.[80]

The intensity of the polarisation within the community, the undiluted anger over the dismissal, seemed to have taken both Kerr and Charteris by surprise. As the furore continued undiminished throughout the next year, the view from the Palace and Fraser on Kerr's resignation began to change. Kerr could sense it, telling Menzies that the reaction then was 'different from previous attitudes'.[81] The Queen was due to make a royal visit in March 1977, and with the prospect of disruptions and demonstrations marring that visit, Kerr's position became untenable.

Kerr's final moment of affirmation, the pinnacle of his royal approbation, came during that royal tour, which he was so proud to host as governor-general. In a ceremony on board the royal yacht *Britannia,* the Queen bestowed on Kerr the highest order of her personal honour, a Knight Grand Cross of the Royal Victorian Order, an honour 'entirely within the Sovereign's personal gift' recognising 'personal service to the monarchy'.[82] It was the last gasp of vice-regal patronage for Kerr. Even as he received the latest of his royal accolades, Kerr knew that by the end of the year he would no longer be governor-general.

Chapter Twelve

'For the sake of the Monarchy'

In the cryptic taxonomy of archives, the relationship between Sir John Kerr and the Queen stretches beyond the Palace letters and into obscure files scattered throughout the National Archives of Australia and elsewhere. The most surprising of these is a new set of letters between Kerr and Charteris in the National Archives of Australia, and the most intriguing is an extraordinary holding of letters between Kerr and the Canadian constitutional theorist Eugene Forsey in the Canadian archives.

From all these archives – in personal letters, Kerr's rambling handwritten notes, and his unguarded personal reflections – a common theme emerges: the involvement of the Palace in every step Kerr took, and every decision he made, regarding the dismissal and its gathering aftermath, including even his own resignation. It is impossible to separate Kerr's decisions from his intractable view of his 'duty' to the monarch and the monarchy, presented to him so clearly in the months before the dismissal by the unctuous Sir Martin Charteris.

Charteris had worked that sense of duty perfectly, most notably in his pointed references to Forsey and the Canadian experience, and his reassurance to Kerr that whatever decision he was to make, it could only do the monarchy good. Kerr's decisions were in this sense entirely bounded by considerations of his view of the interests of the Queen and what was best for the monarchy. There was, quite simply, no decision that Kerr would make without what he saw as the imprimatur of the Palace. How could it have been otherwise? For Kerr, his duty defined his decisions.

Soon after the release of the Palace letters, several previously unpublished letters from one of those obscure files were unexpectedly and quietly released by the Archives, nine years after I first requested it. This file, carrying the incongruous title 'Correspondence between the Prime Minister and the Governor-General on the Governor-General's resignation', contained several letters between Kerr and Charteris that were not included with the Palace letters released by the Archives with such fanfare following the High Court decision. Apart from anything else, this raises the significant question of how many more of these historic letters lie elsewhere in the Archives, imperfectly labelled and unseen, which ought to form part of the broader Palace letters collection.

The newly released documents consist of several anguished letters, drafted and redrafted by Kerr to Charteris in 1977 in the months before his reluctant resignation, and a single letter from Charteris in reply. They tell a poignant story of personal decline. These letters provide a snapshot of the distressed end of Kerr's term as governor-general, of his deteriorating relationship with the Palace, and of his dramatic turn against Malcolm Fraser, as those who had encouraged and cajoled him in the months before the dismissal began to move against him.[1]

In the early months after the dismissal, in the afterglow of the successful revival of the reserve powers of the Crown, Kerr describes the view from the government, and 'encouraged' by the Palace, that he 'should, indeed, must stay'. It is essential that he 'avoid appearing to concede error' in any way about his dismissal of Whitlam.[2] As Kerr navigates the shifting fortunes in his position, a detailed handwritten note prepared by him in April 1976 reveals the role of 'the Palace', and Prince Charles, as part of a select group of informal advisors with whom he discussed his future as governor-general.[3] Kerr sought advice from Prince Charles, the Palace, Sir Robert Menzies, Sir Anthony Mason, prime minister Fraser, and Sir Garfield Barwick. They had all urged him to remain as governor-general because, '(1) what I did was the right thing to do and (2) resignation … would leave the impression that I regretted what I did'.[4]

Despite the private professions of support and encouragement, as the months pass and the protests against him continue, Kerr perceives a change. Privately, he writes of his growing fear that 'the Government, or some of its members, may get tired of defending me … and encourage me to go'.[5] And if they did, Kerr would not go easily. He would not even consider resigning without a new position to go to.[6] In a sign of his faltering judgment as his concern for his position grows, Kerr imagines that Fraser might consider appointing him as Australia's high commissioner to the United Kingdom. 'London might be the best place to spend a few years', he muses.[7] It is hard to understand how Kerr could have entertained the idea that after such intense political controversy, he could be appointed to a plum diplomatic role by the government he had installed in office just months earlier.

In an extraordinary letter to Charteris in late 1976, when his relationship with Fraser is already splintering, Kerr raises the possible use of the reserve powers against the government. Kerr writes that Fraser faces several options for the next election, including a half-Senate election, or an early election for the House of Representatives. He sets out the possibility, raised by some commentators, that 'because of my view that the Governor-General has a real discretion', he ought to consider whether there is a case for invoking the reserve powers to deny Fraser such an early election. 'Forsey has written, as we know, a whole book about it', Kerr reminds Charteris, with the air of one with a shared understanding that these powers exist and are available to him.[8]

Charteris's response is emphatic, and quite unlike his benign insistence on the existence of the reserve powers, and even of their possible beneficial use, just the previous year. 'I hope that this possibility will not arise, both for your own sake and also I think for the sake of the Crown', he writes, firmly closing off that discussion.[9]

By 1977, Kerr's behaviour at public events was also becoming a liability. That was the year he landed face-down in the mud at the Tamworth Show as he attempted to place the winning medallion around the prized cow 'Lovedale Posh', all of it captured by a waiting photographer. The front-page images of the governor-general pinioned under the cow's hoof won a Walkley Award.[10] There was a memorable repeat performance at the Melbourne Cup later that year when Kerr, in an ill-fitting top hat and tails, struggled to remain upright as he awarded the cup to the owners of the winning horse. It was a sad sight of a public decline (now a much-watched YouTube clip called, 'the Governor-General drunk at the Melbourne Cup').

Kerr's inadvertent burning of the carpet at Victoria's Government House during a short visit, when he tripped over the heater in the middle of the night and woke to find the carpet smouldering, no doubt also caused ripples of anxiety in vice-regal circles.[11] And so, it is hardly surprising that by 1977 the Queen had joined the list of those who wished the governor-general to make an early retirement. In little more than a year he had gone from saving the Queen from embarrassment to being the embodiment of that embarrassment. Kerr's greatest fear under Whitlam, his removal from office, would now ensue under Malcolm Fraser.

Kerr's forced resignation was, to him, the ultimate betrayal by Fraser, whose political fortunes during the 1975 crisis his unprecedented actions had assured. The newly released cache of letters and drafts to Charteris is a raw display of devastation. In an extraordinarily indiscreet draft letter, Kerr writes that Fraser had never given him the support that 'I have been entitled to have', and that now, 'victory achieved', Fraser is 'happy for me to go'.[12] The well-honed vituperation that Kerr once deployed against Whitlam he turns towards Fraser, 'a stern, distant, arrogant man determined to rule completely and not able to relax in conversation with me as Mr Whitlam was able to do'.[13] Whitlam is now, apparently, not so bad after all.

Distraught at the prospect of losing his position, Kerr unleashes a bitter denunciation of Fraser for having changed 'his views about November 1975'. In these draft letters to Charteris, he writes that Fraser 'has forgotten how it all came about, has persuaded himself that … it was all done by his great leadership, strength and dominant will to which I had to succumb. This was certainly not the case.'[14] Kerr's own view of those events is quite different: it is one in which he played the central role in doing his 'duty', while Fraser was 'a worried man' who needed persuading by his colleagues 'to keep his nerve and not worry about me not doing my duty'.[15]

In a remarkable exposition of his interactions with the then leader of the opposition in November 1975, Kerr again describes Fraser as having 'almost forgotten the real story of the Supply crisis and his fear that I might not act as he hoped I would. … he was very worried about my character and ability to do what he could see then to be my duty'.[16] Although Kerr denies having spoken to opposition members at the time, he writes that his close friends Sir John Atwill, the president of the Liberal Party, and Robert Ellicott, the shadow attorney-general, had assured Fraser that if the crisis continued, Kerr would act as he did and do 'his duty'.

That Kerr and Fraser were in contact before the dismissal is now well known. They had spoken during the morning of 11 November 1975 and agreed to the terms on which Kerr would appoint him prime minister, and, as revealed in *The Dismissal Dossier* in 2017, they were communicating through Fraser's private office telephone the week before Kerr dismissed the government. Fraser told me that Kerr had spoken to him about dismissing the government and had asked what Fraser would do as the 'incoming person'. 'He said, "No decision has been made but *if*". I believe that was a totally legitimate question; he was going to take a significant action, and he had a right to know what attitude the incoming person would have.'[17] Fraser told Kerr that if he did not act against Whitlam, Fraser would say publicly that the reserve powers, if 'not used in the present crisis would be destroyed forever'.[18]

With the timing of his resignation by the end of 1977 now agreed by everyone except Kerr himself, he digs in. First, he wants a sinecure, the promise of 'some constructive work'. It should be recognised, he tells Charteris, that he has 'made a number of sacrifices in recent years and that, not of course by way of reward but by way of recognition, I should be seen to be going on to "fresh fields"'.[19] This was a matter he would pursue with Fraser, who in 1978 appointed Kerr to the newly resurrected position of Australia's ambassador to UNESCO, in which he lasted one day before resigning.[20]

Second, Kerr will not make a final decision about his resignation without the Queen's 'approval', and for this, he tells Charteris, he requires an audience with the Queen. Perhaps he is hoping that she will urge him to remain, as she had in the months after the dismissal, or perhaps it is just his final 'duty' to the monarch that he 'seek her approval' for his own resignation. Regardless, Kerr is insistent.[21] Charteris is equally determined that, whatever the reality, there must be no public perception that Kerr's decision to resign has any connection to the Queen, which an audience with her might suggest. Charteris asks him: '[I]f you are known to have received an audience, will it be assumed that you have come to resign?'[22] The warm and jovial correspondent of previous years has become an officious Palace courtier.[23]

In a private letter to Menzies, Kerr makes the Queen's role in his resignation explicit. After conversations during the Queen's visit to Australia, and later in London, Kerr writes that he understood that 'perhaps it was in the interests of the Monarchy and the country' that he make way for a successor.[24] He sees this as 'a matter of duty' although, he writes, if he had been asked to stay on, he would have. Charteris and the Queen both make it clear to Kerr that there must be no overt connection between his resignation and his visit to the Palace.[25]

The charade was exemplified by Kerr's visit, very reluctantly agreed to by Charteris, in June 1977 to the Palace to discuss Kerr's resignation – a decision he would not finalise without her input, and in which she was publicly not involved.[26] As always, Kerr's decision was to be filtered through the interests of the monarch and the monarchy. Two days later, his resignation was finalised with Fraser.[27] Kerr publicly took 'full personal responsibility for the decision', as one in which the Queen had played no part, despite it being pressed upon him during an audience on the royal yacht during the royal visit. As Kerr put it, 'Things crystallised on the yacht.'[28]

Kerr resigned on 7 December 1977 and left Australia the next day. Eugene Forsey was 'thunderstruck'.[29]

Charteris's pointed references to the reserve powers and to Eugene Forsey were the beginning of the end of the Whitlam government, and the start of a longstanding 'epistolary friendship' between Forsey and Kerr.[30] In 1977, Eugene Forsey wrote the epilogue to Kerr's royally vetted autobiography, *Matters for Judgment*, and the circle was complete.

From his apparently casual mention of Forsey weeks before the dismissal – 'I believe he lays it down as a principal [sic] that if Supply is refused this always makes it constitutionally proper to grant a dissolution' – Charteris returns to the Canadian example of the use of the reserve powers of the Crown, for so long championed by Forsey, in his final letters to Kerr just days before the dismissal.[31] Forsey's strong views on the reserve powers were well known; he was seen as 'very pro-monarchy' and 'very conservative in constitutional matters', which Charteris knew only too well from his own personal connection.[32] Charteris did not at this point tell Kerr that Forsey was a friend; nor did he reveal that they were already in contact.[33]

In 1974, with the British Labour Party's Harold Wilson heading a minority government, Charteris and Forsey had corresponded on the question of whether the Queen retained any discretion 'in the matter of dissolution'.[34] Charteris had confirmed to Forsey that 'some discretion remains to the Crown in the United Kingdom', a view from the Palace which would have been of great interest in both the United Kingdom and Australia had it been known at the time.[35]

Forsey was the go-to constitutional theorist on the reserve powers, used by Charteris, the FCO, and the Canadian High Commission for advice, including on the Australian political situation. With Forsey, they knew what they would get. The question is, would Kerr? A remarkable holding of previously unexplored letters between Kerr and Forsey reveals just how significant that constitutional prompt from Charteris was.[36] Kerr tells Forsey that a 'highly placed person' had drawn Forsey's name to his attention: 'As a result of this, before the supply crisis I borrowed your book from the Canadian High Commissioner and both before and during the crisis studied it carefully.'[37] Kerr was greatly assisted by his liaison with the Canadian High Commission in Canberra for the receipt of material by Forsey on the crisis. The high commission also passed on to Kerr letters by Forsey in the Canadian press about the political situation in Australia.[38] These were important, as Kerr told Forsey: 'Your writings gave me important guidance in reaching my conclusion'.[39]

The most disturbing thing about Charteris's recommendation of Eugene Forsey is not that the Queen's private secretary interposed a conservative, pro-monarchist theorist in the deliberations of the Australian governor-general during a historic political crisis; it is that Forsey *was ignorant about a key element of the crisis*. Forsey believed there was no such thing as a half-Senate election and 'could find no mention of such an election in the Australian constitution', advising the Canadian High Commission and the FCO as such, and analysing the political situation in Australia in the context of that ignorance.[40]

Three weeks *after* the dismissal, Forsey realised his error after his research advisor told him, 'I have solved the mystery of the half-Senate dissolution.'[41] Forsey himself flippantly told Kerr, 'My newspaper letters were much less than satisfactory on one point: the "half-Senate election", which puzzled me completely ... If I had read the text of the Constitution more carefully, I should, of course, have been able to enlighten myself.'[42]

The fate of an Australian government was being discussed by a Canadian theorist who hadn't 'read the text of the Constitution more carefully', and therefore could not recognise the half-Senate election, neatly rendering invisible the prime minister's advice to the governor-general to call it. This was the person to whom the Queen's private secretary had pointed the governor-general for guidance, rather than to his formal legal advisors – the attorney-general and the solicitor-general – both of whom knew a thing or two about the text of the Australian Constitution. It was the ultimate act of imperial condescension and, worse, ignorance.

One month after his dismissal by the governor-general, Gough Whitlam spoke to the British high commissioner, Sir Morrice James, in Canberra. '[W]ith no particular heat', James recounted,

Whitlam had said that 'it had come as great shock to the whole Labor movement to find that the Crown's reserve powers of (he had thought) long ago could be resuscitated at this late stage to the advantage of those forces here who were opposed to social progress.'[43] The belated release of the Palace letters – some of the most significant historical records in our Archives – has revealed with appalling clarity how this was done.

For forty-five years the Palace has maintained that the Queen played no part in Kerr's decision to dismiss the government, that as a constitutional monarch the Queen remains strictly neutral on political matters. And for forty-five years the Queen's own embargo over her correspondence with the governor-general prevented us from knowing otherwise. A four-year legal battle, and a remarkable High Court decision, have finally allowed this critical part of our history to be known. The Palace fought for decades to keep this history hidden from public view, through both the Queen's embargo over the letters and the utterly unconscionable vetting of Kerr's memoirs, and our history, to omit any mention of his 'unofficial exchanges' with Charteris in relation to the dismissal.

The Palace letters have shattered these claims of royal neutrality and non-involvement, revealing the intensely political nature of the correspondence – none more so than on the existence and use of the reserve powers: assuring Kerr that they existed, assuaging his concerns that their use might damage the monarchy, and giving the royal imprimatur to a Canadian theorist whose knowledge of the Australian political situation was deeply flawed.

The institutional context is equally significant: the Queen knew from September 1975 that Kerr was considering dismissing the government, that he was remaining 'silent' to the prime minister, that he was prepared to act against his constitutional advisors, and that he had failed to warn Whitlam of the possibility of his dismissal. Starkly absent from their discussions was any consideration of Kerr's cardinal duty, to speak to his elected ministers and to ask that most fundamental question, 'What does your prime minister say?' The Palace knew what the Australian prime minister did not.

In this litany of institutional improprieties, these breaches of the essence of the vice-regal relationship are surely the most egregious. The circumstances in which they occurred remain unchanged today, among the lingering colonial entanglements of the imperial aftermath. The Palace continues to claim, just as it did forty-five years ago, that neither Charteris, Prince Charles, nor the Queen 'had any part to play in Kerr's decision to dismiss Whitlam'. This unchanged position, maintained more in faith than in fact, is impossible to reconcile with the history as we now know it.

The pursuit of the Palace letters was always a pursuit of history, of our right to know it, and to know the full story of the dismissal of the Whitlam government. We can neither know our history nor learn from it if we cannot see the documents that would reveal it to us. The Palace letters now take their place among the most critical documents in the history of the dismissal, and the story they tell of deception, collusion, and intrigue is as disturbing as it is undeniable. The lessons they tell are of independence, accountability, and transparency. The tensions they reflect, between responsible parliamentary government and an unarticulated residual power of the Crown, are at the heart of both Australia as a constitutional monarchy and the dismissal. They can never be fully resolved until we complete the post-colonial project of national autonomy, as an Australian republic with an Australian head of state, and in control of our own history.

Acknowledgements

The Palace letters case was a mighty team effort. It could never have happened without the support of an exceptional legal team: Antony Whitlam QC at the Federal Court with Tom Brennan, Brett Walker SC with Tom Brennan at the Full Federal Court and the High Court of Australia, and with James Whittaker, senior partner at Corrs Chambers Westgarth, instructing throughout. I thank them for their commitment to this case and to their concern for public access underpinning it. I also thank Tim Bunker and Chris Marshall at Corrs Chambers Westgarth for being a ready point of contact at all times.

The campaign to release the Palace letters, and to end the Queen's embargo over our own historic records, attracted hundreds of supporters through the crowd-funding campaign *Release the Palace Letters*, which ran in parallel to the court case. I am immensely grateful to every one of them for their generosity and for their personal support and encouragement at every stage. It was a great pleasure to meet many of these determined supporters in person at the court hearings, and I thank them all for their dedication and belief in this case and for their commitment to ensuring an open, public history of the dismissal of the Whitlam government.

No one was more important to this project from its earliest days than Terri King, from PitchProjects. I am indebted to Terri for her calm and expert management at every stage. Grata founder and director, Isabelle Reinecke, supported the case at a critical point, and I thank Grata for their support. I am grateful to the dedicated staff at the National Archives of Australia, the National Library of Australia, the Whitlam Institute, the National Archives UK, and the Library and Archives of Canada for their great assistance over many years in accessing these records. John Menadue published many of my initial assessments of the matters traversed in this book in *Pearls & Irritations*, has kindly granted permission for their use here, and has been a steadfast supporter of the campaign to release the Palace letters. Dr Allison Cadzow proved expert and insightful research assistance. I thank my agent, Jenny Darling, for her advice and encouragement in bringing the book to fruition.

Henry Rosenbloom, Scribe's founder, has been an exemplary editor and publisher, patient and instructive in perfect measure. I am grateful for his enthusiasm and commitment to this book, and for his astute and expert guidance.

My greatest thanks go to Daryl Dellora for his unstinting support along every step of this excellent journey.

This book is dedicated to my mother, Barbara Hocking, the first barrister briefed in the Mabo case, who was there before me.

Notes

In these notes and the bibliography, the following abbreviations are used:
Federal Court of Australia: FCA
Federal Court of Australia Full Court: FCAFC
High Court of Australia: HCA
National Archives of Australia: NAA
National Library of Australia: NLA
Hocking v Director-General of the National Archives of Australia:
  Hocking v Director-General NAA

Chapter One: 'In the shades of history'

1 This research began in 2006 as an Australian Research Council linkage grant with the NLA and the NAA.
2 Michael Bobelian, 'Robert Caro, pre-eminent biographer, tells us how he does what he does', *National Book Review*, 9 April 2019.
3 'Decision on Access: Statement of Reasons', NAA to Jenny Hocking, 2 August 2011; Sir John Kerr, 'Personal Papers', NAA M4513.
4 In 2005, the Labor member for Banks, Daryl Melham, had referred to these letters in a Question in Writing, asking the minister responsible for the Archives whether they were to be released with the cabinet papers of the Whitlam government the following year, and if not why not. The minister replied that the letters were 'personal and confidential' and not for release. *Hansard*, House of Representatives, 12 September 2005, p. 177.
5 NAA to Jenny Hocking, 3 August 2011.
6 Paul Kelly, 'Kerr unmasks Mason from the grave', *The Australian*, 29 August 2012.

7 Sir Anthony Mason, 'It was unfolding like a Greek tragedy', *Sydney Morning Herald*, 27 August 2012.

8 C.J. Brennan, 'Speech on Swearing In as Chief Justice', HCA, 21 April 1995.

9 Editorial, 'The governor-general, the judge and the dismissal', *The Australian*, 28 August 2012.

10 Sir John Kerr, 'Statement of reasons', 11 November 1975, NAA A1209, 1975/2448.

11 David Smith is the other; he has repeatedly refused to speak to me, despite numerous requests.

12 Jenny Hocking, *Gough Whitlam: his time*, p. 497.

13 Barwick, G. to Kerr, J., 11 November 1982, 'Barwick, the Rt Hon Sir Garfield, Part 1', NAA M4526 4 Part 1; Kerr, J. to Barwick, G., 22 November 1982, 'Barwick, the Rt Hon Sir Garfield, Part 1', NAA M4526 4 Part 1.

14 'What we do', National Archives of Australia naa.gov.au, About Us.

15 William Heseltine recalls that Whitlam rang Buckingham Palace shortly before 8.00 am London time, three hours after the official secretary, David Smith, had rung to inform them. In Malcolm Quekett, 'No wake-up call for Queen over dismissal', *West Australian*, 12 April 2011.

16 Hilary Mantel, 'Why I became a historical novelist', *The Guardian*, 3 June 2017.

Chapter Two: 'I never had any doubts'

1 John Kerr, *Journal*, 1980, NAA M4523 1 Part 17.

2 Sir Garfield Barwick, Billy Snedden, Phil Lynch, Jim Killen, Peter Nixon, and Tony Eggleton were just some of the rotating pool of visitors. See Jenny Hocking, *Gough Whitlam*, p. 410

3 Malcolm Quekett, 'No wake-up call for Queen over dismissal', *West Australian*, 12 April 2011.

4 William Atkins, 'Syncopal kick: on the trauma of exile', *Times Literary Supplement*, 25 October 2019 https://www.the-tls.co.uk/articles/anthology-literature-exile-naffis-sahely/.

5 Kerr to Sir Walter Crocker, 15 March 1979, NAA M4526 11 Part 1.

6 Report of the Imperial Conference, 1930.

7 John Kerr, 'Miscellanous handwritten notes', NAA M4523 1 Part 16.

8 John Kerr, *Journal*, 4 February 1980, pp. 79–80; NAA M4523 1 Part 17.

9 John Kerr, 'Extracts from letters dated 20 September 1975, 17 October 1975, 20 October 1975, 6 November 1975, 11 November 1975, and 20 November 1975', NAA 4523 1 Part 7.

Chapter Three: 'Australia owns its history'

1 Tom Brennan, 'Australia owns its history', 13 Wentworth Chambers, 10 November 2015.

2 Jenny Hocking to Tom Brennan, 8 December 2015.

3 Jenny Hocking to NAA, 10 December 2015.

4 NAA to Jenny Hocking, 17 December 2015.

5 Stephen Murtagh, deputy official secretary to the governor-general, to Professor Jenny Hocking, 1 October 2015.

6 Tom Brennan to Jenny Hocking, 31 December 2015.

7 John Kerr, *Matters for Judgment*, p. 329.

8 NAA to Jenny Hocking, 3 August 2011.

9 Tom Brennan interview, 31 August 2020.

10 An eighth letter was released under FOI in 2020, NAA FOI131.

11 David Smith to John Kerr, 3 June 1978, NAA M4520 2.

12 John Kerr to David Smith, 24 March 1981, NAA M4520 2.

13 David Smith to John Kerr, 3 June 1978, NAA M4520 2.

14 David Smith to John Kerr, 23 December 1977, released by the Archives under Notice to Produce, Hocking v Director-General NAA, 27 January 2017.

15 Legal documents with the author.

16 Madeleine Morris, 'The Palace Letters: New fight to release correspondence between Queen, G-G in lead-up to Whitlam dismissal', ABC, 21 October 2016.

Chapter Four: Archival manoeuvres in the dark

1 George Brandis to John Kerr, 'Australia Day', 1987, Brandis, George, NAA M4526 5.

2 Dan Harrison and Jonathan Swan, 'Attorney-General George Brandis: People have a right to be bigots', *Sydney Morning Herald*, 24 March 2014.

3 Brandis, George, Senate *Hansard*, 10 November 2000. Markwell was later an executive director of the Menzies Centre and an advisor to Liberal minister for education Christopher Pyne. Harley, later a 'trouble-shooter for BHP' and a Liberal Party vice-president, was a great-grandson of Alfred Deakin and had worked for Liberal leader Billy Snedden. See *A Dissident Liberal: the political writings of Peter Baume*, by Peter Baume. John Wanna and Marija Taflaga (eds), 2015; Mark Baker, 'The art of compromise: George Brandis', *The Age*, 6 July 2013. 'Bright group of young Australians', Kerr to Barwick, 1 July 1985, 'Barwick, the Right Honourable Sir Garfield', NAA M4526 4 Part 2.

4 Brandis, Harley and Markwell jointly edited *Liberals Face the Future: essays on Australian Liberalism* in 1984.

5 John Kerr to Don Markwell, 1 April 1985, Markwell, D.G., Part 3, NAA M4526 30 Part 3.

6 Kep Enderby to Jenny Hocking at the launch of *Gough Whitlam* by Kevin Rudd, Sydney, 28 August 2012.

7 John Kerr, 'Matters arising from meeting on 6 July 1985', Markwell, D.G., Part 4, NAA M4526 30 Part 4.

8 John Kerr, 'Matters arising from meeting on 6 July 1985'.

9 Kerr died in Sydney on 24 March 1991, but his death was not reported until after his burial the following day. His family did not request a state funeral. 'Sir John Kerr dies alone: the storm goes on', *Canberra Times*, 26 March 1991, p. 1.

10 Malcolm Turnbull, *The Spycatcher Trial*, 1989.

11 'A fierce battle is on to release secret letters to the Queen about the dismissal of Gough Whitlam', news.com.au, 1 August 2017.

12 Jenny Hocking, *The Dismissal Dossier*, Chapters 1, 3.

13 In Marc Parry, 'Uncovering the brutal truth about the British empire', *The Guardian*, 18 August 2016.

14 Kerr/Smith letters in Jennifer Hocking Exhibits, Hocking v Director-General NAA; Sir John Kerr, 'Introduction to Annotated Copy of Palace Letters', M4523 1 Part 15.

15 Hocking v Director-General NAA, FCA Case Management Hearing.

16 Hocking v Director-General NAA, FCA Case Management Hearing.

17 NAA, FOI131 no. 2, 2.1.

18 Stephen Brady, official secretary to the Governor-General, to
Christopher Geidt, private secretary to the Queen, 1 February 2017, in
submission of Mark Fraser, official secretary to the Governor-General,
3 February 2017.

19 Submission of Mark Fraser, 3 February 2017.

20 NAA, FOI131.

21 Submission of David Fricker, 3 February 2017.

22 Submission of Mark Fraser, 3 February 2017.

23 Submission of David Fricker, 24 March 2017; FOI131 no. 23, 23.1
Government House to Buckingham Palace, 3 March 2017.

24 Legal documents with the author.

25 Anne-Marie Schwirtlich to Stephanie Bashford, 30 January 2003;
Maggie Shapley to Stephanie Bashford, 17 November 2003.

26 Stephanie Bashford Instrument of Deposit, 29 March 2004.

27 Hocking v Director-General NAA, FCA, 14 February 2017.

28 Hocking v Director-General NAA, FCA, 14 February 2017.

29 Legal documents with the author.

30 Stephanie Bashford Instrument of Deposit, 9 March 2017.

Chapter Five: 'Mr Whitlam … would inevitably suspect the U.K.'s involvement'

1 M. James, 'Report: Immigration, Anglo-Australian Relations',
18 December 1972 in NAA A1838 67/1/3 Part 7; 'Mr Whitlam's visit
to London, April 1973, Omnibus Brief for Secretary of State', 16 April
1973 in FCO 24/1613, Visit of Gough Whitlam, Prime Minister of
Australia, to UK 20–25 April 1973.

2 Letter from J.K. Hickmann, South West Pacific Department, to
D.P. Aiers esq CMG, British High Commission, Canberra, 1 May
1973 in FCO 24/1614, Visit of Gough Whitlam, Prime Minister of
Australia, to UK 20–25 April 1973; 'Australian Domestic Politics:
Possible Intervention of the UK government', in FCO 24/2051 Political
Situation in Australia; FCO to BHC, Confidential, 'The Australian
Constitutional Deadlock', 28 October 1975 in FCO 24/2051 Political
Situation in Australia.

3 Confidential, 'Australian Domestic Politics: Possible Intervention of
the UK Government', 21 October 1975, in FCO 24/2051 Political

Situation in Australia.

4 Confidential, 'Australian Domestic Politics'.

5 Anne Twomey, *The Chameleon Crown*, pp. 78–9; Jenny Hocking, *The Dismissal Dossier: everything you were never meant to know about November 1975 — The Palace Connection*, p. 116.

6 South West Pacific Department, 22 September 1975, 'Australian Constitutional Issues', p. 3, p. 6 in FCO 24/2059, Federal Election in Australia 13 December 1975.

7 Mr Bevan FCO, 'Confidential Memo: Australian domestic politics possible intervention of the UK government', 21 October 1975, FCO 24/2051.

8 Changes in Constitution of Australia, 1974 FCO 24/1931.

9 FCO to Certain Missions, restricted, 'The Australian Constitutional Crisis', 21 November 1975 in FCO 24/2079, Constitutional matters in Australia. Whitlam correctly, if provocatively, had described the state governments as 'governments of British colonies'.

10 Changes in Constitution of Australia, 1974, FCO 24/1931.

11 George Brandis, ' "Green lawfare" and standing: the view from within government', AIAL Forum, December 2017, pp. 12–19.

12 S. Medhora and J. Robertson, 'George Brandis: vigilante green groups destroying thousands of mining jobs', *The Guardian*, 17 August 2015. Brandis sought changes to section 487 of the *Environmental Protection and Biodiversity Act*.

13 FCAFC, Australian Conservation Foundation Incorporated v Minister for the Environment and Energy [2017], 134, 25 August 2017. Justice Griffiths had dismissed the appeal against the minister's approval of Adani on 29 August 2016. See Bill McCredie, 'Climate change challenge against Adani Carmichael coal mine dismissed', Allens: Insights & News, 30 August 2016.

14 Bernard Lagan, 'Ousted PM's son fights to see Queen's secret letters', *The Times*, 2 August 2017; Louise Burke, 'Queen's secret letters could finally solve mystery of Australian prime minister Gough Whitlam's dismissal', *Daily Telegraph*, 1 August 2017; 'Australia as a Republic', *Deutsche Welle*, 29 July 2017.

15 Michelle Brown, 'Gough Whitlam's son leads court case to release Queen's dismissal letters', ABC News, 31 July 2017.

16 FCA transcript, 31 July 2017, p. 9.

17 FCA transcript, p. 30.

18 FCA transcript, p. 28.

19 FCA transcript, p. 33–6.

20 Professor Anne Twomey discusses numerous British and Commonwealth instances of royal letters placed on open access, see 'Peering into the black box of executive power', in Jason NE Varuhas, Shona Wilson Stark (eds), *The Frontiers of Public Law*, 2020.

21 Applicant's Submissions in Reply, p. 6.

22 FCA transcript, pp. 56–7.

23 FCA transcript, p. 55.

24 In 'Fraser to Kerr: "The Queen's letters should remain private"', *The Australian*, 3 August 2017, p. 5.

25 FCA transcript, pp. 89–90.

Chapter Six: Fourteen minutes

1 David Fricker to Mark Fraser, 24 October 2016, NAA FOI131 no. 5.

2 Mark Dreyfus, Federation Chamber debate, 28 November 2016, p. 4629; David Fricker to Jenny Hocking 16 September 2020.

3 David Fricker to Mark Fraser, 24 October 2016, NAA FOI131 no. 5.

4 Prince Philip's full title is: His Royal Highness The Prince Philip, Duke of Edinburgh, Earl of Merioneth, Baron Greenwich, Royal Knight of the Most Noble Order of the Garter, Extra Knight of the Most Ancient and Most Noble Order of the Thistle, Member of the Order of Merit, Knight Grand Cross of the Royal Victorian Order, Grand Master and First and Principal Knight Grand Cross of the Most Excellent Order of the British Empire, Additional Member of the Order of New Zealand, Extra Companion of the Queen's Service Order, Knight of the Order of Australia, Royal Chief of the Order of Logohu, Extraordinary Companion of the Order of Canada, Extraordinary Commander of the Order of Military Merit, Canadian Forces Decoration, Lord of Her Majesty's Most Honourable Privy Council, Member of the Queen's Privy Council for Canada, Personal Aide-de-Camp to His Majesty King George VI, Lord High Admiral of the United Kingdom.

5 Jenny Hocking, 'Archival secrets and hidden histories: Reasserting

the right to public access', *Griffith Review* no. 67, 'Matters of Trust', February 2020. Indicative of the growing 'securitisation' of the Archives, its conceptual shift away from a foundational historical and cultural focus, was its administrative move from the Arts together with the leading national cultural institutions, and into the Attorney-General's Department.

6 Paul Kelly, 'Malcolm Turnbull to try recovering John Kerr's letters to the Queen', *The Australian*, 10 November 2015.

7 'Editorial', 'Legal spat with George Brandis demeans the role of solicitor-general', *Canberra Times*, 9 October 2016; Justin Gleeson SC, 'Submission to the Senate Legal and Constitutional Affairs Committee', 11 May 2016.

8 James Whittaker to the Hon. Malcolm Turnbull, 2 June 2017. A parallel exchange was being played out in the parliament, where the Labor member for Bruce, Julian Hill, was also pursuing Turnbull over his quickly discarded promise to ask the Queen to release the Palace letters. Hill had placed a question on notice in the House of Representatives in February 2017 asking whether the prime minister had approached the Queen seeking the release of the letters and, if so, what her response had been. For the next eight months Turnbull refused to answer, despite being twice prompted by the Speaker to do so.

9 Robert Garran, *Prosper the Commonwealth*, 1957.

10 FCA transcript, 6 September 2017, p. 15.

11 Lord Viscount Sydney was British home secretary (secretary of state for the Home Department) 1783–89 who devised and oversaw the transportation of convicts to New South Wales.

12 FCA transcript, 6 September 2017, p. 16.

13 pp. 21–2.

14 p. 27.

15 p. 55.

16 Alan Missen Papers, NLA MS7528.

17 Alan J. Missen, 'The powers they seek are totalitarian!', *The Argus*, 22 August 1951.

18 Alan Missen, *Diary*, Alan Missen Papers, NLA MS7528.

19 Gerard Henderson, 'Media Watch', The Sydney Institute, 12 July 2019.

20 Anton Hermann, *Alan Missen: Liberal pilgrim*, 1993.

21 Peter Baume, John Wanna, and Marija Taflaga (eds), *A Dissident Liberal: Peter Baume*, 2015.

22 The diary ends in late November 1975. *Diary*, Papers of Alan Missen, NLA MS7528.

23 Anton Hermann, *Alan Missen*, p. 108.

24 Anton Hermann, *Alan Missen*, pp. 106–11.

25 'Countdown to the dismissal', *The Age*, 22 October 2005; Philip Ayres, *Malcolm Fraser*, pp. 293, 299.

26 Alan Reid Papers, Interviews on 1975, NLA MS7796.

27 Jenny Hocking, 'Archival secrets and hidden histories. Reasserting the right to public access', *Griffith Review* no. 67, 'Matters of Trust', February 2020.

28 Twomey in Stephen Easton, 'National Archives "completely dysfunctional" for serious scholarship', *The Mandarin*, 18 April 2019; Doug Dingwall, 'National Archives of Australia to cut 40 jobs in two years as budget tightens', *Sydney Morning Herald*, 21 February 2018.

Chapter Seven: 'Who cares what the Queen thinks?'

1 Hocking v Director-General NAA [2018], FCA 340, p. 3.

2 p. 33, pp. 2–3, p. 10.

3 p. 3.

4 p. 36.

5 See the interjections from Griffiths, J. on Kerr's genuinely 'personal' communications being those 'unrelated to the performance of his office', and on the Palace letters as 'communications engaged in in connection with the performance of their offices'.

6 Hocking v Director-General NAA [2018], FCA 340, p. 26.

7 p. 36.

8 Applicant's Submissions in Reply, pp. 5–7, p. 5.

9 p. 37.

10 pp. 37–9.

11 See ten of the eleven stated reasons, pars 108–118 in Hocking v Director-General NAA [2018], FCA 340, pp. 34–6.

12 Hocking v Director-General NAA [2018], FCA 340, p. 37, p. 3.

13 p. 37.

14 p. 36.

15 p. 36.

16 p. 36.

17 By the end of the case, there were more than thirty articles.

18 Jenny Hocking, 'Archival manoeuvres in the dark', *Pearls & Irritations*, 26 March 2018.

19 Christopher Knaus, 'Palace letters: historian claims National Archives misled her over copies', *The Guardian*, 28 March 2018.

20 On David Fricker declining to comment, see Rod McGuirk, 'Australian court keeps Queen Elizabeth's letters secret', CTV News (Canada), 16 March 2018.

21 David Fricker in Christopher Knaus, 'Palace letters: historian claims National Archives misled her over copies', *The Guardian*, 28 March 2018.

22 Bianca Hall, ' "Uncommonly good": the case of Pell's lawyer, Bret Walker', *The Age*, 10 April 2020.

23 Nick Bonyhady, 'National archives runs up legal bill in face of budget cuts', *Sydney Morning Herald*, 27 October 2019; Julian Hill MP, ALP member for Bruce, Questions on Notice, 28 November 2019.

24 Hocking v Director-General NAA, Notice of Appeal.

25 Legal documents with the author.

26 John Kerr, 'Address at the Cardinal's dinner', 21 August 1975, Papers of Jean Lester, NLA MS Acc05/8.

27 Michael White, 'Kerr's curs', *Justinian*, 17 August 2020.

28 Troy Bramston and Paul Kelly, 'Let's dismiss the conspiracy theories', *The Australian*, 26 December 2015; and 'In defence of the Queen', *The Australian*, 14 April 2018; Troy Bramston on Paul Murray SkyNews, 10 March 2020.

29 Appellant's outline of submissions, pp 1–2.

30 p. 2.

31 FCAFC transcript, 28 November 2018, p. 2.

32 pp. 12–13.

33 p. 18.

34 p. 10.

35 p. 7.

36 p. 57.

37 pp. 24–5.

38 p. 6.

39 p. 5.

40 p. 21.

41 Respondent's outline of submissions, p. 4.

42 FCAFC transcript, 28 November 2018, p. 37.

43 p. 20.

44 p. 33.

45 p. 20.

46 p. 60.

47 p. 73.

Chapter Eight: A royal whitewash of history

1 Richard Ackland, 'Another dismissal', *Justinian*, 11 February 2019.

2 Hocking v Director-General NAA (2019), FCAFC 12. I would pay the Archives' legal costs up to $30,000 under the Protective Cost Order granted by the court.

3 Hocking v Director-General NAA (2019), FCAFC 12, p. 24.

4 p. 25.

5 p. 24.

6 p. 24.

7 Richard Ackland, 'Another dismissal', *Justinian*, 11 February 2019.

8 Richard Ackland, 'Another dismissal'.

9 Hocking v Director-General NAA (2019), FCAFC 12, pp. 27–8.

10 p. 29.

11 p. 28.

12 Jenny Hocking, 'A national humiliation', *Pearls & Irritations*, 21 February 2019.

13 Stewart, Pam; Stuhmcke, Anita et al., 'Litigants and Legal Representatives: a study of special leave applications in the High Court of Australia', *Sydney Law Review*, 2019, 41 (1).

14 Of the applications for special leave to appeal, nearly 60 per cent are denied leave directly, or 'on the papers'.

15 Kerr to Sir Walter Crocker, 15 March 1979, NAA M4526 11 Part 1.

16 John Kerr, *Matters for Judgment*, p. ix.

17 Kerr to Mr H. Jamieson, Allen Allen & Hemsley, 2 June 1978, 'Correspondence re: Publication — Part 1', NAA M4507 30.

18 Jennifer Damrel, chief clerk, Private Secretary's Office, to Kerr, 22 September 1978, NAA M4526 6.

19 Sir Philip Moore to Sir John Kerr, 31 August 1978, Buckingham Palace, NAA M4526 6.

20 Kerr to Moore, 25 September 1978, Buckingham Palace, NAA M4526 6.

21 Jenny Hocking, ' "I never had any doubts about the Palace's attitude": Sir John Kerr's Royal secrets exposed', *Pearls & Irritations*, 11 October 2017.

22 Michelle Brown, 'High Court to determine whether "Palace letters" on Gough Whitlam's dismissal should be released', ABC News, 16 August 2019.

23 Questions on Notice in parliament from Julian Hill MP, the ALP member for Bruce, showed that the Archives had spent over $700,000 contesting the case to that point. The Liberal attorney-general, Christian Porter, joined with the Archives in contesting the case, and from October 2019 his department shared 25 per cent of the Archives' costs at the High Court appeal.

24 Damien Murphy, 'How Barwick lost his would-be country pile', *The Age*, 31 December 2009.

25 Hocking v Director-General NAA, HCA transcript, 4 February 2020.

26 S.A. Hamilton to A.D. Rose, Deputy Secretary Department of the Prime Minister and Cabinet, 20 September 1982 A1209, 1976/1957 Part 8.

27 S.A. Hamilton, Assistant Secretary Parliamentary Branch PM&C to A.D. Rose, Deputy Secretary PM&C, 20 September 1982.

28 David Smith to S.A. Hamilton, 2 September 1982.

29 S.A. Hamilton, Assistant Secretary Parliamentary Branch PM&C to A.D. Rose, Deputy Secretary PM&C, 23 September 1982.

30 S.A. Hamilton, 15 September 1982; Geoffrey Yeend, Head of PM&C, 8 September 1982.

31 Hocking v Director-General NAA, HCA, Application for Special Leave to Appeal, p. 5.

Chapter Nine: 'Constitutionally unthinkable'

1 'First confirmed case of novel coronavirus in Australia', Australian Government Department of Health, 25 January 2020.

2 Christopher Niesche, 'Australia's High Court and Federal Court Close in Response to Spread of COVID-19', Law.com International, 18 March 2020. Accessed 22 August 2020.

3 Jenny Hocking, 'High Court says "Release the Palace letters"', *Pearls & Irritations*, 1 June 2020.

4 Hocking v Director-General NAA, HCA 19 [2020], p. 39.

5 p. 43.

6 p. 2.

7 p. 42.

8 p. 35.

9 p. 66.

10 p. 94.

11 p. 97.

12 pp. 25–6.

13 p. 22.

14 p. 11.

15 p. 44.

16 p. 99.

17 See also 'The big reveal: Jenny Hocking on what the "Palace letters" may tell us, finally, about The Dismissal', *The Conversation*, 13 July 2020.

18 Anne Twomey, 'High Court ruling on "Palace letters" case paves way to learn more about The Dismissal — and our Constitution', *The Conversation*, 29 May 2020.

19 NAA, 'Media Statement on the Palace Letters', 2 June 2020.

20 Caroline Bush and Mathew Bock, 'Two wrongs don't always make a writ', Clayton Utz, 2015.

21 Max Koslowski, 'Palace letters still being declassified by National Archives', *Sydney Morning Herald*, 16 June 2020.

Chapter Ten: 'My continued loyalty and humble duty'

1 David Fricker, 'Release of the Palace letters', 14 July 2020 https://www.facebook.com/watch/live/?v=301823464208623&ref=watch_permalink.

2 Troy Bramston by Twitter at 10.19 am, 14 July 2020.

3 Bernard Lagan, *The Times*, 15 July 2020; Nic White, *Daily Mail*, 14 July 2020.

4 HCA transcript, 4 February 2020, p. 67.

5 Katharine Murphy, 'The Palace letters amount to an act of interference in Australian democracy', *The Guardian*, 14 July 2020.

6 Chris Wallace, '"Palace letters" reveal the palace's fingerprints on the dismissal of the Whitlam government', *The Conversation*, 14 July 2020.

7 Michael Pelly, 'Palace gave Kerr green light to sack Whitlam', *Australian Financial Review*, 14 July 2020.

8 Nick Feik, 'Sunday Reads', *The Monthly*, 19 July 2020.

9 See Kerr's letters of 11 June 1974; 15 August 1974; 21 September 1976.

10 See Charteris's letters of 4 December 1974; September 1974; 19 June 1975.

11 Anne Twomey, 'The High Court and the release of the Palace letters', The Sydney Institute, 4 June 2020.

12 Anne Twomey, 'Keeping the Queen in Queensland', *University of Queensland Law Journal*, 28 (1), 2009, p. 83.

13 See the discussion in Jenny Hocking, 'Government by Double Dissolution', p. 137 and throughout.

14 Jenny Hocking, 'Government by Double Dissolution', p. 135.

15 Kerr to Charteris, 15 August 1974, p. 8. Kerr queried the inclusion of the Petroleum and Minerals Authority (PMA) Bill in the proclamation, as it had been challenged in the High Court. The High Court found that the inclusion of all six bills before the joint sitting did not preclude them from any subsequent legal challenge, at which point any one of them could be invalidated. Only the PMA Act was disallowed, being found not to have met the requisite three-month interval between the first rejection by the Senate and the second passage by the House of Representatives. Jenny Hocking, 'Government by Double Dissolution', p. 138.

16 An earlier assessment of this was published in Jenny Hocking, 'Letters of an insecure and indiscreet John Kerr make a mockery of the claim that the Queen played "no part"', *The Guardian*, 17 July 2020.

17 See, for example, Kerr to Charteris, 22 November 1974, 15 August 1974, 10 December 1974, 4 February 1975, among others.

18 John Kerr, 'The Governor-Generalship in Australia', *Journal of the Indian Law Institute*, vol 17:1 1975, p. 5. Attachment in Kerr to Charteris, 23 February 1976.

19 In Laurie Oakes, *Crash Through or Crash: the unmaking of a prime minister*, 1976, p. 205.

20 Paul Hasluck, 'The office of the Governor-General', Nineteenth Queale Lecture, 1973 in 'The Dismissal — Reference Material — Governor General (appointment, instructions, role and advice)', Personal papers created and maintained by Sir Clarence Harders, NAA M4081 2/20.

21 Sir E.J. Bunting, 'Confidential: Note for File', 25 July 1974, NAA M4081 2/20, The Dismissal — Reference Material — Governor-General.

22 John Kerr, *Matters for Judgment*, p. 1.

23 Attorney-General's Department, 'Governor-General: Leader of the Opposition. Whether the Governor-General should grant an audience to the Leader of the Opposition', 9 August 1974, NAA A432, A1975/7853 Part 2.

24 Anne Twomey, 'Most surprising of the Palace letters shines new light on Whitlam', *The Age*, 15 July 2020.

25 See Charteris's letters between 14 September 1974 and 30 July 1975.

26 Kerr to Charteris, 10 December 1974.

27 Frank Bongiorno, 'The Palace letters unpacked', Webinar Kings College, 29 July 2020.

28 Interview with John Menadue, 24 August 2020.

29 Kerr to Charteris, 10 December 1974, 'It would not be right for me to repeat rumours and gossip but the incidents which have so far been publicly discussed involve the appointment by Dr Cairns as Treasurer to his staff of a Miss Morosi', which Kerr then describes in detail.

30 Kerr to Charteris, 8 November 1974.

31 Melbourne Ports Federal Election 1974. F Crean ALP 60.4 per cent http://psephos.adam-carr.net/countries/a/australia/1974/1974repsvic.txt.

32 Kerr to Private Secretary, Buckingham Palace, telegram, 19 December 1974.

33 John Kerr, *Journal*, 1980, 'Personal and Confidential Papers of Sir John Kerr', NAA M4523 1 Part 17, p. 132.

34 Paul Hasluck, 'The office of the Governor-General', p. 12.

35 Sir Morrice James to K.M. Wilford FCO, Confidential, 18 October 1974, 'Australia: Constitutional Issues', UK Archives PREM 16/6/1.

36 'Lady Kerr dies after a brief illness', *Sydney Morning Herald*, 10 September 1974, p. 1.

37 Kerr to Charteris, 3 July 1975 and attached *Canberra Times* editorial.
38 David Lee, 'The Palace letters — what you need to know', 15 July 2020 adfa.edu/au.
39 Michael White, 'Kerr's curs', *Justinian*, 17 August 2020.
40 Paul Rodan, 'Sir John's lack of candour', *Inside Story*, 22 July 2020; Kerr's *Journal* entry in Jenny Hocking, *Gough Whitlam*, p. 312.
41 Paul Kelly and Troy Bramston, 'In defence of the Queen', *The Australian*, 14 April 2018.

Chapter Eleven: 'You will do it good'

1 'Confidential Sir Michael Palliser's visit to Australia', 15–18 October 1975 in FCO 24/2032, Visits of Foreign and Commonwealth Office officials to South West Pacific area, includes visit of Sir Michael Palliser, Permanent Under-Secretary of State, to Australia and New Zealand, 15–21 October 1975; Charteris to Kerr, 2 September 1974.
2 Anne Twomey, *The Chameleon Crown*, pp. 78–9; Jenny Hocking, *The Dismissal Dossier,* pp. 115–19.
3 Mr Barder BHC to Mr Bevan FCO, 17 October 1975, FCO 24/2079.
4 Australian Constitution section 11, 'The Senate may proceed to the dispatch of business, notwithstanding the failure of any State to provide for its representation in the Senate'.
5 Mr Bevan FCO, confidential: 'Australian Domestic Politics possible intervention of the UK government', 21 October 1975, FCO 24/2051.
6 'Confidential Sir Michael Palliser's visit to Australia', 15–18 October 1975 in FCO 24/2032, Visits of Foreign and Commonwealth Office officials to South West Pacific area, includes visit of Sir Michael Palliser, Permanent Under-Secretary of State, to Australia and New Zealand, 15–21 October 1975.
7 'Cancelled visit of Sir Michael Palliser, Permanent Under-Secretary of State for Foreign and Commonwealth Affairs', FCO 28/27887.
8 Jenny Hocking, *The Dismissal Dossier,* p. 125.
9 Gerard Henderson, 'Whitlam dismissal bombshell is nothing more than a fizzer', Sydney Institute, 18 July 2020; Gerard Henderson, 'Media Watch', Sydney Institute, 24 July 2020.
10 *Canberra Times*, 17 October 1975, p. 5.
11 Kerr to Charteris, 30 September 1975.

12 Australian Constitution, section 13, 'Rotation of Senators'.

13 Frykberg, I., 'Uneasiness on both sides', *Sydney Morning Herald*, 17 October 1975, p. 1.

14 Kerr to Charteris, 17 October 1975.

15 Kerr to Charteris, 17 October 1975; my emphasis.

16 Sir Morrice James to FCO, 'Australian political situation', 15 October 1975, FCO 24/2051.

17 The territories were to have two senators each for the first time following the passage of the *Senate (Representation of Territories) Act* at the joint sitting in August 1974.

18 Four new senators and two replacement senators would take their places immediately; the remaining senators would take up their places in July 1976.

19 Alan Reid, *The Whitlam Venture*, p. 354.

20 An earlier assessment of this discussion appears in Jenny Hocking, 'The question avoided by Kerr and the Palace, "What does your Prime Minister say?"', *Pearls & Irritations*, 24 July 2020.

21 Guy Rundle, 'Yes the Queen did have a hand in the Dismissal', *Crikey*, 15 July 2020.

22 Under-secretary of state for external affairs, Ottawa 2 Canadian High Commission, Canberra, 'Conversation with Senator Eugene Forsey', 28 November 1975, FCO 24/2052.

23 In Christopher Dummitt, *'Je me souviens* Too: Eugene Forsey and the Inclusiveness of 1950s' British Canadianism', *Canadian Historical Review*, 100, 3, September 2019; Frank Milligan, *Eugene A. Forsey: an intellectual biography*.

24 Charteris to Kerr, 8 March 1976.

25 Thomson, James A., 'Reserve Powers of the Crown', [Book Review], *University of New South Wales Law Journal*, vol. 13, no. 2, May 1991, pp. 420–7.

26 Eugene Forsey, *The Royal Power of Dissolution of Parliament in the British Commonwealth*, 1943, Chapter 1.

27 H.V. Evatt, *The King and His Dominion Governors*, p. 62.

28 See, for example, B.S. Markesinis, 'The Royal Prerogative Re-visited', *Cambridge Law Journal*, 32 (2) 1973; L.F. Crisp, *Australian National Government*, 1967 edn, p. 364.

29 L.F. Crisp, *Australian National Government*, p. 364.

30 Maurice Byers in *Power, Parliament and the People*, 1997.

31 Whitlam, *The Truth of the Matter*, p. 116; Ellicott statement, 17 October 1975. See also Sir John Kerr, Notes relevant to legal opinions and advice available to Governor-General in connection with the Constitutional Crisis, NAA 4524 8.

32 Kerr to Charteris, 20 October 1975.

33 Kerr to Charteris, 22 October 1975.

34 Jenny Hocking, *Gough Whitlam*, pp. 296–7.

35 The Opinion was prepared by Byers as solicitor-general, was signed by Enderby, and was awaiting Byers' signature. Attorney-General of Australia and Solicitor-General of Australia, Joint Opinion, 4 November 1975, NAA M4081 2/6.

36 John Kerr, 'Conversation with Sir Anthony Mason', Personal and confidential papers of Sir John Kerr, NAA M4523 1 Part 14.

37 In J.B. Paul, 'The Life of a Political Lawyer', *Quadrant*, 22 August 2016.

38 John Kerr, 'Conversation with Sir Anthony Mason'; Anthony Mason, 'Statement by Sir Anthony Mason', *Sydney Morning Herald*, 27 August 2012.

39 Helen Irving, 'Advisory Opinions, the Rule of Law, and the Separation of Powers', *Macquarie Law Journal*, 6 (4), p. 105; Jenny Hocking, 'Government by double dissolution', p. 141.

40 Jenny Hocking, *Gough Whitlam*, pp. 298–9.

41 John Kerr, 'Miscellaneous handwritten notes', NAA M4523 1 Part 16.

42 Anne Twomey, 'In Kerr's words: how 1975 played out', *Australian Financial Review*, 15 July 2020; Rod McGuirk, 'Queen's Australia rep was assured of power before '75 crisis', *Washington Post*, 14 July 2020.

43 David Lee, 'The Palace letters — what you need to know', 15 July 2020 adfa.edu/au.

44 Charteris to Kerr, 17 November 1975; Bill Denny in Jenny Hocking, *Gough Whitlam*, p. 335.

45 Anne Twomey, 'Most surprising of the Palace letters shines new light on Whitlam', *The Age*, 14 July 2020.

46 'Notice of motion written by Gough Whitlam, 11 November 1975', Double Dissolution of Parliament, 11 November 1975, NAA A1209 1975/2448.

47 Margaret Whitlam in *Gough Whitlam*, p. 338.

48 Gordon Scholes interview with Gary Sturgess, 2010, NLA.

49 Scholes interview with Sturgess.

50 *House of Representatives Practice*, 7th edn., Canberra, 2018, p. 51.

51 J.R. Kerr to J.B. Paul, 5 October 1982, J.B. Paul, NAA M4526 38 Part 1.

52 Under the terms of the *Parliamentary Presiding Officers Act 1965*, the Speaker remains in office until the election of a successor.

53 Letter from the Hon. Gordon Scholes to the Queen, 12 November 1975, NAA A1209 1975/2448.

54 Kerr to Charteris, 22 January 1976.

55 Anthony Mason, 'Statement by Sir Anthony Mason'.

56 Kerr to Charteris, 22 January 1976.

57 Kerr, J.R., 'Statement of Reasons'; John Kerr, 'Statement by the Governor-General', Miscellaneous drafts following 11 November 1975, including a statement by His Excellency and draft of a letter to Mr Whitlam, NAA M4524 1 Part 10.

58 David Smith, 'Address. Senate Chamber', Old Parliament House, Canberra, 7 November 2004.

59 This series of events is described in Jenny Hocking, *Gough Whitlam*, pp. 338–40.

60 Charteris to Scholes, 17 November 1975 [my emphasis].

61 Mungo MacCallum, 'The Queen's plausible denial is risible', *Pearls & Irritations*, 20 July 2020.

62 John Kerr, *Matters for Judgment*, p. 381; Jenny Hocking, *Gough Whitlam*, pp. 376–7.

63 Charteris to Kerr, 9 January 1976.

64 Charteris to Kerr, 16 February 1976.

65 Charteris to Kerr, 30 December 1975, Buckingham Palace, NAA M4526, item 6.

66 Royal Charters and Statutes of The Most Venerable Order of the Hospital of St John of Jerusalem (2004), p. 12.

67 *Canberra Times*, 'Medal designs approved', 12 February 1976, p. 1; David I. Smith, 'For Press', 11 February 1976. NAA M4512 2.

68 Philip Ziegler, *Mountbatten*, p. 657; Kerr to Barwick, 1 July 1985, 'Barwick, the Right Honourable Sir Garfield', NAA M4526 4 Part 2; Kerr to Charteris, 2 March 1976.

69 Jenny Hocking, *Gough Whitlam*, p. 354; Kerr to Barwick, 1 July 1985, 'Barwick, the Rt Hon Sir Garfield, Part 1', 'Barwick, the Right Honourable Sir Garfield', NAA M4526 4 Part 2.

70 Charteris to Kerr, 25 November 1975; 17 November 1976.

71 Charteris to Kerr, 21 April 1976.

72 See Leslie Katz, 'The double dissolution', Letter to the editor, *Current Affairs Bulletin*, July 1976, p. 30; Professor Colin Howard, 'Dismissal of Mr Whitlam', Letter to the editor, *The Times*, 18 November 1975.

73 Professor Colin Howard, 'Dismissal of Mr Whitlam', Letter to the editor, *The Times*, 18 November 1975.

74 Charteris to Kerr, 31 March 1976.

75 Kerr to Charteris, 22 January 1976, with an illegible word in the ellipsis.

76 Kerr to Charteris, 20 November 1975.

77 Kerr to Charteris, 19 February 1976; Kerr to Charteris, 23 March 1976.

78 Charteris to Kerr, 25 November 1975.

79 Kerr to Menzies, 14 July 1977, 'Menzies [Robert Menzies] correspondence', NAA M4524 1 Part 4; Charteris to Kerr, 25 November 1975.

80 Kerr to Charteris, 17 November 1975.

81 Kerr to Menzies, 14 July 1977, 'Menzies [Robert Menzies] correspondence', NAA M4524 1 Part 4.

82 'Guide to the Honours', BBC News, 6 June 2019 https://www.bbc.com/news/uk-11990088.

Chapter Twelve: 'For the sake of the Monarchy'

1 There are three drafts of a letter from Kerr to Charteris, 5 May 1977; a draft letter from Kerr to Charteris dated 9 April 1977; Kerr to Charteris, 8 June 1977; Charteris to Kerr, 12 May 1977, together with correspondence with Malcolm Fraser regarding Kerr's formal resignation letter, 8–10 June 1977. It is unclear why these letters were not included in the original cache of Palace letters in the Archives. 'Correspondence between the Prime Minister and the Governor-General on the Governor-General's resignation', NAA M4524 31.

2 John Kerr, 'The Queen's visit and the protection of the Governor-General', The Queen's visit and the Governor-General, NAA M4524, 28.

3 John Kerr, 'Assessment of position up to the Queen's visit and relevant conversations [enclosed in an envelope marked "Conversations with the Prime Minister and others about security, future planning and related matters during April 1976" and signed by John R. Kerr]', NAA M4524 34.

4 John Kerr, 'Assessment of position'.

5 John Kerr, 'Assessment of position'.

6 John Kerr, 'Assessment of position'.

7 John Kerr, 'Assessment of position'.

8 Kerr to Charteris, 26 October 1976.

9 Charteris to Kerr, 18 November 1976.

10 Jenny Hocking, *The Dismissal Dossier*, p. 240.

11 Kerr to Sir Henry Winneke, 18 August 1977, 'Correspondence with State Governors', NAA M4529 2005.

12 Draft letter, Kerr to Charteris, 9 April 1977, 'Correspondence between the Prime Minister and the Governor-General on the Governor-General's resignation', NAA M4524, 31.

13 Kerr to Charteris, 9 April 1977.

14 Kerr to Charteris, 9 April 1977.

15 Kerr to Charteris, 9 April 1977.

16 Kerr to Charteris, 9 April 1977.

17 Interview with Malcolm Fraser, 19 June 2007.

18 Kerr to Charteris, 20 November 1975, p. 4.

19 Kerr to Charteris, 5 May 1977, 'Correspondence between the Prime Minister and the Governor-General on the Governor-General's resignation', NAA M4524 31.

20 Fraser resurrected the position of Australia's ambassador to UNESCO the following year, after letting it lapse for the previous two years, in order to appoint Kerr to it. Kerr lasted one day before resigning in the face of an extraordinary public and political outcry over his appointment. Gough Whitlam was appointed as the ambassador in 1983, a term followed by his election to the UNESCO executive board. See Jenny Hocking, *Gough Whitlam*, pp. 396–9.

21 Kerr to Charteris, 5 May 1977; Kerr to Charteris, 9 May 1977, 'Correspondence between the Prime Minister and the Governor-General on the Governor-General's resignation', NAA M4524 31.

22 Charteris to Kerr, 12 May 1977, 'Correspondence between the Prime

Minister and the Governor-General on the Governor-General's resignation', NAA M4524 31.

23 Charteris to Kerr, 12 May 1977.

24 Kerr to Menzies, 14 July 1977, 'Menzies [Robert Menzies] correspondence', NAA M4524 1 Part 4.

25 Kerr to Charteris, 5 May 1977; Kerr to Charteris, 9 May 1977.

26 Charteris to Kerr, 12 May 1977.

27 Fraser to Kerr, 10 June 1977, 'Correspondence between the Prime Minister and the Governor-General on the Governor-General's resignation', NAA M4524 31.

28 Kerr to Menzies, 14 July 1977.

29 Forsey to Kerr, 8 August 1977, Forsey Papers, Library and Archives Canada.

30 *Canada from Afar: The Daily Telegraph book of Canadian obituaries*, 'Eugene Forsey', p. 76.

31 Charteris to Kerr, 24 September 1975; Charteris to Kerr, 5 November 1975.

32 Professor Peter Hogg in Mike Steketee, 'Kerr's action "fully justified" authority says', *Canberra Times*, 3 December 1978, p. 11.

33 Charteris refers to Forsey as a 'friend' in a letter after the dismissal, Charteris to Kerr, 8 March 1976.

34 Forsey to Charteris, 23 May 1974.

35 Charteris to Forsey, 21 May 1974, Forsey Papers, Library and Archives Canada.

36 Forsey Papers.

37 Kerr to Forsey, 13 September 1977.

38 Kerr to Forsey, 8 April 1976.

39 Kerr to Forsey, 16 June 1978.

40 Under-secretary of state for external affairs, Ottawa to Canadian High Commission, Canberra, 'Conversation with Senator Eugene Forsey', 28 November 1975, FCO24/2015.

41 Eglington to Forsey, 8 December 1975, Forsey Papers.

42 Forsey to Kerr, 16 April 1976, Forsey Papers.

43 Morrice James to Bevan, FCO, 'Footnotes to the constitutional crisis', 20 December 1975 FCO 24/2052.

Bibliography

Archival sources

National Archives of Australia

The Palace Letters
Correspondence between Sir John Kerr and The Queen, AA 1984/609.
Copies of correspondence between Sir John Kerr and The Queen, M4513.

Personal papers of Sir John Kerr
Drafts of *Matters for Judgment* and related material, M4507.
Correspondence re: publication — Part 1, M4507 30.

Private and confidential papers relating to the constitutional crisis of 1975, M4523
Conversation with Sir Anthony Mason, M4523 1 Part 14.
Extracts from letters, M4523 1 Part 7.
Introduction to annotated copy of the Palace correspondence, M4523 1 Part 15.
Journal, 1980, M4523 1 Part 17.
Miscellaneous handwritten notes, M4523 1 Part 16.

Notes and papers on the constitutional crisis of 1975 and the political events that followed, M4523

Assessment of position up to the Queen's visit and relevant conversations [enclosed in an envelope marked 'Conversations with the Prime Minister and others about security, future planning and related matters during April 1976' and signed by John R Kerr], M4524, 34.

Correspondence between the Prime Minister and the Governor-General on the Governor-General's resignation, M4524, 31.

Miscellaneous drafts following 11 November 1975, including a statement by His Excellency and draft of a letter to Mr Whitlam, M4524 1 Part 10.

The Queen's visit and the position of the Governor-General, NAA M4524, 28.

Personal correspondence of Sir John Kerr, alphabetical series Archdale-Yeend M4526

Barwick, the Rt Hon Sir Garfield, M4526 4 Part 1.

Brandis, George, M4526 5.

Buckingham Palace, M4526 6.

Crocker, Sir Walter, M4526 11 Part 1.

Markwell, Don, M4526 30 Parts 3, 4, 6, 7.

Carrick, Sir John, M4526.

Paul, J.B., M4526 38 Parts 1, 2.

Menzies [Robert Menzies] correspondence, M4524 1 Part 4.

Smith, David I., M4526 49.

Wootten, Hal, M4526 59.

Personal correspondence with State Governors, M4529

Personal papers created and maintained by Sir Clarence Harders, M4081

Byers, Sir Maurice QC, solicitor-general, and Kep Enderby, attorney-general, Opinion of Solicitor-General and Attorney-General regarding exercise of the Governor General's powers in constitutional crisis, M4081 2/6.

The Dismissal — Advice — Opinion of Solicitor General and Attorney

General regarding exercise of the Governor General's powers in
constitutional crisis, M4081 2/6.
The Dismissal — Reference Material — Governor-General, M4081 2/20.

Other
Access to the records of the Governor-General's Office and of
Parliamentary Depts, A3437 A1975/551.
Dismissal of Prime Minister by Governor-General [Folder marked
'Cabinet'], A432 A1975/7853 Part 2.
Double Dissolution of Parliament, 11 November 1975, A1209 1975/2448.
Miscellaneous papers concerning the functions of the governor-general
[Sir Paul Halsuck], M1767, 8.
National Archives Legislation, A1209 1976/1957 Part 8.
Mr Whitlam's visit to London, April 1973, Omnibus Brief for Secretary of
State A1838 67/1/3 Part 7.
Personal Papers of Prime Minister Fraser] Correspondence, '1978K',
M1256 1978K.
NAA Freedom of Information log, FOI131 2020.

Library and Archives Canada
Papers of Eugene A. Forsey.

National Archives [UK]
Australia: Constitutional Issues: Australian honours system; States' access
to Monarch', PREM 16/6/1.
Cancelled visit of Sir Michael Palliser, Permanent Under-Secretary of State
for Foreign and Commonwealth Affairs, FCO 28/2787.
Changes in Constitution of Australia 1974, FCO 24/1931.
Constitutional matters in Australia: includes disagreement between State
and Federal Governments over proposed revised Privy Council Appeals
Abolition Bill, FCO24/2074.
Constitutional matters in Australia: includes disagreement between State
and Federal Governments over proposed revised Privy Council Appeals
Abolition Bill, FCO24/2076.
Constitutional matters in Australia: includes disagreement between State
and Federal Governments over proposed revised Privy Council Appeals

Abolition Bill; constitutional crisis following dismissal of Gough Whitlam, Labor Prime Minister, by Sir John Kerr, Governor-General; and statute law repeals in Australian States, FCO 24/2079.

Extent of seabed rights of Australian States: petitions from Governments of Queensland and Tasmania to HM The Queen for reference to Judicial Committee of Privy Council, FCO 24/2015.

Federal Election in Australia, 13 December 1975, FCO 24/2059.

Political situation in Australia: includes constitutional crisis following dismissal of Gough Whitlam, Labor Prime Minister of Australia, by Sir John Kerr, Governor-General, 11 November 1975, FCO 24/2051.

Political situation in Australia: includes constitutional crisis following dismissal of Gough Whitlam, Labor Prime Minister of Australia, by Sir John Kerr, Governor-General, 11 November 1975, FCO 24/2052.

Visit of Gough Whitlam, Prime Minister of Australia, to UK, 20–25 April 1973, FCO 24/1613.

Visit of Gough Whitlam, Prime Minister of Australia, to UK, 20–25 April 1973, FCO 24/1614.

Visits of Foreign and Commonwealth Office officials to South West Pacific area, includes visit of Sir Michael Palliser, Permanent Under-Secretary of State, to Australia and New Zealand, 15–21 October 1975, FCO 24/2032.

National Library of Australia
Papers of Alan Missen, MS7528.
Papers of Jean Lester, MS Acc05/8.

University of Adelaide
Sir Walter Crocker Papers, MSS327 C938p.
Sir Marcus Laurence Oliphant Papers, MSS92 O4775p.

Whitlam Institute within Western Sydney University
The Whitlam Prime Ministerial Collection.

Court material

Judgments

Hocking v Director-General of the National Archives of Australia [2020], HCA 19.

Hocking v Director-General of the National Archives of Australia [2019], FCAFC 12.

Hocking v Director-General of National Archives of Australia [2018], FCA 340.

Transcripts

Transcripts of hearings in the FCA and the FCAFC with the author.

Transcripts HCA, Hocking v Director-General of the National Archives of Australia, Case S262/2019 4 February 2020, 5 February 2020.

Legal documents relating to Hocking v Director-General of the National Archives of Australia with the author.

Books

Philip Ayres, *Malcolm Fraser: a biography*, Heinemann, Melbourne, 1987.

Peter Baume, John Wanna, and Marija Taflaga (eds), *A Dissident Liberal: the political writings of Peter Baume*, ANU Press, Canberra, 2015.

George Brandis, Tom Harley, and Don Markwell (eds), *Liberals Face the Future: essays on Australian Liberalism*, Oxford University Press, Melbourne, 1984.

Michael Coper and George Williams (eds), *Power, Parliament and the People*, Federation Press, Leichhardt, 1997.

Canada from Afar: the Daily Telegraph *book of Canadian obituaries*, Dundurn Group, Toronto, 1996.

Crisp, L.F., *Australian National Government*, Longman Cheshire, Melbourne, 1967 edn.

Evatt, Dr Herbert Vere, *The King and His Dominion Governors* (1936), Routledge, London, 1967 edn.

Eugene A. Forsey, *The Royal Power of Dissolution of Parliament in the British Commonwealth*, Oxford University Press, Toronto, 1968.

Robert Garran, *Prosper the Commonwealth*, Angus & Robertson, Sydney, 1958.

Anton Hermann, *Alan Missen: Liberal pilgrim*, Poplar Press, Woden, 1993.

Jenny Hocking, *The Dismissal Dossier: everything you were never meant to know about November 1975 — the Palace connection*, Melbourne University Press, Carlton (2015), 2017.

—, *Gough Whitlam: his time*, 2nd edn, Melbourne University Publishing, Carlton (2012), 2014.

—, 'Gough Whitlam's 1974 re-election: "Government by double dissolution"' in Jenny Hocking and Tim Rowse (eds) *Making Modern Australian: Gough Whitlam's 21st century agenda*, Monash University Publishing, Melbourne, 2017.

Paul Kelly, *November 1975*, Allen & Unwin, North Sydney, 1995.

John Kerr, *Matters for Judgment*, Macmillan, South Melbourne, 1978.

Frank Milligan, *Eugene A. Forsey: an intellectual biography*, University of Calgary Press, Calgary, 2004.

Laurie Oakes, *Crash Through or Crash: the unmaking of a prime minister*, Drummond, Melbourne, 1976.

Malcolm Fraser and Margaret Simons, *Malcolm Fraser: the political memoirs*, Melbourne University Publishing, Carlton, 2015.

Malcolm Turnbull, *The Spycatcher Trial*, Mandarin, Richmond, 1989.

Anne Twomey, *The Chameleon Crown*, Federation Press, Sydney, 2006.

—, 'Peering into the Black Box of Executive Power: Cabinet Manuals, Secrecy and the Identification of Convention' in Jason Varuhas and Shona Wilson Stark (eds), *The Frontiers of Public Law* (Bloomsbury, 2020), pp. 399–428.

Gough Whitlam, *The Truth of the Matter*, 3rd edn, Melbourne University Publishing, Carlton, 2005.

Philip Ziegler, *Mountbatten: the official biography*, Harper & Row, New York, 1985.

Articles

Richard Ackland, 'Another dismissal', *Justinian*, 11 February 2019.

William Atkins, 'Syncopal kick: on the trauma of exile', *Times Literary Supplement*, 25 October 2019.

George Brandis, '"Green lawfare" and standing: the view from within government', *IAL Forum*, December 2017, pp. 12–19.

Tom Brennan, 'Australia owns its history', 13 Wentworth Chambers, 10 November 2015.

Caroline Bush and Mathew Bock, 'Two wrongs don't always make a writ', Clayton Utz *Administrative Law Updater*, 18 February 2015.

Carroll, J., Bush, C., Cuthbert, N., and Grivas, R., 'The Palace letters and you', Clayton Utz *Administrative Law Updater*, 3 September 2019.

Christopher Dummitt, '*Je me souviens* too: Eugene Forsey and the Inclusiveness of 1950s' British Canadianism', *Canadian Historical Review* 100, 3, September 2019.

Easton, S,. 'National Archives "completely dysfunctional" for serious scholarship', *The Mandarin*, 18 April 2019.

Talitha Fishburn, 'An opening for the Palace Letters: No dismissal in respect of The Dismissal', *Law Society of NSW Journal*, no. 68, July 2020: 78-79.

Paul Hasluck, 'The office of the Governor-General', Nineteenth Queale Lecture, 1973.

Jenny Hocking, 'Archival secrets and hidden histories — Reasserting the right to public access', *Griffith Review* 67, 'Matters of Trust', February 2020.

—, 'At Her Majesty's pleasure: Sir John Kerr and the royal dismissal secrets', *Australian Book Review*, 4, 20 April 2020.

—, 'Relics of colonialism: the Whitlam dismissal and the Palace letters', *Griffith Review* 59, 'Commonwealth Now', January 2018.

Colin Howard, 'Dismissal of Mr Whitlam', Letter to the editor *The Times*, 18 November 1975.

Helen Irving, 'Advisory Opinions, the Rule of Law, and the Separation of Powers,' *Macquarie Law Journal* 6 (4).

Leslie Katz, 'The double dissolution', Letter to the editor, *Current Affairs Bulletin*, July 1976.

A. Berriedale Keith, 'The Imperial Conference of 1930', *Journal of Comparative Legislation and International Law*, vol. 13, no. 1 (1931), pp. 26-42.

John Kerr, 'The Governor-Generalship in Australia', *Journal of the Indian law Institute* vol 17:1 1975.

Christopher Knaus, 'Palace letters: historian claims national archives misled her over copies', *The Guardian*, 28 March 2018.

Max Koslowski, 'National Archives may not survive unless funding doubles, warns council', *Canberra Times*, 18 July 2019.

Hilary Mantel, 'Why I became a historical novelist', *The Guardian*, 3 June 2017.

B.S. Markesinis, 'The Royal Prerogative Re-visited', *Cambridge Law Journal* 32 (2) 1973.

Anthony Mason, 'Statement by Sir Anthony Mason', *Sydney Morning Herald*, 27 August 2012.

—, 'It was unfolding like a Greek tragedy, *The Age*, 27 August 2012.

Katharine Murphy, 'The Palace letters amount to an act of interference in Australian democracy', *The Guardian*, 14 July 2020.

M. Nawaz, 'Palace Letters are Commonwealth Records: a victory for democratic transparency', *Australian Public Law*, 10 June 2020.

Malcolm Quekett, 'No wake-up call for Queen over dismissal', *West Australian*, 12 April 2011.

Jennifer Robinson, 'Palace letters highlight undemocratic secrecy', *The Saturday Paper*, 23 February 2019.

Paul Rodan, 'Sir John's lack of candour', *Inside Story*, 22 July 2020.

Stewart, Pam; Stuhmcke, Anita et al, 'Litigants and Legal Representatives: a study of special leave applications in the High Court of Australia', *Sydney Law Review* (2019) 41(1).

Anne Twomey, 'Keeping the Queen in Queensland,' *University of Queensland Law Journal*, 28 (1) 2009.

—, 'Editorial', *Australian Law Journal*, 93 (4) 2019.

Chris Wallace, '"Palace letters" reveal the Palace's fingerprints on the dismissal of the Whitlam government', *The Conversation*, 14 July 2020.

Michael White, 'Kerr's curs', *Justinian*, 17 August 2020.

Dismissal documents

Sir Garfield Barwick, 'Letter from Chief Justice to Governor-General, 10 November 1975', *Canberra Times*, 19 November 1975.

Sir Maurice Byers QC, solicitor-general, and Kep Enderby, attorney-general, 'Law officers' opinion during supply dispute' (dated 4 November 1975), *Canberra Times*, 20 November 1975.

Sir John Kerr, 'Letter of dismissal 11 November 1975'. Original letter held by the Whitlam Institute, Western Sydney University.

—, 'Statement of reasons by the Governor-General', 11 November 1975, NAA A1209, 1975/2448.

—, 'Proclamation', 11 November 1975, in Kerr, *Matters for Judgment*,
pp. 372–3.

Gordon Scholes, 'Speaker's letter to Her Majesty Queen Elizabeth II',
12 November 1975 in NAA A1209, 1975/2448, Double Dissolution of
Parliament, 11 November 1975.

The Queen's reply, sent through Charteris, is in Kerr, *Matters for Judgment*,
pp. 374–5.

Gough Whitlam, 'Letter advising half-senate election', 11 November 1975,
in NAA A1209, 1975/2448 Double Dissolution of Parliament,
11 November 1975.

—, 'Notice of motion of no confidence against the Fraser government
and confidence in the Whitlam government after the dismissal', draft
motion 11, November 1975, NAA M4628, 2.

Other

Justin Gleeson SC, submission to the Senate Legal and Constitutional
Affairs Committee, 11 May 2016.

The Crown and Us: the story of the Royals in Australia, ABC-TV, 2019.

Report of Imperial Conference of British Empire 1926, reproduced in 'The
Imperial Conference', *The Round Table*, vol. 17 1927, pp. 225–41.

Report of Imperial Conference of British Empire 1930 in 'Imperial
Conference, 1930. Summary of Proceedings', *Journals of the House of
Representatives* New Zealand. Session I-II, A-06, Appendix, 1931.

Balfour Declaration 1926, FoundingDocs https://www.foundingdocs.gov.
au/resources/transcripts/cth11_doc_1926.pdf